„DURCH EINSATZ UND KOMPETENZ, DURCH MUT UND PASSION ERWÄCHST AUS JEDEM ERFOLG EIN MOMENT FÜR DIE EWIGKEIT.“

“AS A RESULT OF COMMITMENT AND SKILL, COURAGE AND PASSION, EVERY SUCCESS PRODUCES A MOMENT FOR ETERNITY.”

Chris Reinke

AUDI SPORT CUSTOMER RACING 2017

VERLAG PUBLISHING HOUSE

Adrenalin Verlag GmbH
Bernhard-Nocht-Str. 99, D-20359 Hamburg
Tel. +49 40 300682-70
E-Mail info@adrenalin-verlag.com
www.adrenalin-verlag.com

REDAKTION, PRODUKTION EDITING, PRODUCTION

Speedpool, Hamburg
www.speedpool.com

FOTOS UND ANIMATIONEN PICTURES AND ANIMATIONS

ACI Sport/Photo 4, ADAC Motorsport, Kevin Adolf, AUDI AG, Audi China, Audi Hong Kong, Audi Sport Italia, Berzerkdesign, Dirk Bogaerts, Stevie Borowik, Jan Brucke/VLN, Euan Cameron, Malte Christians/ Hoch Zwei, Marat Daminov, Georges Decoster, Jakob Ebrey, Edd Ellison, Roger Frauenrath, Petr Frýba, Petr Gabriel, Gary Graham, Chris Green, Gruppe C GmbH, Flo Hagena, Matthew Hansen, Patrick Hecq, KC Ho, Mark Horsburgh, Michinao Ishibashi, Burkhard Kasan, Paul Khoo/Rewind Images, Ferdi Kräling Motorsport-Bild GmbH, Klaus Kuhne, Michael Kunkel/Hoch Zwei, Thomas Lam, Jean Michel Le Meur, Jacques Letihon, Dave Maries, Media 77, David Paul Morris, Nuno Oliveira, Nuno Organista, Jörn Pollex/Hoch Zwei, Ahmed S. Rayan, Tobias Sagmeister, Stefan Sauer, Michael Schulz, Speedpool GmbH, Michael Stahlschmidt, Matt Stark, Super Taikyu Series, Sutton Images, Timothy Tan/Rewind Images, TCR China, TCR Middle East, TCR Russia, Eduardo Viera/ MotorCanario.com, Farid Wagner, John Wardzynski, Tony Welam, Michael Wells, Heng Ying, Ineke Zondag

AUTOR AUTHOR

Alexander von Wegner

RECHERCHE, REDAKTION RESEARCH, EDITORIAL STAFF

Johan Laubscher

ENGLISCH ENGLISH

Helga Oberländer

DRUCK PRINTING

Blattwerk Hannover GmbH
Gedruckt in Deutschland, Dezember 2017
Printed in Germany, December 2017

In Kooperation mit Audi Sport customer racing
In cooperation with Audi Sport customer racing

ISBN 978-3-943861-41-9

adrenalin

VORWORT PREFACE

LIEBE LESERINNEN, LIEBE LESER,

die Saison 2017 bleibt für Audi Sport customer racing unvergesslich. Unserem rasch wachsenden Kundenkreis und den Rennfahrern sowie all der Energie der gesamten Mannschaft von Audi Sport customer racing ist es zu verdanken, dass wir sportlich und wirtschaftlich zwölf außerordentliche Monate hinter uns haben. Der neue Audi RS 3 LMS hat sich so gut verkauft, dass wir bereits im Juli das 100. Auto vorgestellt haben. In Nordamerika, Europa und Asien hat sich dieser TCR-Tourenwagen fest etabliert und weltweit seine ersten Titel eingefahren. Eine geradezu unglaubliche Serie ist uns im Langstrecken-Rennsport geglückt. Nach Siegen bei den 24-Stunden-Rennen auf dem Nürburgring, in Spa und bei den 12 Stunden von Imola hat sich der Audi R8 LMS auch beim Petit-Le-Mans-Rennen in Road Atlanta und den California 8 Hours durchgesetzt und die Intercontinental GT Challenge gewonnen. Zudem haben die Teams weltweit zahlreiche Sprint-Titel mit unserem Spitzenmodell eingefahren. Bereits in den Startlöchern steht der neue Audi R8 LMS GT4. Lassen Sie uns gemeinsam in eine faszinierende Zukunft schauen und die spektakuläre Saison mit einem großartigen Rückblick abschließen, zu dem das vorliegende Jahrbuch einlädt.

DEAR READERS,

The 2017 season will remain an unforgettable one for Audi Sport customer racing. Thanks to our fast-growing customer base and the race drivers, as well as all the energy of the entire Audi Sport customer racing team, we can look back on twelve exceptional months both in terms of racing and business. The new Audi RS 3 LMS has been selling so well that we presented the 100th car as early as in July. In North America, Europe and Asia, this touring car has become firmly established and has clinched its first titles around the world. In endurance racing, we achieved a near-incredible string of success. Following victories in the 24-hour races at the Nürburgring, at Spa and in the 12 Hours of Imola, the Audi R8 LMS prevailed as well in the Petit Le Mans race at Road Atlanta and the California 8 Hours, and won the Intercontinental GT Challenge. In addition, the teams around the globe have clinched numerous sprint titles with our top-end model. Now ready to be deployed is the new Audi R8 LMS GT4. Please join us in looking at a fascinating future and in closing the spectacular season with an outstanding retrospective which this yearbook invites you to enjoy.

Chris Reinke, Leiter Audi Sport customer racing Head of Audi Sport customer racing

Welcome to the world of Audi Sport customer racing

BORN ON THE TRACK.
BUILT FOR THE ROAD.
BLAUPUNKT
MICHELIN
BOSCH
Pikes Peak
AUTO HILL CLIMB
Audi Sport
Audi Sport.
Castrol
Eibach
montaplast
Audi Sport
customer racing
1
Audi Sport
Audi Sport
R8 LMS GT3

Living legends

The sun always shines in California

Asphalt cowboy

Sunset glow

We want you!

Larger than life

RENNSPORT-QUARTETT

RACING QUARTET

Vier Rennwagen bietet Audi Sport customer racing inzwischen an: den Audi TT cup für den Markenpokal und die drei zu erwerbenden Modelle Audi RS 3 LMS, Audi R8 LMS GT4 und Audi R8 LMS GT3. Das GT3-Modell fährt auch im Audi R8 LMS Cup

Audi Sport customer racing's offering encompasses four race cars: the Audi TT cup for the one-make cup and the three models, Audi RS 3 LMS, Audi R8 LMS GT4 and Audi R8 LMS GT3, available for purchase. The GT3 car competes in the Audi R8 LMS Cup as well

AUDI TT CUP

BEWÄHRTER CUP-RACER

Frontantrieb, 310 PS als Standard und 30 PS zusätzlich über Push-to-Pass, eine hochwertige Sicherheitsausrüstung und ein modernes Doppelkupplungsgetriebe, das über Schaltwippen am Lenkrad betätigt wird: Der Audi TT cup war die optimale Basis für den von 2015 bis 2017 ausgetragenen Audi Sport TT Cup.

PROVEN CUP RACER

Front-wheel drive, 310 hp of standard output, plus an extra 30 hp via push-to-pass, high-end safety equipment and a modern double-clutch transmission operated via paddle shifts in the steering wheel: the Audi TT cup provided the optimal basis for the Audi Sport TT Cup held between 2015 and 2017.

FAHRZEUG

Fahrzeugtyp	Cup-Fahrzeug nach Audi Sport TT Cup-Reglement
Aufbau	Rohkarosserie in Stahl-/Aluminium-Hybrid-Bauweise mit eingeschweißter Stahl-Sicherheitszelle (nach FIA-Reglement)

MOTOR

Bauart	Reihen-Vierzylinder-Ottomotor mit Benzindirekteinspritzung, Abgasturboaufladung mit Ladeluftkühlung, Vierventil-Technik, zwei obenliegende Nockenwellen, DOHC
Abgasreinigung	Lambdasonde vor Turbine (zylinderselektive Erkennung), Stahl-Rennkatalysator
Motormanagement	Simos 18
Motorschmierung	Nasssumpf
Hubraum	1.984 ccm
Leistung	228 kW (310 PS) / 250 kW (340 PS) Mehrleistung durch Push-to-Pass-System für Überholvorgänge abrufbar
Drehmoment	Über 400 Nm bei 1.600 bis 4.300 U/min

ANTRIEB/KRAFTÜBERTRAGUNG

Antriebsart	Frontantrieb, Traktionskontrolle (ASR)
Kupplung	Zwei elektrohydraulisch betätigte Lamellen-kupplungen im Ölbad
Getriebe	6-Gang-Doppelkupplungsgetriebe S tronic mit Wippenschaltung
Differenzial	Aktives elektrohydraulisches Vorderachs-Sperrdifferenzial
Antriebswellen	Gleichlaufgelenkwellen

FAHRWERK/LENKUNG/BREMSE

Lenkung	Elektrische Progressivlenkung
Fahrwerk Vorderachse	McPherson-Federbeinachse mit unteren Stahl-Dreiecksquerlenkern, Alu-Schwenklager, Stahl-Hilfsrahmen, Federbeine mit Schraubenfedern und einstellbaren Stoßdämpfern, einstellbarer Stabilisator
Fahrwerk Hinterachse	Vierlenker-Hinterachse, Stoßdämpfer mit Schraubenfedern (coil-over-Anordnung), Stahl-Hilfsrahmen, Alu-Radträger, einstellbarer Stabilisator
Bremsen	Hydraulische Zweikreis-Bremsanlage mit einstellbarer Bremsdruckverteilung (Vorderachse/Hinterachse), Stahl-Bremsscheiben vorn und hinten, Renn-ABS
Felgen	Aluminium-Felgen, vorn und hinten 10 x 18 Zoll
Reifen	260-660/18 oder vergleichbar

ABMESSUNGEN/GEWICHT

Länge	4.260 mm
Breite	1.994 mm
Höhe	1.282 mm
Mindestgewicht	1.125 kg
Tankinhalt	100 l

AUSSTATTUNG

Feuerlöschsystem	Audi Sport
Sitzsystem	Audi Sport customer racing PS 1 Protection Seat
Betankungssystem	Serie mit Sicherheitsventil
Elektrik	Serie, für Motorsportzwecke angepasst

CAR

Vehicle type	Cup vehicle according to Audi Sport TT Cup Regulations
Body	Body-in-white featuring a steel/aluminum hybrid design with welded-in steel safety cell (according to FIA Regulations)

ENGINE

Type	Four-in-line gasoline engine with gasoline direct injection, exhaust gas turbocharger with intercooler, four-valve technology, double overhead camshaft, DOHC
Exhaust emission control system	Oxygen sensor upstream of turbine (cylinder-selective sensor signal), steel racing catalytic converter
Engine management	Simos 18
Engine lubrication	Wet sump
Cubic capacity	1,984 cc
Power output	228 kW (310 hp) / 250 kW (340 hp) Boost for overtaking maneuvers accessible through Push-to-pass system
Torque	Over 400 Nm at 1,600 to 4,300 rpm

DRIVETRAIN/TRANSMISSION

Type of drive	Front wheel drive, traction control (ASR)
Clutch	Two electro-hydraulically operated wet-type multi-plate clutches
Transmission	6-speed dual-clutch S tronic with paddle shifting
Differential	Active electro-hydraulic front axle limited-slip differential
Driveshafts	Constant velocity joint shafts

SUSPENSION/STEERING/BRAKES

Steering	Electric progressive steering
Front suspension	McPherson struts with lower steel wishbones, aluminum swivel bearing, steel subframe, struts with coil springs and adjustable dampers, adjustable stabilizer
Rear suspension	Four-link rear suspension, dampers with coil springs (coil-over-configuration), steel subframe, aluminum uprights, adjustable stabilizer
Brakes	Hydraulic dual-circuit brake system with adjustable brake pressure distribution (front axle/rear axle), steel brake discs front and rear, racing ABS
Rims	Aluminum rims, front and rear, 10 x 18 inches
Tires	260/660-18 or comparable

DIMENSIONS/WEIGHT

Length	4,260 mm
Width	1,994 mm
Height	1,282 mm
Minimum weight	1,125 kg
Tank capacity	100 l

EQUIPMENT

Fire extinguisher	Audi Sport
Seat system	Audi Sport customer racing PS 1 Protection Seat
Refueling system	Production-level with safety valve
Electrical system	Production-level, modified for motorsport purposes

AUDI RS 3 LMS

EINSTEIGER-TOURENWAGEN

Bis zu 350 PS, zwei Getriebevarianten mit Doppelkupplung oder sequenzieller Betätigung, ein hochwertiges, einstellbares Rennsport-Fahrwerk, die gute Aerodynamik und ein Sicherheitskonzept, das über dem Klassenstandard liegt, zeichnen den Audi RS 3 LMS aus. Er entsteht im Konzernverbund am Standort Martorell in Spanien und markiert den Einstieg in die attraktive Welt des TCR-Tourenwagen-Sports.

ENTRY-LEVEL TOURING CAR

Up to 350 hp, two transmission versions with double-clutch or sequential operation, a high-end, adjustable racing suspension, good aerodynamics and a safety concept exceeding the standards in its class are the hallmarks of the Audi RS 3 LMS. It is produced within the corporate group at the the Martorell site in Spain and marks the entry level into the attractive world of touring car racing.

FAHRZEUG

Fahrzeugtyp	Tourenwagen gemäß TCR-Reglement
Aufbau	Verstärkte Stahlkarosserie mit eingeschweißter Stahl-Sicherheitszelle
Karosserie	Kohlefaser, Glasfaser und Stahlblech

MOTOR

Bauart	Reihen-Vierzylinder-Ottomotor mit Benzindirekteinspritzung, Abgasturboaufladung mit Ladeluftkühlung, Vierventil-Technik, zwei obenliegende Nockenwellen, DOHC, quer vor der Vorderachse angeordnet
Abgasreinigung	Lambdasonde vor Turbine (zylinderselektive Erkennung), Stahl-Rennsportkatalysator
Motormanagement	Continental Simos 18
Motorschmierung	Nasssumpf
Hubraum	1.984 ccm (Bohrung x Hub 82,5 x 92,8 mm)
Leistung	Bis zu 257 kW (350 PS) bei 6.200 U/min
Drehmoment	Bis zu 460 Nm bei 2.500 U/min

ANTRIEB/KRAFTÜBERTRAGUNG

Antriebsart	Frontantrieb
Kupplung	Gesinterte Mehrscheiben-Kupplung
Getriebe	Sequenzielles 6-Gang-Renngetriebe, wahlweise 6-Gang-Doppelkupplungs-Getriebe S tronic mit Wippenschaltung
Differenzial	Lamellen-Sperrdifferenzial, aktives Sperrdifferenzial bei S tronic
Antriebswellen	Gleichlaufgelenkwellen

LENKUNG

Lenkung	Elektrische Zahnstangenlenkung mit modifizierter Soft- und Hardware, höhen- und längsverstellbares Lenkrad

FAHRWERK/BREMSE

Fahrwerk Vorderachse	McPherson-Federbeinachse mit unteren Stahl-Dreiecksquerlenkern, Alu-Schwenklager, Stahl-Hilfsrahmen, Federbeine mit Schraubenfedern und einstellbaren Stoßdämpfern, Fahrzeughöhe, Spur und Sturz stufenlos einstellbar, Stabilisator in drei Stufen einstellbar
Fahrwerk Hinterachse	Vierlenker-Hinterachse, Stoßdämpfer mit Schraubenfedern (Coil-over-Anordnung), Stahl-Hilfsrahmen, Alu-Radträger, Fahrzeughöhe, Spur und Sturz stufenlos einstellbar, Stabilisator in drei Stufen einstellbar
Bremsen	Hydraulische Zweikreis-Bremsanlage, einstellbare Bremsdruckverteilung (Vorderachse/Hinterachse), Stahl-Bremsscheiben vorn (378 x 34 mm) und hinten (272 x 12 mm)
Felgen	Aluminium-Felgen, vorn und hinten 10 x 18 Zoll
Reifen	27/65 x 18

ABMESSUNGEN/GEWICHT

Länge	4.589 mm
Breite	1.950 mm
Höhe	1.340 mm
Radstand	2.665 mm
Gewicht	1.180 kg (1.215 kg bei S tronic)
Tankinhalt	100 l

FAHRLEISTUNGEN

0–100 km/h	Ca. 4,5 Sekunden
Höchstgeschwindigkeit	265 km/h (245 km/h bei S tronic)

AUSSTATTUNG

Feuerlöschsystem	OMP
Sitzsystem	Audi Sport customer racing Protection Seat PS 3
Betankungssystem	Serie mit Sicherheitsventil
Elektrik	Serie, für Motorsportzwecke angepasst

CAR

Vehicle type	Touring car according to TCR regulations
Structure	Reinforced steel body with weld-in steel safety cell
Body	Carbon fiber, glass fiber and sheet steel

ENGINE

Type	Four-in-line gasoline engine with direct injection, exhaust gas turbocharger with intercooler, four-valve technology, double overhead camshaft, DOHC, transversely mounted front engine
Exhaust emission control system	Oxygen sensor upstream of turbine (cylinder-selective sensor signal), steel racing catalytic converter
Engine management	Continental Simos 18
Engine lubrication	Wet sump
Cubic capacity	1,984 cc (bore x stroke 82.5 x 92.8 mm)
Power	Up to 257 kW (350 hp) at 6,200 rpm
Torque	Up to 460 Nm at 2,500 rpm

DRIVETRAIN/TRANSMISSION

Type of drive	Front wheel drive
Clutch	Sintered multi-plate clutch
Transmission	Sequential 6-speed racing transmission, optional 6-speed double-clutch transmission S tronic with paddle shifters
Differential	Multi-plate limited-slip differential, active limited slip differential for S tronic
Driveshafts	Constant velocity joint shafts

STEERING

Steering	Electric rack and pinion steering with modified soft- and hardware, steering wheel adjustable in heigth and longitudinal direction

SUSPENSION/BRAKES

Front suspension	McPherson struts with lower steel wishbones, aluminum swivel bearing, steel subframe, struts with coil springs and adjustable dampers, infinitely variable ride height, toe and camber, three-way adjustment of stabilizer
Rear suspension	Four-link rear suspension, dampers with coil springs (coil-over-configuration), steel subframe, aluminum uprights, infinitely variable ride height, toe and camber, three-way adjustment of stabilizer
Brakes	Hydraulic dual-circuit braking system with adjustable brake pressure distribution (front axle/rear axle), steel brake discs front (378 x 34 mm) and rear (272 x 12 mm)
Rims	Aluminum rims, front and rear 10 x 18 inches
Tires	27/65 x 18

DIMENSIONS/WEIGHT

Length	4,589 mm
Width	1,950 mm
Height	1,340 mm
Wheelbase	2,665 mm
Weight	1,180 (1,215 kg with S tronic)
Fuel tank capacity	100 l

PERFORMANCE

0–100 km/h	Approx. 4.5 seconds
Top speed	265 km/h (245 km/h with S tronic)

EQUIPMENT

Fire extinguisher	OMP
Seat system	Audi Sport customer racing Protection Seat PS 3
Refueling system	Production version with safety valve
Electrical system	Production version, modified for use in racing

AUDI R8 LMS GT4

LEISTUNGSTRÄGER IN DER GT4-KLASSE

Der GT4-Rennsport ist die ideale Bühne für Gentlemen und Amateure, die aus kleineren Klassen aufsteigen und gerne Sportwagen fahren wollen. Der 495 PS starke Mittelmotor-Rennwagen ist direkt vom Serienmodell abgeleitet, teilt sich rund 60 Prozent der Baugruppen mit ihm und führt einen hohen Sicherheitsstandard in der GT4-Kategorie ein.

HIGH PERFORMER IN THE GT4 CLASS

GT4 racing is the ideal stage for gentlemen and amateurs who would like to move up from smaller classes and drive sports cars. The 495-hp mid-engine race car has been derived directly from the production model, shares some 60 percent of the assemblies with it and introduces a high safety standard in the GT4 category.

FAHRZEUG

Fahrzeugtyp	Sportwagen gemäß GT4-Reglement
Aufbau	Audi Space Frame (ASF) in Aluminium-CFK-Verbundbauweise mit eingeschweißter und verschraubter Stahl-Sicherheitszelle
Karosserie	Faserverbundwerkstoffe und Aluminium
Sicherheitskonzept	Energieaufnehmende Crashstrukturen, Feuerlöschsystem gemäß FIA Standard 8865-2015, Audi Sport customer racing Protection Seat PS 3, FT3-Sicherheitstank, Bergungsluke im Dach

MOTOR

Bauart	90°-V10-Motor mit kombinierter Saugrohr- und Benzindirekteinspritzung, 4 Ventile pro Zylinder, vier obenliegende Nockenwellen, Abgasreinigung mit Lambdasonde vor KAT, Metallkatalysatoren
Motormanagement	2 x Bosch MED 17 (Master-Slave-Konzept)
Motorschmierung	Trockensumpf
Hubraum	5.200 ccm
Leistung	Variabel per Restriktor bis zu 364 kW (495 PS) *
Drehmoment	Über 550 Nm *
Tankinhalt	110 l (Minimum)
Betankungssystem	Betankungssystem für Langstrecken-Rennsport, optional Schnellbefüllung

ANTRIEB/KRAFTÜBERTRAGUNG

Kraftübertragung	Heckantrieb, Traktionskontrolle (ASR), ESC
Kupplung	Zwei elektrohydraulisch betätigte Lamellenkupplungen im Ölbad
Getriebe	7-Gang-Doppelkupplungsgetriebe S tronic mit Wippenschaltung
Differenzial	Mechanisches Sperrdifferenzial
Antriebswellen	Gleichlaufgelenkwellen

FAHRWERK/LENKUNG/BREMSE

Lenkung	Elektrohydraulische Zahnstangen-Lenkung
Verstellung	Höhen- und längsverstellbare Lenksäule
Lenkrad	Multifunktional
Fahrwerk	Vorn und hinten Doppelquerlenker, 2-Wege-Gasdruckstoßdämpfer, Fahrzeughöhe, Spur, Sturz und Stabilisator einstellbar
Bremsen	Hydraulische Zweikreis-Bremsanlage, GT3-Stahl-Bremsscheiben vorn und hinten
Felgen	5-Loch-Aluminium-Guss-Felgen, vorn: 11 x 18 Zoll ET 63; hinten: 12 x 18 Zoll ET 56
Reifen	Vorn: 305/645 R18; hinten: 325/680 R18

ABMESSUNGEN/GEWICHT

Länge	4.467 mm
Breite	1.990 bzw. 2.037 mm **
Höhe	1.240 mm
Radstand	2.650 mm
Homologationsgewicht	1.460 kg

* GT4-Konfiguration, abhängig von SRO Balance of Performance (BOP).
** wie Audi R8 Coupé: ohne bzw. mit Außenspiegeln.

VEHICLE

Vehicle type	Sports car complying with GT4 regulations
Chassis	Audi Space Frame (ASF) in aluminum-CFRP-composite design with weld-in and bolted steel safety cell
Bodywork	Fiber composite materials and aluminum
Safety concept	Energy absorbing crash structures, fire extinguisher system according to FIA Standard 8865-2015, Audi Sport customer racing Protection Seat PS 3, FT3 safety fuell cell, rescue hatch

ENGINE

Type	90° V 10 engine with combined multi-point and gasoline direct injection, 4 valves per cylinder, four double overhead camshafts, emission control by upstream oxygen sensor, metal catalytic converters
Engine management	2 x Bosch MED 17 (master-slave concept)
Engine lubrication	Dry sump
Cubic capacity	5,200 cc
Power output	Variable by restrictor up to 364 kW (495 HP) *
Torque	Over 550 Nm *
Fuel tank capacity	110 l (minimum)
Refueling system	refilling system eligible for endurance racing, quick refilling as an option

DRIVETRAIN/TRANSMISSION

Type of drive	Rear-wheel drive, traction control (ASR), ESC
Clutch	Two electrohydraulically operated wet-type multi-plate clutches
Transmission	7-speed double-clutch S tronic transmission with paddle shifters
Differential	Mechanical limited-slip differential
Drive shafts	Constant-velocity joint shafts

SUSPENSION/STEERING/BRAKES

Steering	Electrohydraulic rack-and pinion steering
Controls	Height and length adjustable safety steering column
Steering wheel	multi-function
Suspension	Double wishbones front and rear, 2-way gas pressure dampers, ride height, toe, camber and stabilizers adjustable
Brakes	Hydraulic dual-circuit braking system, GT3 steel brake discs front and rear
Wheels	5-hole cast aluminum wheels, front: 11" x 18" ET 63; rear: 12" x 18" ET 56
Tires	Front: 305/645 R18; rear: 325/680 R18

WEIGHT/DIMENSIONS

Length	4,467 mm
Width	1,990 or 2,037 mm **
Height	1.240 mm
Wheelbase	2,650 mm
Homologation weight	1,460 kg

* GT4 configuration, depending on SRO Balance of Performance (BOP).

** like Audi R8 Coupé: without/with side view mirrors.

AUDI R8 LMS GT3

SPITZENSPORTLER

Der Audi R8 LMS GT3 in der zweiten Generation markiert die Spitze im Kundensportprogramm. Der bis zu 585 PS starke Hochleistungssportwagen mit seinem umfassenden Sicherheitskonzept gewinnt auf nationaler und internationaler Ebene Titel und setzte 2017 bei großen Langstreckenrennen einmal mehr die Maßstäbe.

TOP-CLASS SPORTS CAR

The second generation of the Audi R8 LMS GT3 marks the pinnacle of the lineup in the customer racing program. The high-performance sports car delivering up to 585 hp with its comprehensive safety concept has been winning titles on national and international levels and in 2017 set standards in major endurance races once again.

FAHRZEUG

Fahrzeugtyp	Sportwagen nach Reglement FIA GT3
Aufbau	Audi Space Frame (ASF) in Aluminium-CFK-Hybridbauweise mit tragendem Stahl-Überrollkäfig, Karosserieanbauteile aus CFK und Aluminium
Sicherheitskonzept	Energieabsorbierende Aluminium- und CFK-Crashstrukturen vorn und hinten. Sicherheitskonzept erfüllt FIA-LMP1-Crashanforderungen, Sicherheitssitz Audi Sport PS 3, Bergungsluke im Dach

MOTOR

Bauart	V10-Motor, 90-Grad-Zylinderwinkel, 4 Ventile pro Zylinder, DOHC, Benzin-Direkteinspritzung, Abgasreinigung durch zwei Abgas-Rennkatalysatoren
Motormanagement	Bosch Motorsport Motronic MS6.4
Motorschmierung	Trockensumpf
Hubraum	5.200 ccm
Leistung	Variabel per Restriktor bis zu 430 kW (585 PS)*
Drehmoment	Über 550 Nm

ANTRIEB/KRAFTÜBERTRAGUNG

Antriebsart	Heckantrieb, Traktionskontrolle (ASR)
Kupplung	Elektrohydraulisch betätigte 3-Scheiben-Rennkupplung (ECA)
Getriebe	Sequenzielles, pneumatisch betätigtes 6-Gang-Sportgetriebe mit Wippenschaltung
Differenzial	Sperrdifferenzial, Vorspannung einstellbar
Antriebswellen	Gleichlaufgelenkwellen

FAHRWERK/LENKUNG/BREMSE

Lenkung	Servounterstützte Zahnstangenlenkung
Fahrwerk	Vorn und hinten Einzelradaufhängung, Doppelquerlenker, Federbeine mit Schraubenfedern und einstellbaren Stoßdämpfern sowie einstellbaren Stabilisatoren vorn und hinten
Bremsen	Hydraulische Zweikreis-Bremsanlage, Stahl-Bremsscheiben vorn (380 x 34 mm) und hinten (355 x 32 mm), Renn-ABS
Felgen	Schmiedefelgen aus Aluminium, vorn 12,5 x 18 Zoll, hinten 13 x 18 Zoll
Reifen	Vorn 30-68/18, hinten 31-71/18

ABMESSUNGEN/GEWICHT

Länge	4.583 mm
Breite	1.997 mm
Höhe	1.171 mm
Mindestgewicht	1.225 kg
Tankinhalt	120 l

AUSSTATTUNG

Bedienelemente	In Höhe und Länge verstellbare Sicherheitslenksäule, schnellverstellbares, auf Rails gelagertes Fußhebelwerk
Feuerlöschsystem	Audi Sport
Sitzsystem	Audi Sport customer racing PS 3

* festgelegt durch Balance of Performance (BoP) der Serien-Veranstalter.

CAR

Vehicle type	Sports car complying with FIA GT3 regulations
Chassis	Audi Space Frame (ASF) in aluminum-CFRP hybrid construction with stressed steel roll-cage, bodywork parts from CFRP and aluminum
Safety concept	Energy absorbing aluminum and CFRP crash structures front and rear. Safety concept fulfils FIA LMP1 crash requirements, Audi Sport PS 3 safety seat, rescue hatch in the roof

ENGINE

Type	90 degree V10 engine, 4 valves per cylinder, DOHC, gasoline direct injection, emission control by two exhaust gas race catalytic converters
Engine management	Bosch Motorsport Motronic MS6.4
Engine lubrication	Dry sump
Cubic capacity	5,200 cc
Power	Variable by restrictor up to 430 kW (585 hp)*
Torque	Over 550 Nm

DRIVETRAIN/TRANSMISSION

Type of transmission	Rear wheel drive, traction control (ASR)
Clutch	Electro hydraulically operated three-plate racing clutch (ECA)
Gearbox	Sequential, pneumatically activated six-speed performance transmission with paddle shift
Differential	Limited-slip rear differential, variable preload
Driveshafts	Constant velocity sliding tripod universal joints

SUSPENSION/STEERING/BRAKES

Steering	Servo-assisted rack and pinion steering
Suspension	Front and rear independent suspension. Double wishbones, damper struts with coil springs and adjustable dampers as well as adjustable front and rear anti-roll bars
Brakes	Hydraulic dual-circuit braking system, steel brake discs front (380 x 34 mm) and rear (355 x 32 mm), race ABS
Wheels	Forged aluminum wheels, front 12.5 x 18 inches, rear 13 x 18 inches
Tires	Front 30-68/18, rear 31-71/18

DIMENSIONS/WEIGHT

Length	4,583 mm
Width	1,997 mm
Height	1,171 mm
Minimum weight	1,225 kg
Tank capacity	120 l

EQUIPMENT

Controls	Height and length-adjustable safety steering column, quick adjust rail-mounted pedal box
Fire extinguisher	Audi Sport
Seating system	Audi Sport customer racing PS 3

*established by Balance of Performance (BoP) of the series organizers.

MEDIA SHUTTLE
motorsport network
8
L. Engstler
TCR Germany
LIQUI MOLY
78
F. Danz
DEKRA
K. Poulsen
5
S. Goede
9
R. Poulsen
4
J. Söhmar
11
koppcon
STOCK
Plattn
V&F Analyse- und Messtechnik GmbH
T. Kramwinkel
82
J. Rodrigues
27
BRAGA
ultimate
PAJURANTA
71
ISOVER
Niedertscheider
83
D. Calcum
36
Hankook

GANZ SCHÖN VIEL LOS

QUITE A BIT GOING ON

Aufstellung als Suchbild: Wie viele Audi RS 3 LMS sind am Vorstart der ADAC TCR Germany erkennbar? Neun vollständig, dazu fünf im Anschnitt. Und das sind erst 14 der 16 eingeschriebenen Teilnehmer, die auf die Vier Ringe setzen. Die TCR-Klasse boomt – nicht nur in Europa

Lineup as a picture puzzle: How many Audi RS 3 LMS cars are discernible before the start of the ADAC TCR Germany? Nine in full plus five in partial view. And these are just 14 of the 16 registered entrants relying on the four rings. The TCR class is booming – not just in Europe

Geschenkt gibt's nichts: Hinter Niels Langeveld drängelt die Konkurrenz im Millimeterabstand
No such thing as a free lunch: competitors behind Niels Langeveld are tailgating with millimeter gaps

Sheldon van der Linde (Zweiter von links) war 2017 siegfähig. Ebenso Niels Langeveld (rechts daneben) – sehr zur Freude von racing-one-Teamchef Martin Kohlhaas (ganz rechts)
Sheldon van der Linde (pictured second from left) was in contention for victory in 2017. So was Niels Langeveld (pictured to his right) – much to the delight of racing-one team principal Martin Kohlhaas (pictured at far right)

Bei mehr als 40 Teilnehmern zählte jedes Hundertstel. Sheldon van der Linde vor Sandro Kaibach
With more than 40 entrants, every hundredth mattered. Sheldon van der Linde in front of Sandro Kaibach

DER GROSSE BOOM

Das internationale TCR-Konzept hält die richtige Antwort zum richtigen Zeitpunkt bereit: Eine Einstiegsklasse mit Rennwagen im Wert von rund 100.000 Euro, volle Starterfelder und packender Tourenwagensport, der für heiße Duelle steht – das wollen die Fans sehen. In vielen Ländern Europas, aber auch in anderen Regionen boomt diese Klasse, die Promoter Marcello Lotti ins Leben gerufen hat. In Deutschland hat sich das Starterfeld der ADAC TCR Germany von rund 20 Teilnehmern in der ersten Saison 2016 auf über 40 im zweiten Jahr glatt verdoppelt. Den Löwenanteil trugen 2017 erstmals die Kundenteams von Audi bei: Zum Saisonauftakt in Oschersleben bereicherten 16 Exemplare des RS 3 LMS das Feld, in Zandvoort waren sogar 18 neue Rennwagen mit den Vier Ringen dabei.

BIG BOOM

The international TCR concept has the right answer at the right time: an entry-level class with race cars worth about 100,000 euros, full fields and gripping touring car racing that stands for fierce duels – that's what the fans would like to see. In many European countries, as well as in other regions, this class which promoter Marcello Lotti has incepted is booming. In Germany, the ADAC TCR Germany's field has no less than doubled from about 20 entrants in the 2016 inaugural season to more than 40 in the second year. For the first time, the customer teams from Audi contributed the lion's share in 2017. At the Oschersleben season opener, 16 RS 3 LMS cars expanded the field and at Zandvoort even 18 new race cars with the four rings were on track.

Teamchef Bernd Hohaus setzte mit German Flavours zwei Audi für Thomas Kramwinkel und Sven Markert ein (oben). Projektleiter Alexander Hecker, Techniker Pierre Arnaud, der Technische Projektleiter Detlef Schmidt und Verkaufsmanager Garreth Greif betreuen für Audi Sport customer racing die Kunden (Mitte). Manfred Wollgarten und Timo Frings von PROsport Performance mit Rennfahrer Max Hofer (unten)
Team principal Bernd Hohaus with German Flavours fielded two Audi cars for Thomas Kramwinkel and Sven Markert (top). Project leader Alexander Hecker, engineer Pierre Arnaud, technical project leader Detlef Schmidt and sales manager Garreth Greif take care of customers (center) for Audi Sport customer racing. Manfred Wollgarten and Timo Frings from PROsport Performance with race driver Max Hofer (bottom)

KNALLHARTES GESCHÄFT

Acht verschiedene Sieger von vier Marken in 14 Rennen bei sieben Veranstaltungen – das war die Bilanz in der ADAC TCR Germany 2017. Audi war dabei die einzige Marke, bei der sich die Siege auf drei Fahrer aus drei Teams verteilten. Der Südafrikaner Sheldon van der Linde gewann am Sachsenring und erreichte als bester Audi-Pilot Tabellenrang drei. Sein Team AC 1927 Mayen e. V. im ADAC erzielte die Vizemeisterschaft in der Teamwertung. Niels Langeveld von racing one feierte in Oschersleben und in seiner niederländischen Heimat Zandvoort je einen Sieg. Der Finne Antti Buri von LMS Racing versprühte am Nürburgring den Sieger-Champagner. Und der Österreicher Simon Reicher vom Certainty Racing Team beendete die Saison auf Platz zwei der Rookie-Wertung.

TOUGH BUSINESS

Eight different winners from four brands in 14 races at seven events – that's how the ADAC TCR Germany ended in 2017. Audi was the only brand with victories going to three drivers from three teams. South African Sheldon van der Linde was vicorious at the Sachsenring and as the best Audi driver achieved position three in the standings. His team, AC 1927 Mayen e. V. im ADAC, clinched the vice-championship in the teams' classification. Niels Langeveld from racing one celebrated a victory each at Oschersleben and on home soil at Zandvoort in the Netherlands. Finn Antti Buri from LMS Racing sprayed the winner's champagne at the Nürburgring. And Austrian Simon Reicher from Certainty Racing Team finished the season in second place of the rookie classification.

Die Teamchefs Andreas und Markus Gummerer setzten mit Target Competition bis zu vier Audi RS 3 LMS ein (links). Einen davon fuhr Gosia Rdest (darunter)

Team principals Andreas and Markus Gummerer fielded up to four Audi RS 3 LMS cars with Target Competition (pictured left). One of them was driven by Gosia Rdest (pictured below)

Misha van Mil von Certainty Racing mit Nachwuchspilot Simon Reicher (rechts oben). Sein Team setzte ein zweites Auto für Dillon Koster ein (rechts)

Misha van Mil from Certainty Racing with up-and-coming driver Simon Reicher (pictured right above). His team entered a second car for Dillon Koster (pictured right)

Aust-Motorsport-Teamchef Frank Aust mit Sandro Kaibach und Robert Brezina

Aust Motorsport team principal Frank Aust with Sandro Kaibach and Robert Brezina

Der Finne Antti Buri gewann am Nürburgring mit LMS Racing (links und unten)

The Finn Antti Buri won at the Nürburgring with LMS Racing (pictured left and below)

Kevin Arnold startete in der DMV GTC
Kevin Arnold competed in the DMV GTC

Bonk Motorsport war auf der Nordschleife zu Hause
Bonk Motorsport was at home on the Nordschleife

LMS Engineering bestritt VLN-Läufe und das 24-Stunden-Rennen
LMS Engineering contested VLN rounds and the 24-hour race

Tom Lautenschlager mit spektakulärem Fahrstil in der ADAC TCR Germany
Tom Lautenschlager with spectacular driving style in the ADAC TCR Germany

Møller Bil gelang der erste Sieg des Audi RS 3 LMS in der VLN
Møller Bil achieved the first victory of the Audi RS 3 LMS in the VLN

Tom Lautenschlager aus der ADAC TCR Germany hat einen Vorfahren im Motorsport – Ur-Urgroßonkel Christian Lautenschlager war 1908 erster deutscher Grand-Prix-Sieger
Tom Lautenschlager from the ADAC TCR Germany has an ancestor in motorsport – his great-great granduncle, Christian Lautenschlager, was the first German Grand Prix winner in 1908

MEHRERE BÜHNEN IN DEUTSCHLAND

Neben der ADAC TCR Germany nutzten die Teams weitere Einsatzgebiete in Deutschland. In der VLN Langstrecken-Meisterschaft Nürburgring waren Bonk Motorsport, LMS Engineering und Møller Bil zu sehen. Møller Bil aus Norwegen feierte beim sechsten Lauf den ersten VLN-Klassensieg des Audi RS 3 LMS. Kevin Arnold startete in der DMV GTC und gewann am Jahresende die Klasse 4 der Dunlop-60-Wertung. Das Unternehmen Paravan seines Vaters Roland Arnold hat sich spezialisiert auf behindertengerechte Fahrzeugumbauten. Es nutzt den Audi RS 3 LMS künftig zur Erprobung neuartiger Lenkungssysteme ohne Lenksäule. Das Team GT3 Kasko Motorsport schließlich bestritt ein RCN-Rennen auf dem Nürburgring.

SEVERAL STAGES IN GERMANY

In addition to the ADAC TCR Germany, the teams used other fielding opportunities in Germany. In the VLN Endurance Championship Nürburgring, Bonk Motorsport, LMS Engineering and Møller Bil were seen on track. Møller Bil from Norway in round six celebrated the first VLN class victory of the Audi RS 3 LMS. Kevin Arnold competed in the DMV GTC and at the end of the year won Class 4 of the Dunlop 60 classification. Paravan, his father Roland Arnold's company, specializes in vehicle conversions for people with disabilities. In the future, it will use the Audi RS 3 LMS to test innovative steering systems without steering columns. Finally, Team GT3 Kasko Motorsport contested an RCN race at the Nürburgring.

Nico Kankkunen erhielt bei LMS Racing Tipps von Vater Juha, dem viermaligen Rallye-Weltmeister
Nico Kankkunen at LMS Racing received advice from his father, Juha, the four-time rally world champion

Tobias Brink vertraute in Schweden auf den Audi RS 3 LMS
Tobias Brink relied on the Audi RS 3 LMS in Sweden

Joonas Lappalainen stieg als Sieger des Audi Sport TT Cup in die TCR Scandinavia auf
Joonas Lappalainen as the winner of the Audi Sport TT Cup was promoted to the TCR Scandinavia

Mikaela Åhlin-Kottulinsky fuhr in Schweden den Audi RS 3 LMS und in Deutschland den R8 LMS
Mikaela Åhlin-Kottulinsky drove the Audi RS 3 LMS in Sweden and the R8 LMS in Germany

TCR IN NORD UND SÜD

In den nordischen Ländern war die TCR Scandinavia die erste Adresse für rund 20 Tourenwagen-Piloten. Die meist kurzen und engen Strecken waren für den Audi RS 3 LMS kein Vorteil. Erfolgreichster der fünf Audi-Privatiers war der Schwede Tobias Brink mit je einem dritten Platz zu Beginn in Knutstorp und beim Finale in Mantorp. Sein Landsmann Reuben Kressner steuerte in Falkenberg einen dritten Platz bei, der Finne Joonas Lappalainen bestieg in Anderstorp die dritte Stufe auf dem Podest. Brink Motorsport erreichte Platz drei in der Teamwertung. Giacomo Altoè errang beim Finale in Monza den ersten Sieg für Audi in der TCR Italy. Max Mugelli von Pit Lane Competizioni war als Vierter bester Audi-Pilot in der Tabelle vor dem Bulgaren Plamen Kralev in einem Audi von Kraf Racing.

Joonas Lappalainen im finnischen Alastaro vor Antti Buri, Tobias Brink und Nico Kankkunen
Joonas Lappalainen at Alastaro, Finland, trailed by Antti Buri, Tobias Brink and Nico Kankkunen

Max Mugelli war ein regulärer Teilnehmer in der TCR Italy (rechtes Bild und gelbes Auto im linken Bild). Simon Reicher (weiß-blaues Auto) gab ein Gastspiel, Enrico Bettera (rot-silber) startete sporadisch

Max Mugelli was a regular entrant in the TCR Italy (pictured right and yellow car pictured left). Simon Reicher (white-blue car) drove as a guest and Enrico Bettera (red-silver) raced sporadically

TCR IN THE NORTH AND SOUTH

In the Nordic countries, the TCR Scandinavia was the number one series for some 20 touring car campaigners. The typically short and narrow tracks did not provide the Audi RS 3 LMS with any advantage. The most successful of the five Audi privateers was the Swede Tobias Brink having clinched a third place at the beginning at Knutstorp and in the finale at Mantorp. His compatriot Reuben Kressner contributed a third place at Falkenberg, the Finn Joonas Lappalainen mounted the third step of the podium at Anderstorp. Brink Motorsport achieved third place in the teams' classification. Giacomo Altoè in the finale at Monza clinched first place for Audi in the TCR Italy. Max Mugelli from Pit Lane Competizioni in position four was the best Audi driver in the standings, trailed by the Bulgarian Plamen Kralev in an Audi from Kraf Racing.

Giacomo Altoè errang den ersten Sieg des Audi RS 3 LMS in der TCR Italy (links und unten)

Giacomo Altoè clinched the first victory of the Audi RS 3 LMS in the TCR Italy (left and below)

DIVERSE RENNFORMATE

Die TCR Benelux mit sechs Veranstaltungen in Belgien und den Niederlanden entschied sich für ein ungewöhnliches Rennformat: In einem einstündigen Rennen mit Fahrerwechsel teilten sich zwei Fahrer ein Auto. Anschließend folgten vier 20-minütige Sprints, von denen jeder Fahrer zwei bestritt. Der Niederländer Mika Morien erreichte als bester Audi-Pilot Gesamtrang sieben und Platz vier der Junior-Wertung, sein Team Bas Koeten Racing fuhr auf Rang drei vor sechs weiteren Mannschaften in der Teamwertung. In der TCR Ibérico mit bis zur vier Läufen pro Wochenende errangen die Portugiesen Rafael Lobato/Patrick Cunha den Vizetitel, in der TCR Portugal erreichten sie Platz drei im Audi RS 3 LMS vom Team Sporting Clube de Braga. In der FIA ETCC gelang dem Bulgaren Plamen Kralev beim Finale in Most ein Sieg.

DIVERSE RACE FORMATS

The TCR Benelux with six events in Belgium and the Netherlands opted for an unusual race format in which two drivers shared a car in a one-hour race with driver change. This was followed by four 20-minute sprints, two of which were contested by each driver. The Dutchman Mika Morien as the best Audi driver achieved position seven overall and fourth place in the Junior classification. His team, Team Bas Koeten Racing, came third, trailed by six other squads in the teams' classification. In the TCR Ibérico with up to four races per weekend, the Portuguese Rafael Lobato/Patrick Cunha claimed the runner-up title and in the TCR Portugal, they achieved position three in the Audi RS 3 LMS from Team Sporting Clube de Braga. In the FIA ETCC, the Bulgarian Plamen Kralev managed taking a victory in the finale at Most.

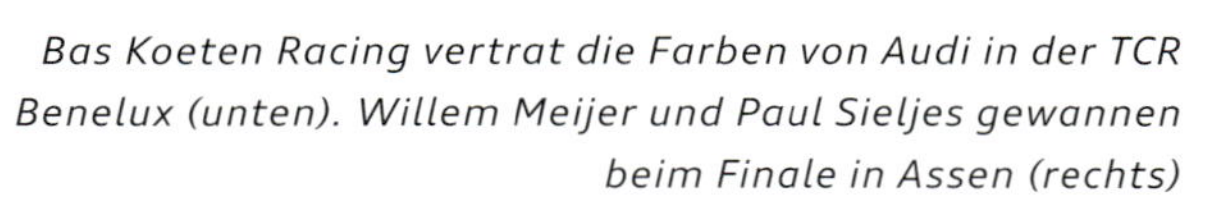

Bas Koeten Racing vertrat die Farben von Audi in der TCR Benelux (unten). Willem Meijer und Paul Sieljes gewannen beim Finale in Assen (rechts)

Bas Koeten Racing represented Audi's colors in the TCR Benelux (bottom). Willem Meijer and Paul Sieljes won in the finale at Assen (right)

Rafael Lobato (oben Mitte) und Patrick Cunha erzielten den Vizemeistertitel in der TCR Ibérico (darunter)
Rafael Lobato (top, center) and Patrick Cunha achieved the vice-championship title in the TCR Ibérico (pictured below)

Stefano Comini gewann mit Comtoyou Racing beim Auftakt der TCR Benelux in Spa zwei Rennen, Teamkollege Sheldon van der Linde ein weiteres
Stefano Comini with Comtoyou Racing won two races in the TCR Benelux season opener at Spa and his teammate, Sheldon van der Linde, another one

Plamen Kralev gewann beim Finale der FIA ETCC in Most
Plamen Kralev won in the finale of the FIA ETCC at Most

Mario Altoè vom Adria International Raceway übernahm insgesamt zehn Audi RS 3 LMS von Chris Reinke, Leiter Audi Sport customer racing
Mario Altoè from Adria International Raceway took over a total of ten Audi RS 3 LMS from Chris Reinke, Head of Audi Sport customer racing

Bereits im Juli 2017 war das 100. Exemplar des Audi RS 3 LMS aufgebaut
The 100th Audi RS 3 LMS car was assembled as early as in July 2017

INTERNATIONALE HIGHLIGHTS

Verschiedene Teams betätigten sich auch in internationalen Serien. Comtoyou Racing verpflichtete Vorjahresmeister Stefano Comini und den Belgier Frédéric Vervisch für die TCR International Series. Nach drei Siegen und fünf dritten Plätzen erreichte der Tessiner Tabellenplatz drei. In der 24H Touring Car Endurance Series errang Pit Lane Competizioni beim Auftakt einen Pokal. Alberto Vescovi/Roberto Ferri/Zach Arnold/Enrico Bettera/John Filippi erreichten bei den 24 Stunden von Silverstone den zweiten Platz. Einen weiteren europäischen Langstreckenerfolg fuhr Bonk Motorsport ein. Hermann Bock und Max Partl entschieden die TCR-Kategorie der 12 Stunden von Mugello für sich. Weltweit war die Nachfrage so groß, dass Audi Sport customer racing bereits im Juli den 100. Audi RS 3 LMS baute. Allein zehn Exemplare gingen an den Adria International Raceway, der damit die TCR Academy und die ab 2018 ausgetragene TCR Academy Endurance Series bestückte.

Pit Lane Competizioni in der 24H Touring Car Endurance Series in Silverstone
Pit Lane Competizioni in the 24-Hour Touring Car Endurance Series at Silverstone

Alberto Vescovi mit Pit Lane Competizioni in Silverstone
Alberto Vescovi with Pit Lane Competizioni at Silverstone

Bonk Motorsport gewann seine Klasse bei den 12 Stunden von Mugello
Bonk Motorsport won its class in the Mugello 12 Hours

INTERNATIONAL HIGHLIGHTS

Various teams were active in international series as well. Comtoyou Racing signed last year's champion Stefano Comini and the Belgian Frédéric Vervisch for the TCR International Series. Following three victories and five third places, the Swiss from Ticino achieved third place in the standings. In the 24-Hour Touring Car Endurance Series, Pit Lane Competizioni won a trophy at the opening event. Alberto Vescovi/Roberto Ferri/Zach Arnold/Enrico Bettera/John Filippi achieved second place in the Silverstone 24 Hours. Another European endurance racing success was clinched by Bonk Motorsport. Hermann Bock and Max Partl decided the TCR category of the Mugello 12 Hours in their favor. Global demand was so high that Audi Sport customer racing built the 100th Audi RS 3 LMS as early as in July. As many as ten of the cars went to Adria International Raceway that provided them to the TCR Academy and the TCR Academy Endurance Series to be held starting in 2018.

In der TCR International Series betätigte sich das Team Comtoyou Racing von Jean-Michel Baert aus Belgien (rechts). Fahrer waren Frédéric Vervisch (im Bild links stehend) und Stefano Comini (sitzend)
In the TCR International Series, Team Comtoyou Racing of Jean-Michel Baert from Belgium (right) was active. The drivers were Frédéric Vervisch (left, standing) and Stefano Comini (sitting)

ORIENT-EXPRESS

ORIENT EXPRESS

In verschiedenen Regionen von Osteuropa bis nach Asien war der Audi RS 3 LMS auf Anhieb ein Erfolgsgarant

In various regions from Eastern Europe to Asia, the Audi RS 3 LMS was an immediate guarantee for success

AKHMAT RACE 2017
176
TAIF-NK
SMP RACING
YOKOHAMA
ЛЕНТА

Dmitry Bragin verteidigte als Vorjahresmeister seine Startnummer 1 im Audi RS 3 LMS erfolgreich

Dmitry Bragin as the previous year's champion successfully defended the number 1 on his Audi RS 3 LMS car

Dmitry Bragin (Mitte) gewann die TCR Russia 2017 und nach dem Finale mit Irek Minnakhmetov auch das Akhmat Race (vorherige Doppelseite)

Dmitry Bragin (middle) won the 2017 TCR Russia and, following the finale, the Akhmat Race with Irek Minnakhmetov as well (pictured in preceding spread)

NEUES TERRAIN

Russland war bislang ein weißer Fleck auf der Landkarte von Audi Sport customer racing. Das änderte sich in der Saison 2017 grundlegend. Vorjahresmeister Dmitry Bragin, Irek Minnakhmetov, Marat Sharapov und Timur Shigaboutdinov traten mit vier Audi RS 3 LMS in der TCR Russia an. Zwar wechselte Bragin zwischenzeitlich für drei Veranstaltungen auf einen Seat, doch 144 seiner 241 Punkte erzielte der Russe mit Audi. Vier Siege feierte er mit dem RS 3 LMS von Taif Motorsport und gewann den Titel beim Finale auf dem Kazanring im Audi. Bereits im Januar hatte der Audi RS 3 LMS seinen ersten Langstreckensieg erreicht: James Kaye/Julian Griffin/Erik Holstein/Finlay Hutchison gewannen die TCR-Klasse bei den 24 Stunden von Dubai.

NEW GROUND

Russia had so far been a blank spot on Audi Sport customer racing's map. That fundamentally changed in the 2017 season. The previous year's champion, Dmitry Bragin, Irek Minnakhmetov, Marat Sharapov and Timur Shigaboutdinov competed in the TCR Russia with four Audi RS 3 LMS. Although Bragin switched to a Seat for three events, the Russian scored 144 of his 241 points with Audi. Four victories he celebrated in the RS 3 LMS of Taif Motorsport and won the title in the finale at the Kazanring in an Audi. The Audi RS 3 LMS had achieved its first endurance racing victory as early as in January: James Kaye/Julian Griffin/Erik Holstein/Finlay Hutchison won the TCR class in the Dubai 24 Hours.

Irek Minnakhmetov war zweitbester Audi-Pilot in Russland

Irek Minnakhmetov was the second-best Audi campaigner in Russia

Cadspeed Racing with Atech setzte den Audi RS 3 LMS bei den 24 Stunden von Dubai ein
Cadspeed Racing with Atech fielded the Audi RS 3 LMS in the Dubai 24 Hours

James Kaye gewann mit seinen Teamkollegen in Dubai
James Kaye won with his teammates in Dubai

In der japanischen Super Taikyu Series waren zwei Audi RS 3 LMS am Start
In the Japanese Super Taikyu Series, two Audi RS 3 LMS were on the grid

Jasper Thong mit der Nummer 5, Sieger der TCR Asia in Zhuhai, und Tong Siu Kau mit der Nummer 8 im Hintergrund vertraten die Farben von Audi Hong Kong
Jasper Thong in car number 5, winner of the TCR Asia at Zhuhai, and Tong Siu Kau in car number 8 in the background represented the colors of Audi Hong Kong

AUF TITELKURS IN ASIEN

Ganz unterschiedlich verlief die Saison für die Audi-Kundenteams in Japan, China und in der TCR Asia. Das BRP Audi Mie Team erreichte Klassenplatz drei in der japanischen Super Taikyu Series vor dem Audi Team DreamDrive. In der TCR Asia erreichte Jasper Thong Gesamtrang sechs und Position zwei in der Cup-Klasse. In der TCR China dominierte das New Faster Team. Nach vier von fünf Veranstaltungen hatte Andy Yan bis zum Redaktionsschluss sechs Siege im Audi RS 3 LMS gefeiert. Er führte die Tabelle mit 51 Punkten Vorsprung vor Teamkollege Huang Chu Han an, der seinerseits vier Mal ganz oben auf dem Podest stand. Deng Bao Wei vom Team Leo 109 Racing gelang als Zweitem in Ningbo ebenfalls ein Podiumsplatz. Die Entscheidung fällt beim Finale der Serie am 31. Dezember in Guangdong.

Andy Yan (Zweiter von rechts) und Huang Chu Han (rechts) waren führend in China
Andy Yan (second from right) and Huang Chu Han (right) were leading in China

Das New Faster Team gab in China mit dem Audi RS 3 LMS den Ton an
New Faster Team called the shots in China in the Audi RS 3 LMS

Huang Chu Han stand in der TCR Asia in Zhuhai auf dem Podium (oben). Martin Kühl, Leiter Audi Sport customer racing Asia, im Gespräch mit Jasper und Shaun Thong (unten)

Huang Chu Han was on podium in TCR Asia at Zhuhai (top). Martin Kühl, Head of Audi Sport customer racing Asia, in conversation with Jasper and Shaun Thong (bottom)

ON COURSE FOR THE TITLE IN ASIA

The Audi customer teams in Japan, China and in the TCR Asia experienced the season in completely different ways. BRP Audi Mie Team achieved third place in class in the Japanese Super Taikyu Series trailed by Audi Team DreamDrive. In the TCR Asia, Jasper Thong took position six overall and two in the Cup class. In the TCR China, the New Faster Team was dominant. After four of five events, Andy Yan had celebrated six victories in the Audi RS 3 LMS before the editorial deadline. He was leading the standings with a 51-point advantage over his teammate, Huang Chu Han, who had mounted the top of the podium himself four times. Deng Bao Wei from Team Leo 109 Racing on coming second at Ningbo achieved a podium finish as well. The decision will be made in the series' finale at Guangdong on December 31.

Deng Bao Wei erzielte mit dem Team Leo 109 Racing in der TCR China einen Podiumsplatz

Deng Bao Wei with Team Leo 109 Racing achieved a podium place in the TCR China

Audi Sport
uine Parts
freem
PIRELLI
WC
World Challenge
PFAFF

PAUL POSITION

PAUL POSITION

Paul Holton kam, sah und siegte. Genau genommen kehrte er mit wertvollen Erfahrungen aus einer Saison im Audi Sport TT Cup in die USA zurück. Damit stand er beim Know-how in Sachen Frontantrieb auf der Pole-Position. In der Debütsaison des Audi RS 3 LMS gewann der Junior den Titel in der TC-Klasse der Pirelli World Challenge

Paul Holton came, saw and conquered. In fact, he returned to the United States with valuable experience gained from a season in the Audi Sport TT Cup that put him on pole position in terms of front-wheel drive know-how. In the debut season of the Audi RS 3 LMS, the junior won the title in the TC class of the Pirelli World Challenge

TITEL IM DEBÜTJAHR

Paul Holton aus Orlando in Florida begann die Saison in der TC-Klasse der Pirelli World Challenge mit einem Sieg und einem zweiten Platz in Virginia. Auf seiner Lieblingsstrecke in Mosport folgte der nächste Triumph, in Lime Rock ergaben sich zwei zweite Plätze. Wegen des Ballastgewichts nach den Erfolgen war der Audi in Utah und Austin chancenlos. Beim Finale in Laguna Seca aber schlug Holton zurück: Zweimal Startplatz eins, zwei schnellste Rennrunden, zwei Siege, Titelgewinn mit 27 Punkten Vorsprung. Jason Coupal von Berg Racing erzielte als Zweiter in Mosport ein weiteres Podestergebnis für Audi. Anthony Geraci im RS 3 LMS von S.A.C. Racing verbuchte Platz vier als bestes Saisonresultat.

TITLE IN THE DEBUT YEAR

Paul Holton from Orlando, Florida, began the season in the TC class of the Pirelli World Challenge with a victory and a second place in Virginia. The next triumph followed on his favorite track, at Motorsport, and two second places were the results at Lime Rock. Due to the ballast weight following these successes, the Audi was chanceless in Utah and Austin. In the finale at Laguna Seca, however, Holton fought back: two pole positions, two fastest race laps, two victories and the title win with a 27-point advantage. Jason Coupal from Berg Racing as the runner-up at Mosport clinched another podium result for Audi. Anthony Geraci in an RS 3 LMS from S.A.C. Racing recorded fourth place as his best result of the season.

Jason Coupal im Audi Nummer 9 von Berg Racing, mit der Nummer 30 Travis Washay von Indian Summer Racing und mit der Nummer 69 Anthony Geraci von S.A.C. Racing
Jason Coupal in the number 9 Audi from Berg Racing, Travis Washay from Indian Summer Racing in number 30 and Anthony Geraci from S.A.C. Racing in number 69

Drei Tage nach seinem 21. Geburtstag gewann Paul Holton den Titel

Three days after his 21st birthday, Paul Holton won the title

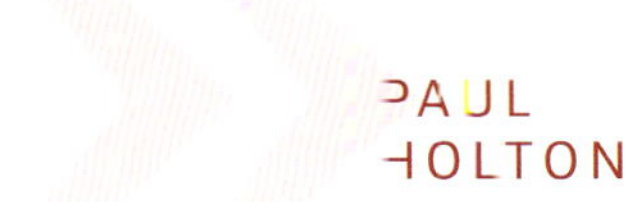

PAUL
HOLTON

Uns ist ein toller Start gelungen, denn schon beim Auftaktwochenende haben wir den ersten Sieg eingefahren. Nach den nächsten Erfolgen mussten wir viel Gewicht einladen und waren chancenlos, doch die beiden Siege beim Finale und der Titel waren perfekt. Das Reglement hat den Audi RS 3 LMS deutlich eingebremst, da unsere Gegner noch keine TCR-Rennwagen besitzen. Viele Fans und Rennfahrer freuen sich aber schon darauf, dass diese echten Tourenwagen bald in größeren Stückzahlen nach Amerika kommen.

We managed a fantastic start because we clinched our first victory right on the opening weekend. Following the next successes, we had to take a lot of weight on board and were chanceless, but the two victories in the finale and the title were perfect. The regulations clearly restrained the Audi RS 3 LMS because our opponents do not own any TCR race cars yet. However, many fans and race drivers are already looking forward to these true touring cars coming to America soon in larger volumes.

Paul Holton feierte mit Audi Sport customer racing USA und dem Team C360R seinen Titel in Kalifornien (unten). Travis Washay im Audi RS 3 LMS (darunter)

Paul Holton celebrated his title in California with Audi Sport customer racing USA and Team C360R (below). Travis Washay in the Audi RS 3 LMS (bottom)

DEUTSCHE BOTSCHAFTER

GERMAN AMBASSADORS

Audi prägte die einzige weltweit ausgetragene GT-Rennserie deutlich. Die Marke aus Deutschland verteidigte ihren Vorjahrestitel erfolgreich, während Markus Winkelhock mit zwei Gesamtsiegen zum ersten Mal die Fahrerwertung gewann. Die lange Reise um die Welt führte die Piloten von Australien über Europa nach Amerika

Audi clearly shaped the only worldwide GT racing series. The German brand successfully defended its title from the previous year while Markus Winkelhock on clinching two overall victories won the drivers' classification for the first time. The long journey around the world took the campaigners from Australia via Europe to America

Audi Sport
AUDI R8 SPYDER.
ARRIVING SOON.
THE AUDI
CUTTING.
Audi Sport
Audi Sport
Audi Sport
SUPABARN
FARMER'S MARKET
LIVE WELL for LESS
KFC
AUDI R8 SPYDER.
ARRIVING SOON.

PRIVATSACHE PRIVATE AFFAIR

Die Intercontinental GT Challenge begann im Februar in Australien. Statt der erhofften Ausbeute für die Audi-Sport-Piloten aber freuten sich die Privatiers am Mount Panorama über zwei Podiumsplätze in ihrer Klasse

The Intercontinental GT Challenge began in Australia in February. Instead of the expected results for the Audi Sport drivers, the privateers celebrated two podium places in their classes at Mount Panorama

GROSSE ERWARTUNGEN

Sieben Audi bei den 12 Stunden von Bathurst, darunter die beiden Rennwagen von Jamec Pem Racing mit professionellen Fahrerbesetzungen, weckten Hoffnungen. In einem von vielen Unfällen geprägten Rennen musste die große Audi-Fangemeinde in Australien aber bereits in Runde sieben den ersten Rückschlag hinnehmen: Frank Stippler zahlte als Neuling Lehrgeld und verunfallte noch im Morgengrauen auf dem Berg. Sein Auto war nicht mehr reparabel. In der vierten Rennstunde fiel Christopher Mies im Schwesterauto der Attacke eines Konkurrenten zum Opfer. Nach dem zeitraubenden Wechsel von Fahrwerksteilen und einer Aufholjagd erreichte er mit Christopher Haase und dem australischen Tourenwagen-Ass Garth Tander das Ziel auf Platz 13.

GREAT EXPECTATIONS

Seven Audi cars in the Bathurst 12 Hour, including the two race cars of Jamec Pem Racing with professional driver lineups, inspired hopes. However, in a race marked by many accidents, the large Audi fan community in Australia had to accept the first setback as early as on lap seven. As a rookie, Frank Stippler learned the hard way and had an accident on the mountain at the break of dawn. His car was not repairable. Four hours into the race, Christopher Mies in the sister car fell victim to an attack by a rival. Following a time-consuming change of suspension components and a comeback drive, he came 13th together with Christopher Haase and Australian touring car ace Garth Tander.

Markus Winkelhock und Robin Frijns kamen nach dem Unfall ihres Teamkollegen Frank Stippler gar nicht zum Fahren

Markus Winkelhock and Robin Frijns did not get to drive at all after the accident of their teammate Frank Stippler

Jamec Pem Racing brachte zwei Audi R8 LMS zum Mount Panorama
Jamec Pem Racing brought two Audi R8 LMS cars to Mount Panorama

Sieben Audi waren 2017 in Bathurst am Start
Seven Audi cars were on the grid at Bathurst in 2017

Freude beim Wiedersehen: Markus Winkelhock nahm sich die Zeit für seinen langjährigen, treuen australischen Fan Callum Burgess
Happy reunion: Markus Winkelhock took time to chat with his longstanding, loyal Australian fan Callum Burgess

Der Audi R8 LMS Nummer 5 führte zur Halbzeit die Am-Wertung an
The number 5 Audi R8 LMS was leading the Am classification at the race's midpoint

STARKE AMATEURE

Für Aufsehen sorgte der Audi R8 LMS mit der Nummer 5 bereits im Qualifying. Nathan Antunes gelang mit dem Team GT Motorsport als einzigem Audi-Fahrer der Einzug in das Zeitfahren der zehn Besten – als Amateur. Für die Startaufstellung sicherte er sich Platz drei in der Am-Klasse. Im Rennen arbeiteten sich Antunes, Elliot Barbour und Greg Taylor bis zur Rennmitte an die Spitze ihrer Wertung vor. Das Team lag auf Gesamtrang fünf, als nach einem Ausritt Folgeschäden auftraten. So musste Greg Taylor mit seinen Mitstreitern die Hoffnungen begraben, seinen Klassensieg aus dem Vorjahr wiederholen zu können.

STRONG AMATEURS

The number 5 Audi R8 LMS attracted attention as early as in qualifying. Nathan Antunes with Team GT Motorsport was the only Audi driver to make it into the top ten qualifying – as an amateur. For the starting grid, he secured position three in the Am class. In the race, Antunes, Elliot Barbour and Greg Taylor advanced to the top spot in their classification halfway through the race. The team was running in fifth overall when an off-track excursion led to subsequent damage. As a result, Greg Taylor and his teammates had to bury their hopes of repeating his class victory from the year before.

Privatier Nathan Antunes, links neben Elliot Barbour und Greg Taylor, kam als einziger Audi-Pilot ins Shoot-out-Qualifying

Privateer Nathan Antunes, pictured left alongside Elliot Barbour and Greg Taylor, was the only Audi driver to make it into the qualifying shootout

Ash Samadi, Marc Cini und Dean Fiore schafften es aufs Podium
Ash Samadi, Marc Cini and Dean Fiore finished on podium

POKALE FÜR DIE PRIVATIERS

Zwei weitere Kunden des Melbourne Performance Centre retteten die Ehre der Audi-Piloten. Die beiden Neuseeländer Daniel Gaunt und Matt Halliday fuhren mit dem Australier Ash Samadi auf Platz zwei der Pro-Am-Wertung für gemischte Fahreraufgebote. Den dritten Platz in dieser Wertung sicherte sich der langjährige Audi-Kunde Marc Cini zusammen mit seinen australischen Landsleuten Dean Fiore und Lee Holdsworth. Der Neuseeländer Simon Evans schließlich kam mit den Australiern James und Theo Koundouris sowie Marcus Marshall in einem weiteren Audi R8 LMS für das Team Supabarn als Elfter ins Ziel.

TROPHIES FOR THE PRIVATEERS

Two other customers of the Melbourne Performance Centre proved to be the saving grace for the Audi driver squad. The two New Zealanders Daniel Gaunt and Matt Halliday together with Australian Ash Samadi took second place in the Pro-Am classification for mixed driver lineups. Third place in this classification was secured by longstanding Audi customer Marc Cini together with his Australian compatriots Dean Fiore and Lee Holdsworth. Finally, New Zealander Simon Evans together with Australians James and Theo Koundouris and Marcus Marshall in another Audi R8 LMS finished eleventh for Team Supabarn.

Dean Fiore, Lee Holdsworth und Marc Cini auf Platz drei (auf dem Podium links), Matt Halliday, Daniel Gaunt und Ash Samadi auf Platz zwei in der Pro-Am-Klasse (rechts)

Dean Fiore, Lee Holdsworth and Marc Cini in position three (pictured left on podium), Matt Halliday, Daniel Gaunt and Ash Samadi in second place of the Pro Am class (right)

Das Team Hallmarc fuhr auf Platz drei in der Pro-Am-Wertung

Team Hallmarc came third in the Pro-Am classification

SAINTÉLOC AROUND THE CLOCK

Der zweite Lauf zur Intercontinental GT Challenge brachte den Durchbruch für die Audi-Sport-Piloten. Die späteren Sieger der 24 Stunden von Spa sind von Platz 19 gestartet. Sie lagen nachts mehr als eine Runde zurück. Sie galten als die Underdogs. Und doch haben Jules Gounon, Christopher Haase und Markus Winkelhock mit dem Audi Sport Team Saintéloc in Belgien gewonnen. Sie wussten früh, worum es bei diesem Rennen ging

Round two of the Intercontinental GT Challenge marked the breakthrough for the Audi Sport campaigners. The subsequent winners of the Spa 24 Hours started from position 19. At night, they had a deficit of more than one lap. They were regarded as the underdogs. But in spite of this, Jules Gounon, Christopher Haase and Markus Winkelhock won in Belgium with Audi Sport Team Saintéloc. They knew early on what this race was all about

SEBASTIEN CHETAIL

Was für ein fantastisches Ergebnis! Seit vielen Jahren schon setzen wir den Audi R8 LMS als Privatteam ein. In diesem Jahr hat Audi Sport customer racing uns unterstützt und uns ein Auto anvertraut. Das gesamte GT-Team unter Leitung von Fred Thalamy, alle Mechaniker und unsere Renningenieure Nicolas Drouelle und Nicolas Chomat haben ihr Bestes gegeben. Taktisch klug, intelligent und schnell haben auch die Fahrer agiert. So haben wir den ersten 24-Stunden-Sieg in unserer Teamgeschichte erreicht.

What a fantastic result! We've been fielding the Audi R8 LMS as a privateer team for many years. This year, Audi Sport customer racing supported us and entrusted us with a car. The entire GT team headed by Fred Thalamy, all the mechanics and our race engineers, Nicolas Drouelle and Nicolas Chomat, gave their best. Tactically clever, intelligent and fast is how the drivers acted as well. That's how we achieved the first 24-hour victory in our team's history.

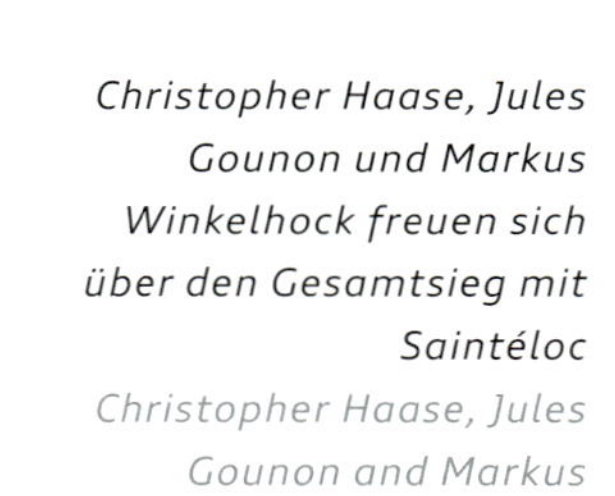

Christopher Haase, Jules Gounon und Markus Winkelhock freuen sich über den Gesamtsieg mit Saintéloc

Christopher Haase, Jules Gounon and Markus Winkelhock celebrate overall victory with Saintéloc

Zehn Audi R8 LMS umfasste das Aufgebot. Hintere Reihe: I.S.R. Racing und Saintéloc Racing. Mittlere Reihe: Belgian Audi Club Team WRT, Audi Sport Team WRT und Team WRT. Vordere Reihe: Audi Sport Team WRT, Audi Sport Team Saintéloc, Audi Sport Team I.S.R.

The lineup encompassed ten Audi R8 LMS cars. Back row: I.S.R. Racing and Saintéloc Racing. Middle row: Belgian Audi Club Team WRT, Audi Sport Team WRT and Team WRT. Front row: Audi Sport Team WRT, Audi Sport Team Saintéloc, Audi Sport Team I.S.R.

VORSICHTIG SCHNELL

Als Markus Winkelhock am Rennsonntag auf das Siegerpodest stieg, durfte er stolz sein: Schon zum zweiten Mal hat er mit Audi die 24 Stunden von Spa gewonnen, hinzu kommen drei 24-Stunden-Pokale vom Nürburgring – macht fünf Langstreckensiege mit dem Audi R8 LMS. Seine beiden Teamkollegen Christopher Haase und Jules Gounon gewannen zum ersten Mal in Spa. Für den 22 Jahre alten Franzosen war es sogar der erste 24-Stunden-Sieg überhaupt. Und er machte dem 37 Jahre alten Routinier Winkelhock ein Kompliment: „Markus hat uns alle vor dem Start darauf eingeschworen, keine Strafen zu kassieren. Das war goldrichtig.“ Hintergrund: Die Rennleitung hatte angekündigt, das Überfahren der Streckenbegrenzungen streng zu ahnden. Tatsächlich tappten viele Teams in diese Falle, während die Startnummer 25 des siegreichen Trios ohne Strafe und sogar nur mit einer einzigen Verwarnung durchkam. Für das Audi Sport Team Saintéloc von Gründer Sébastien Chetail und Manager Fred Thalamy war es der erste 24-Stunden-Rennsieg der Teamgeschichte.

CAUTIOUSLY QUICK

When Markus Winkelhock mounted the podium on Sunday of the race, he had every reason to be proud. For the second time, he won the Spa 24 Hours with Audi, in addition to having clinched three 24-hour trophies at the Nürburgring – resulting in a total of five endurance racing victories in the Audi R8 LMS. His two teammates, Christopher Haase and Jules Gounon, were victorious at Spa for the first time. For the 22-year-old Frenchman, this was even his first ever 24-hour victory. And he paid the 37-year-old seasoned campaigner a compliment: “Before the start, Markus cautioned us not to risk any penalties. That was exactly right.” The reason behind this was that the race directors had announced that they would impose severe penalties for driving over the track barriers. As it was, many teams fell into this trap whereas car number 25 of the victorious trio finished without any penalties and with just one caution. For Audi Sport Team Saintéloc of founder Sébastien Chetail and manager Fred Thalamy, this marked their first 24-hour race victory in the team’s history.

Das Audi Sport Team I.S.R. musste verschiedene Rückschläge ertragen
Audi Sport Team I.S.R. suffered several setbacks

Die Nummer 1 teilten sich Antonio García, Nico Müller und René Rast
Car number 1 was shared by Antonio García, Nico Müller and René Rast

André Lotterer, Dries Vanthoor und Marcel Fässler waren schnell, aber glücklos
André Lotterer, Dries Vanthoor and Marcel Fässler were fast but without fortune

VIELE STARKE FAHRERTEAMS

Seit Jahren schon ist Spa der größte GT3-Wettbewerb der Welt. 63 Teilnehmer waren diesmal am Start des Rennens zwei Mal rund um die Uhr und setzten auf elf Marken. Audi vertraute 2017 auf eine neue Aufstellung. Neben dem bewährten Audi Sport Team WRT waren erstmals das Team I.S.R. von Igor Salaquarda aus Prag sowie Saintéloc Racing aus St. Etienne in Frankreich werksunterstützt. Darüber hinaus brachte jedes der drei Teams auch private Audi R8 LMS an den Start. Connor De Phillippi/Christopher Mies/Frédéric Vervisch sowie Antonio García/Nico Müller/René Rast waren die Fahrer der unterstützten Autos bei WRT und Pierre Kaffer/Frank Stippler/Kelvin van der Linde bei I.S.R. Zu den privaten Besetzungen zählten unter anderem die beiden Le-Mans-Sieger Marcel Fässler und André Lotterer, die zusammen mit Dries Vanthoor bei WRT ins Lenkrad griffen.

MANY STRONG DRIVER TEAMS

Spa has been the world's major GT3 competition for years. This time, 63 entrants relying on eleven marques were on the grid of the race twice around the clock. Audi, in 2017, was represented with a new lineup. In addition to the seasoned Audi Sport Team WRT, Team I.S.R. of Igor Salaquarda from Prague and Saintéloc Racing from St. Etienne in France were factory-backed for the first time. In addition, each of the three teams put private Audi R8 LMS cars on the grid. Connor De Phillippi/Christopher Mies/Frédéric Vervisch and Antonio García/Nico Müller/René Rast were the drivers of the factory-backed cars at WRT and Pierre Kaffer/Frank Stippler/Kelvin van der Linde at I.S.R. The privateer squads, among others, included the two Le Mans winners Marcel Fässler and André Lotterer who took the wheel together with Dries Vanthoor at WRT.

Connor De Phillippi, Christopher Mies und Frédéric Vervisch waren die zweitbeste Audi-Mannschaft im Ziel
Connor De Phillippi, Christopher Mies and Frédéric Vervisch were the second-best Audi squad to see the checkered flag

RÜCKSCHLÄGE UND CHANCEN

Schon früh verkleinerte sich der Favoritenkreis: Ein Schaden an einem Bremsbelag warf Dries Vanthoor und seine Kollegen auf Platz 45 zurück. Doch aufgeben zählt nicht: Das Trio kämpfte sich bis ins Ziel wieder auf Platz elf vor. Am Abend war die Nummer 2 mit Mies/De Phillippi/Vervisch vorn. Doch dann ergab sich ein Zeitverlust bei einem Boxenstopp, anschließend lag das Auto während einer Safety-Car-Phase in einer unglücklichen Position. So kam am Ende nur Platz fünf heraus. Dahinter reihten sich die Teamkollegen García/Müller/Rast ein. Auch sie hatten das Feld phasenweise angeführt, aber Fehler auf der Strecke bewirkten zwei Sportstrafen. Für Jules Gounon, Christopher Haase und Markus Winkelhock indessen war das Rennen eine riesige Chance. Von Platz 19 gestartet, arbeiteten sie sich langsam vor. Nach einem fünfminütigen Pflichtboxenstopp sowie einem zusätzlichen Halt wegen einer gelockerten Radmutter in der Nacht lagen sie stundenlang mehr als eine Runde zurück. Mit glänzender Taktik, guten fahrerischen Leistungen und erstklassigem Service kämpften sie sich aber ganz nach vorn.

SETBACKS AND OPPORTUNITIES

The circle of favorites shrunk at an early stage. Due to a damaged brake lining, Dries Vanthoor and his teammates dropped to position 45. But nothing ventured, nothing gained: The trio fought back to eleventh place on seeing the checkered flag. At night, number 2 with Mies/De Phillippi/Vervisch was in front. But then some time was lost during a pit stop and afterwards the car was in an unfortunate position during a safety car period, ultimately only coming fifth, trailed by their teammates, García/Müller/Rast. They, too, had been leading the field some of the time but on-track mistakes resulted in two sporting penalties. For Jules Gounon, Christopher Haase and Markus Winkelhock on the other hand the race was a huge opportunity. Having started from position 19, they gradually made up ground. Following a five-minute mandatory pit stop and an additional stop due to a loose wheel nut at night, they were a lap behind for hours. However, with brilliant tactics, good driving performances and top-class service, they battled their way to the very front.

Marcel Fässler, André Lotterer und Dries Vanthoor starteten nach einem Rückschlag eine Aufholjagd

Marcel Fässler, André Lotterer and Dries Vanthoor started a comeback drive following a setback

CALIFORNIA DREAMIN'

Die Intercontinental GT Challenge endete dramatisch: Nach einem harten Wettkampf innerhalb der Marke setzte sich in Laguna Seca das Audi Sport Team Magnus durch. Als drei Wochen später die Absage des Finallaufs in Sepang erfolgte, stand Markus Winkelhock als Titelträger fest

The Intercontinental GT Challenge ended dramatically. Following a fierce in-brand battle, Audi Sport Team Magnus prevailed at Laguna Seca. When the final round at Sepang was cancelled three weeks later, Markus Winkelhock was confirmed as the title winner

Christopher Mies erreichte mit seinen Teamkollegen Platz zwei
Christopher Mies achieved second place with his teammates

Kelvin van der Linde (links), hier mit Bruder Sheldon, gewann in Kalifornien
Kelvin van der Linde (left), pictured here with his brother, Sheldon, won in California

Chris Reinke und Markus Winkelhock bei der IGTC-Preisverleihung
Chris Reinke and Markus Winkelhock at the IGTC Awards Ceremony

KAMPFLINIE IN KALIFORNIEN

Bei den erstmals ausgetragenen California 8 Hours teilte sich Markus Winkelhock im Audi Sport Team Magnus das Cockpit mit seinem deutschen Landsmann Pierre Kaffer und mit Kelvin van der Linde. Das Audi Sport Team Land und das Belgian Audi Club Team WRT waren starke Gegner in den eigenen Reihen, hinzu kamen die Herausforderer der Konkurrenz. Eine Schlüsselrolle spielte einmal mehr Kelvin van der Linde. Der Südafrikaner hatte sich bereits am Nürburgring nach einer souveränen Fahrt am Schluss im Regenchaos den Sieg erkämpft. 20 Minuten vor Ende des Langstreckenrennens in Laguna Seca rang er Markenkollege Christopher Mies aus dem Audi Sport Team Land in einem sportlichen Zweikampf nieder. Nur eine Woche zuvor hatte Kelvins Bruder Sheldon die GTD-Klasse beim Petit-Le-Mans-Rennen gewonnen.

LINE OF BATTLE IN CALIFORNIA

At the inaugural event of the California 8 Hours, Markus Winkelhock in Audi Sport Team Magnus shared the cockpit with his German compatriot Pierre Kaffer and with Kelvin van der Linde. Audi Sport Team Land and Belgian Audi Club Team WRT were strong rivals within their own ranks in addition to being pitted against the challengers from the competition. Once again, Kelvin van der Linde played a key role. Previously, following a drive in commanding style, the South African had clinched victory at the Nürburgring at the end of a chaotic wet race. 20 Minutes before the endurance race at Laguna Seca ended, he defeated fellow Audi driver Christopher Mies from Audi Sport Team Land in a fair sporting duel. Only one week earlier, Kelvin's bother, Sheldon, had won the GTD class in the Petit Le Mans race.

MARKUS WINKELHOCK

Nachdem ich schon fünf 24-Stunden-Rennen und viele andere Läufe mit Audi gewonnen habe, ist der Erfolg in der Intercontinental GT Challenge mein erster Titel mit Audi. Auf dem Weg dahin bekamen wir nichts geschenkt. Bathurst war ein herber Rückschlag, Spa eine anspruchsvolle Aufgabe und Laguna Seca bis zum Schluss offen. Danke an Audi Sport customer racing, an meine drei Teams und alle Teamkollegen. Ein ganz besonders herzliches Dankeschön geht an Kelvin van der Linde. Schon am Nürburgring war er erstklassig, und ohne seine starke Fahrt zum Schluss in Laguna Seca wäre ich nicht Meister geworden.

After having previously won five 24-hour race and many other events with Audi, the success in the Intercontinental GT Challenge is my first title with Audi. We got nothing for free on the way to clinching it. Bathurst was a bitter setback, Spa a challenging task and Laguna Seca open up until the end. I'd like to thank Audi Sport customer racing, my three teams and all my teammates. A particularly sincere thank you goes to Kelvin van der Linde. He was top-notch at the Nürburgring already and without his strong drive in the final stage at Laguna Seca I wouldn't have become champion.

Beim Heimspiel in Laguna Seca feierte das Audi Sport Team Magnus aus Amerika den Sieg
On home soil at Laguna Seca, Audi Sport Team Magnus from America celebrated victory

WRIGHT
WRT
11
44

KURIOSE TITELENTSCHEIDUNG

Die Entscheidung in der Intercontinental GT Challenge fiel denkbar unspektakulär: In einer Pressemitteilung gab die SRO am Freitag, dem 3. November, bekannt, dass das für den 10. Dezember geplante Finale in Sepang wegen Teilnehmermangel entfällt. Damit stand Markus Winkelhock als Champion fest und Audi gewann die Markenwertung. Der Weg an die Tabellenspitze aber war für Winkelhock seit Februar alles andere als leicht. Nach dem Ausfall in Bathurst war sein Punktekonto leer. Der hart erkämpfte Sieg in Spa beförderte den 37 Jahre alten Profi auf Tabellenrang drei. Erst der Rennsieg in Kalifornien sicherte ihm den nötigen Vorsprung vor Christopher Haase und Christopher Mies.

UNUSUAL TITLE DECISION

The decision in the Intercontinental GT Challenge was produced in a rather unspectacular way. In a press release on Friday, November 3, the SRO announced that the finale scheduled at Sepang on December 10 was cancelled due to lack of participation. Consequently, Markus Winkelhock was confirmed as champion and Audi won the manufacturers' classification. However, the way to the top of the standings had been anything but easy for Winkelhock since February. Following his retirement at Bathurst, his tally reflected zero points. The hard-fought victory at Spa moved the 37-year-old pro to position three of the standings. Only the race victory in California secured the necessary advantage for Winkelhock over Christopher Haase and Christopher Mies.

sportscars
Hankook
sportscars
TROCKEN
Partners
Spice
freem

ELLIS IM WUNDERLAND

ELLIS IN WONDERLAND

Ohne Audi wäre Philip Ellis vermutlich nur einer von vielen Studenten, die einen alltäglichen Beruf anstreben. Doch mit den Vier Ringen hat er seine Rennsport-Ambitionen wiederbelebt und den Audi Sport TT Cup als Sprungbrett genutzt

Without Audi Philip Ellis would presumably be just one of many students aspiring to an everyday professional career. However, with the four rings he revived his racing ambitions and used the Audi Sport TT Cup as a springboard

ZWEI PROTAGONISTEN UND VIELE VERFOLGER

Der Brite Philip Ellis und Gosia Rdest aus Polen waren die beiden Einzigen, die schon ein Jahr zuvor im Audi Sport TT Cup dabei gewesen sind. Mit dem Spanier Mikel Azcona und dem Niederländer Milan Dontje kamen zwei erfahrene Talente aus anderen Serien hinzu. Zu den Automobilsport-Anfängern zählten Tommaso Mosca und Fabian Vettel. Vettel? Genau: Der 18 Jahre alte Bruder des viermaligen Formel-1-Weltmeisters begann seine Karriere mit Audi. Seinen größten Erfolg feierte der Heppenheimer am Nürburgring: Von Rang drei gestartet, errang er im Regen den zweiten Platz. Exzellent setzte sich Tommaso Mosca in seinem ersten Jahr im Auto in Szene. Am Norisring und am Nürburgring verbuchte der Italiener jeweils einen zweiten Platz. Als einziger Teilnehmer sammelte er bei jedem Lauf Punkte, gewann die Rookie-Wertung und belegte obendrein Rang drei in der Endabrechnung. Den Titel aber machten Ellis und Azcona untereinander aus.

Fabian Vettel erlebte seine erste Saison im Rennsport (links und Mitte). Vater Norbert maß als Helfer den Luftdruck, Bruder Sebastian begleitete den Einsatz beim Finale interessiert vor Ort (rechts)

Fabian Vettel experienced his first season in racing (left and in the middle). His father, Norbert, checked the tire pressure as his assistant and his brother, Sebastian, watched events on-site at the finale with interest (right)

Der Audi Sport TT Cup 2017 mit Philip Ellis, Milan Dontje, Fabian Vettel, Mikel Azcona, Tommaso Mosca, Drew Ridge, Keagan Masters, Fabienne Wohlwend, Gosia Rdest, Yannik Brandt, Simon Wirth, Kevin Arnold, Josh Caygill und Vivien Keszthelyi

The 2017 Audi Sport TT Cup with Philip Ellis, Milan Dontje, Fabian Vettel, Mikel Azcona, Tommaso Mosca, Drew Ridge, Keagan Masters, Fabienne Wohlwend, Gosia Rdest, Yannik Brandt, Simon Wirth, Kevin Arnold, Josh Caygill and Vivien Keszthelyi

Vizemeister Mikel Azcona, Cup-Sieger Philip Ellis und Rookie-Champion Tommaso Mosca
Vice-champion Mikel Azcona, Cup winner Philip Ellis and rookie champion Tommaso Mosca

TWO PROTAGONISTS AND MANY PURSUERS

Briton Philip Ellis and Gosia Rdest from Poland were the only entrants to have competed in the Audi Sport TT Cup the year before. They were joined by two experienced talents from other series, Spaniard Mikel Azcona and Dutchman Milan Dontje. The auto racing rookies included Tommaso Mosca and Fabian Vettel. Vettel? Exactly, the 18-year-old brother of the four-time Formula 1 World Champion started his career with Audi. The driver from Heppenheim, Germany, celebrated his biggest success at the Nürburgring, clinching second place in a wet race after having started from position three. Tommaso Mosca made an excellent showing in his first year in a car. Both at the Norisring and at the Nürburgring, the Italian took second place. He was the only entrant to score points in each race, won the rookie classification and, to top it off, finished the season in third place overall. The title, though, was decided between Ellis and Azcona.

Das Organisationsteam des Markenpokals: Marco Werner, Manuel Jahn, Christiane Fritz, Projektleiter Philipp Mondelaers, Mirjam Glöckner, Markus Winkelhock sowie Hans Top von ABT Sportsline
The organizational team of the one-make cup: Marco Werner, Manuel Jahn, Christiane Fritz, project leader Philipp Mondelaers, Mirjam Glöckner, Markus Winkelhock and Hans Top from ABT Sportsline

GROSSBRITANNIEN GEGEN SPANIEN

Nach Siegerpokalen 5:6, im Titelkampf 1:0 – so ging der Kampf zwischen Philip Ellis und Mikel Azcona aus. Früh verschaffte sich Ellis mit drei Siegen einen Vorteil, auch wenn die schnelle Polin Gosia Rdest in ihrem dritten Cup-Jahr heftigen Widerstand leistete und in Hockenheim zwei Mal nur knapp geschlagen wurde. Am Norisring begann die Serie des Mikel Azcona: Fünf Siege in sechs Läufen waren ein Wort. Am Nürburgring profitierte der Mann aus Navarra von einem schwachen Wochenende mitsamt Fahrfehler, Unfall und Nullrunde seines Kontrahenten Ellis. Seine so gewonnene Tabellenführung aber verspielte der Spanier am Red Bull Ring. Übermotiviert rodelte er als Führender durchs Kiesbett, zerstörte sich beim Auffahrunfall auf Ellis seinen eigenen Kühler und produzierte tags darauf einen Frühstart. So gewann Ellis den Titel in Hockenheim beim zweitletzten Lauf vorzeitig.

UNITED KINGDOM VS. SPAIN

With a score of 5-6 in terms of winners' trophies and 1-0 in the title race – this is how the battle between Philip Ellis and Mikel Azcona ended. Ellis achieved an advantage early on with three victories even though the fast Pole Gosia Rdest put up fierce resistance in her third Cup year and, at Hockenheim, was beaten by just a narrow margin on two occasions. Mikel Azcona's string of success began at the Norisring. Five victories in six races were an impressive result. At the Nürburgring, the man from Navarre benefited from a weak weekend, including a driving mistake, an accident and a race without points, of his opponent Ellis. The Spaniard, however, forfeited his resulting lead of the standings at the Red Bull Ring. Overly motivated, he took a ride through the gravel trap, destroyed his own radiator in a rear-end collision with Ellis and, on the following day, produced a jump start. Consequently, Ellis won the title early at Hockenheim in the penultimate round.

Drew Ridge aus Australien kam im Lauf der Saison immer besser zurecht und freute sich über zwei Pokale
Drew Ridge from Australia increasingly improved during the course of the season and celebrated two trophies

Fabienne Wohlwend, Gosia Rdest and Vivien Keszthelyi were the three ladies in the Cup

INTERNATIONALER WETTSTREIT

Spannend blieb der Markenpokal bis zum Finale, nicht nur im Titelduell. Den Wettstreit um Platz drei gewann der Italiener Tommaso Mosca mit drei Punkten Vorsprung vor Milan Dontje. Der Niederländer, der den Zustand erfüllter Tiefenentspannung mit einer Dosis Tabak auch dann noch genießt, wenn die anderen zum Vorstart rollen, sammelte vier Pokale. Einmal war er Zweiter, drei Mal Dritter. Hinter Dontje kam der Australier Drew Ridge in seiner ersten Europa-Saison immer besser in Fahrt. Nach zwei Podestergebnissen erreichte er Tabellenrang fünf. Damit schlug er die Polin Gosia Rdest, die beim Auftakt um Siege kämpfte, am Jahresende um vier Punkte. Eine echte Überraschung gelang Keagan Masters. Nachdem der Südafrikaner wegen einer Terminüberschneidung auf dem Nürburgring fehlte, feierte er bei der Rückkehr in Österreich zwei Gesamtsiege. Kein anderer Rookie glänzte mit so guten Einzelleistungen.

INTERNATIONAL COMPETITION

The one-make cup remained a thriller up until the finale, and not just in the duel for the title. The competition for third place was won by Italian Tommaso Mosca with a three-point advantage over Milan Dontje. The Dutchman, who enjoys a state of deep relaxation with a dose of tobacco even when the others begin to line up for the warm-up lap, collected four trophies. Once he came second, three times third. Trailing Dontje, Australian Drew Ridge kept picking up momentum in his first European season. Following two podium finishes, he achieved fifth place in the standings, beating Gosia Rdest from Poland, who was in contention for victories in the opening event, by four points at the end of the year. A real surprise was delivered by Keagan Masters. After the South African had been absent at the Nürburgring due to a clash in dates, he celebrated two overall victories in Austria on his return to the Cup. No other rookie shone with such good individual performances.

Motiv mit Symbolwert: Am Ende schlug der Brite Philip Ellis im Titelkampf den Spanier Mikel Azcona
A picture with symbolic value: in the end, Briton Philip Ellis beat Spaniard Mikel Azcona in the title race

Keagan Masters aus Südafrika blieb der einzige Rookie, der auch Gesamtsiege feierte
Keagan Masters from South Africa remained the only rookie to also celebrate overall victories

PHILIP ELLIS

Die Saison war in erster Linie harte Arbeit, der Titelerfolg sorgte aber auch für Freude. Im Vorjahr habe ich noch die anderen beobachtet, in diesem Jahr richteten sich viele Augen auf meine Strategie. Mir war es wichtig, zum Ende eines Rennens gut zu sein, mein Konkurrent Mikel Azcona gab immer vom Start weg alles. Mein Plan ging auf, und jetzt will ich in den GT-Sport aufsteigen. Es gibt schöne Beispiele für frühere Fahrer aus dem Audi Sport TT Cup, die sich auch in den nächsthöheren Klassen etabliert haben.

The season, above all, was hard work, but the title win was also pleasure. The year before I was still watching the others and this year many eyes were focused on my strategy. For me, it was important to be good at the end of a race whereas my rival, Mikel Azcona, always gave his all right from the start. My plan panned out and now I'd like to move up into GT racing. There are nice examples of former drivers from Audi Sport TT Cup who established themselves in the next higher classes as well.

Zu den vielen prominenten Gästen zählten auch die Skifahrer Benni Raich und Max Franz
The large number of prominent guests included skiers Benni Raich and Max Franz

Lucas di Grassi, Chris Reinke, Frank Stippler und Marcel Fässler bei der Spendenübergabe an Hans Hambücher
Lucas di Grassi, Chris Reinke, Frank Stippler and Marcel Fässler presenting the donation to Hans Hambücher

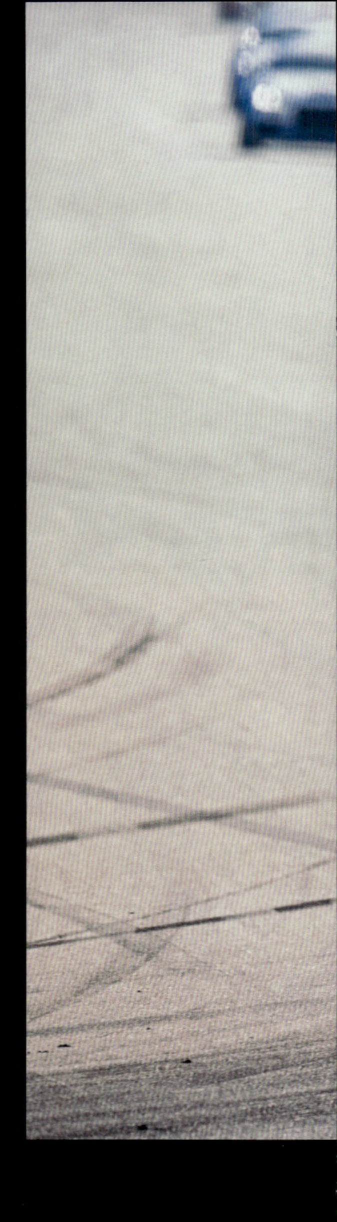

GROSSER AUFTRITT ZUM ABSCHLUSS

Zum Abschluss der Serie nach drei Jahren stiegen in Hockenheim 16 Rennsport-Legenden ins Cockpit. Christian Abt, Filipe Albuquerque, Frank Biela, Dindo Capello, Marcel Fässler, Rahel Frey, Jean-Marc Gounon, Lucas di Grassi, Vanina Ickx, Tom Kristensen, Lucas Luhr, Stéphane Ortelli, Emanuele Pirro, Frank Stippler, Hans-Joachim Stuck und Marco Werner boten beste Unterhaltung beim Race of Legends. Stippler fuhr von Startplatz eins zum Sieg. Dahinter eroberten di Grassi und Fässler die weiteren Podiumsplätze nach einer Aufholjagd von den Rängen zehn und elf. Auch die übrigen prominenten Starter sorgten mit ihren Manövern für viel Jubel und schrieben endlos viele Autogramme. Alle Legenden sammelten zusammen mit Audi Sport customer racing Geld für einen guten Zweck. Die jungen Patienten einer Heilbronner Kinderklinik durften sich am Ende über eine Spende von 25.000 Euro freuen.

GRAND FINALE

To round off the series after three years, 16 racing legends climbed into the cockpit at Hockenheim. Christian Abt, Filipe Albuquerque, Frank Biela, Dindo Capello, Marcel Fässler, Rahel Frey, Jean-Marc Gounon, Lucas di Grassi, Vanina Ickx, Tom Kristensen, Lucas Luhr, Stéphane Ortelli, Emanuele Pirro, Frank Stippler, Hans-Joachim Stuck and Marco Werner delivered first-class entertainment in the Race of Legends. Stippler took a lights-to-flag victory, joined on podium by di Grassi and Fässler who had fought back from positions ten and eleven. The other prominent entrants delivered crowd-pleasing maneuvers as well and signed an endless number of autographs. All legends together with Audi Sport customer racing raised funds for a good cause. At the end of the day, the young patients of a children's hospital in Heilbronn, Germany, were delighted to receive a donation of 25,000 euros.

Tom Kristensen im Interview mit Radio-Le-Mans-Kommentator John Hindhaugh
Tom Kristensen in an interview with Radio Le Mans commentator John Hindhaugh

Frank Stippler gewann das Race of Legends von Startplatz eins
Frank Stippler won the Race of Legends from pole position

Die Autogramme von Lucas di Grassi, Filipe Albuquerque und Co. waren überaus gefragt
The autographs by Lucas di Grassi, Filipe Albuquerque and company were in great demand

NIE AUFGEBEN

NEVER GIVE UP

Der Blancpain GT Series Endurance Cup war 2017 für die Kunden von Audi Sport customer racing eine Achterbahn der Gefühle. Nach vielen Rückschlägen zu Saisonbeginn war das Podium erst ab Sommer erreichbar

The 2017 Blancpain GT Series Endurance Cup was an emotional roller coaster for the Audi Sport customer racing teams. Following numerous setbacks at the beginning of the season, the podium was not achievable until the summer

BLANCPAIN
PRO
75
auto I.S.R.
Audi Sport
Castrol

Beinharte Kämpfe auch zwischen Teamkollegen wie hier beim Belgian Audi Club Team WRT prägten die Saison
Fierce battles even between teammates, like this one of Belgian Audi Club Team WRT, marked the season

UNGESUNDE HÄRTE

Mit bis zu 50 Teilnehmern ist der Blancpain GT Series Endurance Cup weltweit eine der härtesten GT3-Serien. Doch zu viel Kampfgeist schadet: Beim Auftakt in Monza rammte ein Gegner einen Audi des Belgian Audi Club Team WRT in der ersten Runde des Qualifyings so vehement, dass der R8 LMS am ganzen Wochenende nicht mehr zum Einsatz kam. Bei einem Startunfall fiel ein zweiter Audi der Belgier aus. Platz zwölf war das beste Ergebnis. Am zweiten Rennwochenende in Silverstone fehlten dem besten Audi im Qualifying eineinhalb Sekunden zur Spitze, Startplatz 21 war das Ergebnis. Erst beim 1.000-Kilometer-Rennen in Le Castellet erreichte Antonio García mit den beiden DTM-Piloten Nico Müller und René Rast als Dritter das Podium – eine gute Vorbereitung auf die 24 Stunden von Spa.

UNHEALTHY TOUGHNESS

With up to 50 entrants the Blancpain GT Series Endurance Cup is one of the world's toughest GT3 series. An excessive amount of fighting spirit, though, is counterproductive. In the opener at Monza, a rival hit an Audi of Belgian Audi Club Team WRT on lap one of qualifying so hard that the R8 LMS was unable to go out again for the rest of the weekend. In a starting crash, a second Audi of the Belgians was taken out of the race. Position twelve was the best result. On the second race weekend at Silverstone, the best Audi was trailing the front runner by one and a half seconds in qualifying, resulting in grid position 21. Only in the 1.000-kilometer race at Le Castellet, Antonio García together with the two DTM campaigners Nico Müller and René Rast finished on podium in third place – solid preparation for the Spa 24 Hours.

Stuart Leonard, Jake Dennis und Robin Frijns beendeten die Saison als Zweite in Barcelona versöhnlich
Stuart Leonard, Jake Dennis and Robin Frijns as runners-up at Barcelona ended the season on a positive note

Saintéloc Racing war eines der drei Audi-Kundenteams in der Langstreckenrennserie
Saintéloc Racing was one of the three Audi customer teams in the endurance racing series

Das Team von Igor Salaquarda bewies in der Saison 2017 großen Kampfgeist
Igor Salaquarda's team demonstrated a strong fighting spirit in the 2017 season

Thierry Tassin, als Sportlicher Direktor an den Erfolgen des Belgian Audi Club Team WRT beteiligt
Thierry Tassin contributes to the success of Belgian Audi Club Team WRT as its sporting director

AUFHOLJAGD ZUM ENDE

Beim größten GT3-Rennen der Welt in Spa setzte sich ein von Audi Sport customer racing unterstütztes Team durch. Das Audi Sport Team Saintéloc gewann das Rennen zum ersten Mal, und zwar mit Jules Gounon, Christopher Haase und Markus Winkelhock. Die Mannschaft von Sébastien Chetail blieb bei ihrem ersten 24-Stunden-Sieg ohne Strafen. Das Belgian Audi Club Team WRT erzielte sein bestes Saisonergebnis mit Platz zwei von Jake Dennis/Robin Frijns/ Stuart Leonard beim Finale in Barcelona. Auch I.S.R. aus der Tschechischen Republik war in der Saison 2017 erneut als Audi-Kundenteam am Start. Nachdem ein Reifenschaden in Monza fünf Runden vor Schluss Platz zwei vereitelte, blieb der siebte Rang von Filipe Albuquerque, Filip Salaquarda und Clemens Schmid in Le Castellet das beste Ergebnis des Jahres. Beim Finale in Barcelona zeigten Frank Stippler, Kevin Ceccon und Filip Salaquarda mit einer Aufholjagd von Position 38 bis auf Platz acht den großen Kampfgeist des Teams aus Prag.

Den einzigen Saisonsieg in dieser Serie feierte ein Kunde von Audi beim wichtigsten Rennen: Saintéloc gewann mit Unterstützung von Audi Sport customer racing die 24 Stunden von Spa
It was the most important race in which an Audi customer celebrated the only win of the season in this series: Saintéloc, with support from Audi Sport customer racing, won the Spa 24 Hours

Jules Gounon, Christopher Haase und Markus Winkelhock auf dem Weg zum Sieg in Spa
Jules Gounon, Christopher Haase and Markus Winkelhock on the way to victory at Spa

COMEBACK TOWARD THE END

In the world's major GT3 race at Spa, a team supported by Audi Sport customer racing prevailed. Audi Sport Team Saintéloc won the race for the first time, with Jules Gounon, Christopher Haase and Markus Winkelhock. On claiming its first 24-hour victory, Sébastien Chetail's squad remained without penalties. Belgian Audi Club Team WRT, on taking second place with Jake Dennis/Robin Frijns/ Stuart Leonard in the finale at Barcelona, achieved its best result of the season. I.S.R. from the Czech Republic was again on the grid as an Audi customer team in the 2017 season. After a puncture five laps before the end of the race at Monza prevented position two, seventh place achieved by Filipe Albuquerque, Filip Salaquarda and Clemens Schmid at Le Castellet remained the best result of the year. In the finale at Barcelona, Frank Stippler, Kevin Ceccon and Filip Salaquarda with a comeback from position 38 to eight showed the strong fighting spirit of the team from Prague.

P1
2017
R8
S. LEONARD
Snap-on
GrafiWrap
PIRELLI
P ZERO
TOTAL
BLANCPAIN GT SERIES

STARKE SPRINT-LEISTUNG

STRONG SPRINT PERFORMANCE

Stuart Leonard und Robin Frijns gewannen zum ersten Mal zusammen den Blancpain GT Series Sprint Cup. Gleich in mehrerlei Hinsicht war die Saison für die Fahrermannschaften der Kundenteams von Audi eindrucksvoll

Stuart Leonard and Robin Frijns jointly won the Blancpain GT Series Sprint Cup for the first time. The season was impressive for the driver squads of Audi's customer teams in more ways than one

OFFEN BIS ZUM SCHLUSS

Brands Hatch, Sonntagnachmittag, 7. Mai, zweites von fünf Rennwochenenden zum Sprint Cup: Gähnende Leere auf den Punktekonten von Robin Frijns/Stuart Leonard, Will Stevens/Markus Winkelhock und Dries Vanthoor/Marcel Fässler. Dass diese drei Fahrerteams des Belgian Audi Club Team WRT vier Monate später mit nur zwei Punkten Unterschied und besten Titelchancen zum Finale am Nürburgring reisen würden, hat wohl niemand geglaubt. Erst am späten Nachmittag jenes Mai-Sonntages sammelten die drei Mannschaften auf dem Kurs vor den Toren Londons ihre ersten Punkte. Zur Halbzeit in Zolder dann der Durchbruch: Stevens/Winkelhock gewannen vor Clemens Schmid/Filip Salaquarda im Audi R8 LMS von I.S.R. sowie Frijns/Leonard und Fässler/Vanthoor. In Budapest folgte der Sieg von Fässler/Vanthoor vor ihren Teamkollegen Jake Dennis/Pieter Schothorst. Beim Finale schließlich überquerten Frijns/Leonard die Ziellinie vor Winkelhock/Stevens und gewannen so den Titel.

OPEN UP UNTIL THE END

Brands Hatch, Sunday afternoon, May 7, the second of five Sprint Cup race weekends: The tally of Robin Frijns/ Stuart Leonard, Will Stevens/Markus Winkelhock and Dries Vanthoor/Marcel Fässler reflects a yawning void. Arguably, there was no one who thought that four months later these three driver teams from Belgian Audi Club Team WRT would be traveling to the finale at the Nürburgring with a difference of just two points and perfect title chances. It was only in the late afternoon of that Sunday in May that the three squads scored their first points at the venue on the outskirts of London. The breakthrough was subsequently achieved halfway through the season at Zolder when Stevens/Winkelhock won in front of Clemens Schmid/Filip Salaquarda in the Audi R8 LMS from I.S.R. as well as Frijns/Leonard and Fässler/ Vanthoor. At Budapest, the victory of Fässler/Vanthoor, trailed by their teammates Jake Dennis/Pieter Schothorst, followed. Ultimately, in the finale, Frijns/Leonard crossed the finish line ahead of Winkelhock/Stevens, so winning the title.

Pokale und Preisgeld in Zolder für Filip Salaquarda, Clemens Schmid, Will Stevens, Markus Winkelhock, Stuart Leonard und Robin Frijns
Trophies and prize money at Zolder for Filip Salaquarda, Clemens Schmid, Will Stevens, Markus Winkelhock, Stuart Leonard and Robin Frijns

In Belgien dominierten die Kundenteams – WRT vor I.S.R. und WRT
In Belgium, the customer teams prevailed – WRT trailed by I.S.R. and WRT

Marcel Fässler und Dries Vanthoor nach ihrem Sieg in Budapest
Marcel Fässler and Dries Vanthoor after their victory at Budapest

VIELE WEGE FÜHREN ZUM ZIEL

Sie sind beide erste 26 Jahre alt und teilen sich ein Cockpit, doch unterschiedlicher hätten ihre Karrieren kaum verlaufen können. Der Niederländer Robin Frijns stieg Jahr um Jahr bis in die GP2-Kategorie auf, gewann in jeder Saison Rennen und erreichte als Testfahrer die Formel 1, bevor er in den GT3-Sport wechselte. Der Sprint-Titel ist sein fünfter Meisterschaftssieg seit 2010 und der zweite im WRT-Audi nach dem Blancpain-GT-Erfolg 2015. Stuart Leonard sammelte erst vor wenigen Jahren erste Erfahrungen im britischen Clubsport. 2015 gewann er gleich sein erstes 12-Stunden-Rennen mit WRT in Sepang, wenige Wochen später triumphierte er mit den Belgiern bei den 24 Stunden von Dubai. Der Sprint-Erfolg ist der erste Titel seiner Karriere. Das Belgian Audi Club Team WRT dagegen feierte in der Teamwertung nach 2014, 2015 und 2016 den vierten Sprint-Titel in Folge. Ebenso hat die Mannschaft von Vincent Vosse 2011, 2012, 2014 und 2015 die Teamwertung der Endurance Series gewonnen, 2014 und 2015 die GT-Gesamtwertung, 2014 den Sprint-Silver-Cup und 2013 die FIA GT Series.

VARIOUS WAYS OF REACHING A GOAL

Both of them are only 26 years old and they share a cockpit, but their career paths greatly differ from one another. Dutchman Robin Frijns was promoted all the way up to the GP2 category year after year, won races each season and made it into Formula 1 as a test driver before switching to GT3 racing. The Sprint title marks his fifth championship win since 2010 and the second one in the WRT Audi following the 2015 Blancpain GT success. Stuart Leonard only gathered initial experiences in British club racing a few years ago. In 2015, he instantly won his first 12-hour race with WRT at Sepang. A few weeks later, he triumphed with the Belgians in the 24 Hours of Dubai. The Sprint success marks the first title in his career, whereas Belgian Audi Club Team WRT in the teams' classification celebrated its fourth consecutive Sprint title after 2014, 2015 and 2016. In addition, Vincent Vosse's squad in 2011, 2012, 2014 and 2015 won the teams' classification in the Endurance Series, the GT overall classification in 2014 and 2015, the Sprint Silver Cup in 2014 and the FIA GT Series in 2013.

Zwei Väter des Erfolges von WRT: Teamchef Vincent Vosse und Sportdirektor Pierre Dieudonné

Two fathers of WRT's success: Team principal Vincent Vosse and sporting director Pierre Dieudonné

Robin Frijns und Stuart Leonard gewannen den Sprint-Titel beim Finale auf dem Nürburgring mit acht Punkten Vorsprung vor ihren Teamkollegen Will Stevens/Markus Winkelhock
Robin Frijns and Stuart Leonard won the Sprint title in the finale at the Nürburgring with an eight-point advantage over their teammates Will Stevens/Markus Winkelhock

STUART LEONARD

Dieser Titel bedeutet mir sehr viel. Ich habe meine Karriere erst spät begonnen. Markus Winkelhock und Will Stevens waren schon in der Formel 1, Marcel Fässler hat Le Mans gewonnen, Dries Vanthoor fuhr sehr viel Kart. Robin Frijns war ein perfekter Mentor und die Crew von WRT war Spitze. Alle Informationen waren präzise. Ich wusste genau, worauf es ankam. Obwohl Robin zu Saisonbeginn durch eine Knieverletzung beim Fahrerwechsel benachteiligt war und ein Rennen wegen einer Terminüberschneidung verpasst hat, haben wir es zusammen geschafft.

This title really means a lot to me. I only started my career at a late stage. Markus Winkelhock and Will Stevens were already in Formula 1, Marcel Fässler had won Le Mans and Dries Vanthoor was very active in karting. Robin Frijns was a perfect mentor and the WRT crew a class act. All the information was precise. I knew exactly what mattered. Although at the beginning of the season, Robin, due to a knee injury, was disadvantaged in the driver change and missed a race due to a clash in dates we jointly made it.

CERTINA
RAVENOL
motorsport

STARKES FELD

STRONG FIELD

Einmal mehr hat der ADAC in Europa die stärkste nationale GT3-Serie am Start. Im elften Jahr präsentiert sich das ADAC GT Masters mit 28 Startern gesund und voller Abwechslung. Audi war mit zehn R8 LMS im Feld erneut die beliebteste Marke

Once again, ADAC put the strongest national GT3 series in Europe on the grid. In its eleventh year, the ADAC GT Masters with 28 entrants was in good shape and delivered ample variety. Audi, with ten R8 LMS cars in the field, was again the most popular brand

Uwe Geipel erlebte als Teamchef von Yaco Racing keine einfache Saison
For Uwe Geipel as team principal of Yaco Racing, the season was not an easy one

HARTE KÄMPFE IN BESTER NATIONALER SERIE

Wie hart umkämpft die Serie war, zeigen die Zahlen: Drei Siege gingen an den Audi R8 LMS – ebenso viele wie an Corvette und Lamborghini, die anderen Marken mussten sich mit weniger begnügen. Connor De Phillippi und sein Teamkollege Christopher Mies kehrten als Titelverteidiger mit der Nummer 1 zurück. Auch wenn es für den erneuten Erfolg nicht gereicht hat: Dieses Fahrerduo und Montaplast by Land-Motorsport schlugen sich einmal mehr erstklassig. Sie feierten in Zandvoort und am Sachsenring je einen gemeinsamen Sieg. Der Amerikaner und der Deutsche erreichten am Ende Tabellenplatz drei in der Fahrerwertung, Montaplast by Land-Motorsport die zweite Position in der Teamwertung, der Schweizer Jeffrey Schmidt zudem Rang zwei der Junior-Wertung.

FIERCE BATTLES IN BEST NATIONAL SERIES

The statistics show how fiercely competitive the series was. Three victories went to the Audi R8 LMS – and an equal number to Corvette and Lamborghini while the other brands had to settle for less. Connor De Phillippi and his teammate, Christopher Mies, returned in car number 1 as the title defenders. Even though falling short of repeating their success, this driver duo and Montaplast by Land-Motorsport did a more than top-class job once again, celebrating a joint victory at both Zandvoort and at the Sachsenring. In the end, the American and the German achieved position three in the drivers' standings, Montaplast by Land-Motorsport position two in the teams' standings and, in addition, the Swiss Jeffrey Schmidt finished runner-up in the juniors' classification.

Frank Aust freute sich mit seinem Team über den ersten Siegerpokal mit Audi
Frank Aust with his team was pleased to have clinched the first winner's trophy with Audi

Aust Motorsport gewann erstmals mit Kelvin van der Linde/Markus Pommer
Aust Motorsport won for the first time with Kelvin van der Linde/ Markus Pommer

Connor De Phillippi und Christopher Mies feierten zwei Siege
Connor De Phillippi and Christopher Mies celebrated two victories

Im Regen von Zandvoort glückte Christopher Mies/Connor De Phillippi am vierten Rennwochenende der erste Sieg
In the wet race at Zandvoort, Christopher Mies/Connor De Phillippi achieved their first victory on the fourth race weekend

WOLFGANG LAND

Am Saisonbeginn waren wir einfach nicht gut genug. In Österreich haben wir viele Punkte durch Unfälle und technische Defekte verloren. Auf dem Sachsenring waren wir wieder stark, konnten den Rückstand aber nicht mehr aufholen. Christopher Mies und Connor De Phillippi waren einmal mehr herausragend. Und in der Junior-Wertung haben wir mit Jeffrey Schmidt Platz zwei geholt. Unser Saisonhöhepunkt abseits des ADAC GT Masters war natürlich der Sieg bei den 24 Stunden auf dem Nürburgring. Der Defekt nach der langen Führung war dramatisch, es sind Tränen geflossen.
Aber niemand hat aufgegeben und wir haben verdient gewonnen. Es war der größte Sieg in der Geschichte von Land-Motorsport. Wir sind stolz auf die Erfolge mit Audi.

At the beginning of the season, we simply weren't good enough. In Austria, we lost a lot of points due to accidents and technical defects. At the Sachsenring, we were strong again but unable to make up our deficit. Christopher Mies and Connor De Phillippi were outstanding once more. And in the juniors' classification, we clinched position two with Jeffrey Schmidt. Obviously, aside from the ADAC GT Masters, the highlight of our season was our victory in the Nürburgring 24 Hours. The defect following our long lead was dramatic and the squad shed a few tears. But nobody gave up and we took a deserved win. It was the greatest victory in the history of Land-Motorsport. We're proud of the successes with Audi.

Twin Busch Motorsport trat mit Dennis und Marc Busch erstmals im ADAC GT Masters an
Twin Busch Motorsport with Dennis and Marc Busch contested the ADAC GT Masters for the first time

Die Teams Yaco Racing und Audi Sport racing academy erlebten die hohe Leistungsdichte im ADAC GT Masters
Teams Yaco Racing and Audi Sport racing academy experienced the intensive competition in the ADAC GT Masters field

Peter Mücke engagierte sich mit einem Mehrmarken-Team erstmals im ADAC GT Masters und setzte zwei Audi R8 LMS ein, hier mit Mike David Ortmann und Frank Stippler
Peter Mücke fielded a multi-marque team for the first time in the ADAC GT Masters, entering two Audi R8 LMS cars, pictured here with Mike David Ortmann and Frank Stippler

NEWCOMER UND BEWÄHRTE MANNSCHAFTEN

Zum ersten Mal triumphierte das Team von Frank Aust. Kelvin van der Linde und Markus Pommer setzten sich am Nürburgring durch, hinzu kam ein zweiter Platz in Zandvoort. Ohne Sieg verlief dagegen die Saison für Yaco Racing. Philip Geipel und Rahel Frey errangen 2017 im Unterschied zu den beiden Vorjahren keine Pokale. Gleich drei Teams waren neu im ADAC GT Masters. Twin Busch Motorsport, zuvor mit Dennis und Marc Busch auf der Nordschleife erfolgreich, mussten erkennen, dass die Trauben hoch hingen. Die Mannschaft der Audi driving experience wechselte ebenfalls aus der „Grünen Hölle" ins ADAC GT Masters. Unter der Bewerbung der Audi Sport racing academy stellten sich Mikaela Åhlin-Kottulinsky/ Ricardo Feller und ihre Teamkollegen Elia Erhart/ Christopher Höher dem Wettbewerb. Erstmals vertraute das Team von Peter Mücke auf zwei Audi R8 LMS. Mike David Ortmann sammelte als bester Audi-Pilot der Berliner Mannschaft 22 Punkte.

NEWCOMERS AND SEASONED SQUADS

Frank Aust's team triumphed for the first time. Kelvin van der Linde and Markus Pommer prevailed at the Nürburgring, plus the squad achieved a second place at Zandvoort. By contrast, the season ended without any victories for Yaco Racing. In 2017, Philip Geipel and Rahel Frey, unlike the two years before, clinched no trophies. As many as three teams were new in the ADAC GT Masters. Twin Busch Motorsport, previously successful with Dennis and Marc Busch on the Nordschleife, had to realize that the grapes were hanging high on the vine. The Audi driving experience squad switched from the "Green Hell" to the ADAC GT Masters as well. Under the Audi Sport racing academy's entry, Mikaela Åhlin-Kottulinsky/Ricardo Feller and their teammates, Elia Erhart/Christopher Höher, tackled the competition. For the first time, Peter Mücke's team relied on two Audi R8 LMS cars. Mike David Ortmann as the best Audi driver of the Berlin-based outfit scored 22 points.

GROSSE VIELFALT

WIDE VARIETY

Deutschlands große Langstreckenrennserie auf der Nordschleife war einmal mehr das Terrain für viele Audi-Kundenteams. Zum ersten Mal waren alle drei aktuellen Rennwagen von Audi Sport customer racing in der „Grünen Hölle" zu sehen

Germany's major endurance racing series on the Nordschleife was once again a popular field for many Audi customer teams. For the first time, all three current race cars from Audi Sport customer racing were seen on track in the "Green Hell"

Das Team Møller Bil aus Norwegen errang den ersten TCR-Sieg des Audi RS 3 LMS auf der Nordschleife
Team Møller Bil from Norway clinched the first TCR victory of the Audi RS 3 LMS on the Nordschleife

MARKENVIELFALT IN DER EIFEL

Die VLN Langstreckenmeisterschaft Nürburgring ist populär bei Jung und Alt: Klassische Gentleman-Piloten messen sich mit Nachwuchsfahrern, ehemaligen oder aktuellen Profis – Überraschungen eingeschlossen. Vier verschiedene Marken teilten sich 2017 die neun Siege, zwei Mal standen die Fahrer mit den Vier Ringen auf dem Overall ganz oben auf dem Podest. Das Team Montaplast by Land-Motorsport gewann den sechsten Lauf mit Robin Frijns und Connor De Phillippi sowie das achte Rennen mit Dries Vanthoor und Markus Winkelhock. Dieser 7. Oktober ging in die Unternehmensgeschichte des Teams ein: Neben dem VLN-Sieg verbuchte Wolfgang Land am gleichen Tag in Hockenheim einen Erfolg in der DMV GTC und gewann die GTD-Klasse beim Petit-Le-Mans-Rennen in Road Atlanta – jeweils mit einem Audi R8 LMS. In der VLN-Speed-Trophäe erreichte sein Team am Jahresende den zweiten Platz.

Montaplast by Land-Motorsport gewann zwei VLN-Rennen
Montaplast by Land-Motorsport won two VLN races

Klaus Koch, Peter Schmidt und Johannes Siegler im Audi R8 LMS von Car Collection Motorsport beim dritten Saisonrennen

Klaus Koch, Peter Schmidt and Johannes Siegler in the Audi R8 LMS from Car Collection Motorsport in round three

BRAND DIVERSITY IN THE EIFEL

The VLN Endurance Championship Nürburgring is popular with all age groups. Classic gentlemen drivers are pitted against up-and-coming racers, former or current pros – surprises included. Four different marques shared the nine victories in 2017 and on two occasions, drivers with the four rings emblazoned on their suits mounted the very top of the podium. Team Montaplast by Land-Motorsport won round six with Robin Frijns and Connor De Phillippi, plus race eight with Dries Vanthoor and Markus Winkelhock. This seventh day of October went down in the team's history. In addition to the VLN win, Wolfgang Land recorded a success in the DMV GTC at Hockenheim and won the GTD class in the Petit Le Mans race at Road Atlanta – both with an Audi R8 LMS. In the VLN Speed Trophy, his team achieved second place at the end of the year.

DRIES VANTHOOR

Ich habe in dieser Saison so viele tolle Rennen erlebt mit Siegen in der Blancpain GT Series, der Chinesischen GT-Meisterschaft, im Audi R8 LMS Cup und in der VLN. Das VLN-Rennen mit Markus Winkelhock war großartig. Sich im Verkehr zurechtzufinden war schon ganz schön schwierig. Noch anstrengender war es aber, eine zeitlang mit Slicks im Regen zu fahren. Das waren die härtesten Rennkilometer meines Lebens. Ich bin sehr glücklich, mit nur 19 Jahren einen VLN-Gesamtsieg erreicht zu haben.

I've experienced so many fantastic races this season with victories in the Blancpain GT Series, in the Chinese GT Championship, in the Audi R8 LMS Cup and in the VLN. The VLN race with Markus Winkelhock was brilliant. Getting your bearings in traffic was pretty difficult. However, driving on slicks in the rain was even more strenuous. Those were the toughest kilometers of racing in my life. I'm very happy about having achieved an overall VLN victory at just 19 years old.

Teamchef Wolfgang Land mit seinen Siegern Robin Frijns und Connor De Phillippi

Team principal Wolfgang Land with his winners, Robin Frijns and Connor De Phillippi

Erstmals war der Audi R8 LMS GT4 am achten Rennwochenende im Einsatz

For the first time, the Audi R8 LMS GT4 was fielded on the eighth race weekend

ERFOLGE IN DEN KLASSEN

Viele weitere Audi-Kunden engagierten sich ebenfalls in der VLN. Phoenix Racing gelang mit Platz zwei von Frank Stippler und Nicolaj Møller Madsen im sechsten Lauf das beste Saisonergebnis, hinzu kam jeweils ein dritter Platz im fünften Lauf sowie beim Finale. Das Audi Sport Team WRT verbuchte im zweiten Rennen einen dritten Platz. Erstmals vertrauten auch mehrere Teams auf den Audi RS 3 LMS. Das beste Ergebnis gelang dem Team Møller Bil. Es gewann mit den vier Norwegern Håkon Schjærin, Atle Gulbrandsen, Kenneth Østvold und Anders Lindstad beim fünften Lauf die TCR-Klasse. Car Collection Motorsport feierte beim VLN-Debüt des Audi R8 LMS GT4 beim achten Lauf den SP-X-Klassensieg mit Rahel Frey und Christopher Haase.

SUCCESS IN CLASS

There were many other Audi customers active in the VLN as well. Phoenix Racing, in position two clinched by Frank Stippler and Nicolaj Møller Madsen in round six, achieved its best result of the season and additionally took third place in both round five and in the finale. Audi Sport Team WRT in race two posted a third place. For the first time, several teams relied on the Audi RS 3 LMS too. The best result was achieved by Team Møller Bil that was victorious in round five of the TCR class with Norwegians Håkon Schjærin, Atle Gulbrandsen, Kenneth Østvold and Anders Lindstad. Car Collection Motorsport at the VLN debut of the Audi R8 LMS GT4 in round eight celebrated SP-X class victory with Rahel Frey and Christopher Haase.

TURBULENTE SAISON

A TURBULENT SEASON

Audi Sport Italia ging mit einem neuen Fahreraufgebot in die Saison 2017: Der 23 Jahre alte Vittorio Ghirelli teilte sich das Cockpit des Audi R8 LMS mit dem erfahrenen Benoît Tréluyer

Audi Sport Italia entered the 2017 season with a new driver lineup. 23-year-old Vittorio Ghirelli shared the cockpit of the Audi R8 LMS with seasoned campaigner Benoît Tréluyer

adria raceway
Sisal
Matchpoint
NIINIVIRTA
TEN AG Informatik
Zampieri

HOHER ANSPRUCH

Seit 2009 engagiert sich Audi Sport Italia mit dem Audi R8 LMS im heimischen Championat. 26 Rennsiege, 25 Trainingsbestzeiten, 20 schnellste Rennrunden, drei Teamtitel, ein Fahrertitel und zuletzt 2016 die Vizemeisterschaft mit Marco Mapelli unterstreichen, wie erfolgsverwöhnt die Mannschaft von Emilio Radaelli in diesen acht Jahren war. Die neunte GT3-Saison in Folge aber war für das Team aus Nibbiola im Piemont eine Achterbahn der Gefühle. Von Nullrunden bis zu Podestergebnissen und einem Sieg machte das Importeursteam Höhen und Tiefen durch. Der Sieg in Imola am fünften Rennwochenende schmeckte besonders süß. Von Startplatz sieben holte Vittorio Ghirelli zwei Positionen auf, bevor er das Auto an Benoît Tréluyer übergab. Der dreimalige Le-Mans-Sieger aus Frankreich kämpfte sich auf abtrocknender Strecke weiter vor, überholte zwei vor ihm um den Sieg kämpfende Gegner und gewann schließlich mit 3,8 Sekunden Vorsprung.

HIGH EXPECTATIONS

Since 2009, Audi Sport Italia has been active in its home championship with the Audi R8 LMS. 26 race wins, 25 best times in qualifying, 20 fastest race laps, three team titles, one driver title and, most recently in 2016, the runner-up title with Marco Mapelli underscore the type of success Emilio Radaelli's crew enjoyed in these eight years. However, the ninth consecutive GT3 season was an emotional roller coaster for the outfit from Nibbiola in the Piedmont region. From rounds without points through to podium results and a victory, the importer's team went through highs and lows. Its victory at Imola on the fifth race weekend was particularly sweet. Having started from seventh on the grid, Vittorio Ghirelli made up two positions before turning the car over to Benoît Tréluyer. The three-time Le Mans winner from France kept advancing on a drying track, overtook two rivals battling for victory in front of him and ultimately won with a 3.8-second advantage.

Benoît Tréluyer und Vittorio Ghirelli waren beide neu im Team von Audi Sport Italia
Benoît Tréluyer and Vittorio Ghirelli were both new in the team of Audi Sport Italia

Der 23 Jahre alte Vittorio Ghirelli profitierte in seiner ersten Saison im Audi R8 LMS auch vom Erfahrungsschatz von Audi Sport Italia und dem dreimaligen Le-Mans-Sieger Benoît Tréluyer
23-year-old Vittorio Ghirelli in his first season in the Audi R8 LMS also benefited from the wealth of experience of Audi Sport Italia and three-time Le Mans winner Benoît Tréluyer

VITTORIO GHIRELLI

Die Saison war ein wichtiger Schritt, um eine GT-Karriere aufzubauen. Wenn unsere Abstimmung gut war, war der Audi R8 LMS speziell beim Reifenverschleiß besser als die Autos unserer Gegner. Alle Podiumsergebnisse und der Sieg waren das Ergebnis von Aufholjagden, bei denen wir bis zum Schluss starke Rundenzeiten fuhren. Voraussetzung für unsere Erfolge war die Arbeit von Audi Sport Italia. Das ist ein Team, das absolut professionell arbeitet und schon ewig im italienischen Motorsport eine Größe ist.

The season was an important step for building a GT career. When our setup was good, the Audi R8 LMS, especially in terms of tire wear, was better than the cars of our rivals. All podium finishes and the victory were the results of comebacks in which we set strong lap times up until the end. The prerequisite for our successes was the work of Audi Sport Italia. It's a team that works with absolute professionalism and has been established in Italian motorsport for ages.

Ein Sieg und drei zweite Plätze waren die besten Ergebnisse für Vittorio Ghirelli/Benoît Tréluyer
A victory and three second places were the best results for Vittorio Ghirelli/Benoît Tréluyer

Der Audi R8 LMS der ersten Generation war auch in seiner achten Saison noch für Klassensiege gut
The first-generation Audi R8 LMS was still able to clinch class victories even in its eighth season

Michele Merendino und Davide di Benedetto gewannen im bewährten Audi R8 LMS ultra in Monza ihre Klasse
Michele Merendino and Davide di Benedetto in the time-tested Audi R8 LMS ultra won their class at Monza

SCHNELLER GEBRAUCHTWAGEN

Neben dem aktuellen Audi R8 LMS setzte Audi Sport Italia sporadisch auch das Vorgängermodell ein. Am dritten Rennwochenende in Monza feierten die beiden Sizilianer Michele Merendino und Davide de Benedetto damit zwei Klassensiege. In Imola erzielten Gentleman-Pilot Luca Magnoni und sein Teamkollege Luca Rangoni nicht nur einen Klassensieg, sondern kämpften sich in dem sieben Jahre alten GT3-Sportwagen bis auf Platz sechs vor. Damit lagen sie in der Gesamtwertung noch vor Konkurrenten in deutlich aktuelleren Rennwagen. Beim Finale in Mugello folgte ein weiterer Klassenerfolg. Für das bewährte Chassis war es bereits der 24. Sieg, Gesamt- und Klassenerfolge zusammengenommen. In der mehr als 30-jährigen Geschichte von Audi Sport Italia ist dieser Audi R8 LMS das erfolgreichste Auto.

FAST PREVIOUS-GENERATION CAR

In addition to the current Audi R8 LMS, Audi Sport Italia sporadically fielded the preceding model as well. On the third race weekend at Monza, the two Sicilians Michele Merendino and Davide de Benedetto celebrated two class wins in it. At Imola, gentleman driver Luca Magnoni and his teammate, Luca Rangoni, not only scored a class victory but even advanced to position six in the seven-year-old GT3 sports car, so ranking in the overall standings even before competitors in clearly more current race cars. In the finale at Mugello, another success in class followed, marking the 24th victory, overall and class wins included, for the time-tested chassis. In the more than 30-year-history of Audi Sport Italia, this Audi R8 LMS has been the most successful car.

Teamchef Emilio Radaelli engagierte sich im neunten Jahr in Folge im italienischen GT-Sport
Team principal Emilio Radaelli was active in Italian GT racing for the ninth consecutive year

BUNTES TREIBEN

ACTION-PACKED VARIETY

Viele Kundenteams fahren im europäischen Clubsport mit Audi um Pokale. Erfolge bei Sprints, auf Langstreckendistanzen und bei Bergrennen durch Nachwuchsfahrer ebenso wie Gentleman-Piloten unterstreichen die Vielseitigkeit des Audi R8 LMS

Many customer teams compete for trophies in European club racing with Audi. Successes in sprint, endurance and hillclimb races by up-and-coming as well as by gentleman drivers emphasize the versatility of the Audi R8 LMS

Elmar Grimm, Gustav Edelhoff, Ingo Vogler, Dr. Johannes Kirchhoff, Horst Felbermayr, Dimitri Parhofer, Max Edelhoff und Toni Forné auf dem Siegerpodest der 24H Endurance Series in Imola
Elmar Grimm, Gustav Edelhoff, Ingo Vogler, Dr. Johannes Kirchhoff, Horst Felbermayr, Dimitri Parhofer, Max Edelhoff and Toni Forné on the 24H Endurance Series podium at Imola

Das Team Car Collection Motorsport feierte bei den 12 Stunden von Imola den Gesamtsieg sowie Platz eins und zwei in der A6-Am-Klasse
Team Car Collection Motorsport in the Imola 12 Hours celebrated overall victory, plus positions one and two in the A6-Am class

LÄNGE LÄUFT

Die 24H Endurance Series richtet sich mit ihren Langstreckenrennen in erster Linie an Privatiers. Car Collection Motorsport bestritt dort seine bislang erfolgreichste Saison. Dr. Johannes Kirchhoff, Gustav und Max Edelhoff, Elmar Grimm und Ingo Vogler fuhren im Januar bei den 24 Stunden von Dubai im Audi R8 LMS auf Platz drei in der A6-Am-Klasse. Bei den 24 Stunden von Paul Ricard gingen Gesamtrang zwei und Klassenplatz zwei in der Am-Klasse an das Team von Peter Schmidt, ebenso Platz zwei in der TCR-Klasse an einen Audi RS 3 LMS der Mannschaft. Seinen größten Erfolg feierte das hessische Unternehmen am 1. Juli in Imola: Max Edelhoff, Horst Felbermayr, Toni Forné und Dimitri Parhofer gelang als Am-Team nach 12 Stunden der Gesamtsieg vor den Pro-Mannschaften. Auch Position zwei in der Am-Klasse und Gesamtrang sechs gingen an einen Audi R8 LMS von Car Collection Motorsport. Bei den 24 Stunden von Portimão im August erzielte die Mannschaft die Plätze drei und vier in der A6-Am-Klasse und gewann diese Kategorie in Austin im November.

LONG-DISTANCE RUNNERS

The 24H Series with its endurance races primarily addresses privateers. Car Collection Motorsport contested its most successful season there to date. At the Dubai 24 Hours in January, Dr. Johannes Kirchhoff, Gustav and Max Edelhoff, Elmar Grimm and Ingo Vogler in the Audi R8 LMS took third place in the A6-Am class. In the Paul Ricard 24 Hours, position two overall and second place in class went to the team of Peter Schmidt, plus second place in the TCR class went to an Audi RS 3 LMS fielded by the squad. The company from the German state of Hesse celebrated its greatest success at Imola on July 1. After 12 hours, Max Edelhoff, Horst Felbermayr, Toni Forné and Dimitri Parhofer as an Am team achieved overall victory trailed by the Pro squads. Position two in the Am class and sixth place overall went to an Audi R8 LMS from Car Collection Motorsport as well. In the Portimão 24 Hours in August, the squad achieved positions three and four in the A6-Am class and won this category at Austin in November.

PETER SCHMIDT

Wir sind mit der Saison 2017 absolut zufrieden. Neben dem ersten Gesamtsieg einer Gentleman-Fahrerbesetzung in Imola gewann unser Junior Max Edelhoff eindrucksvoll die Rookie-Wertung. Einige langjährige Kunden wie auch neue Fahrer erreichten zahlreiche Podestplätze. Das gilt für die 24H Endurance Series, aber auch die 24 Stunden auf dem Nürburgring mit Platz zwei in der Pro-Am-Wertung. Die Fahrer und unsere gesamte Mannschaft sorgten dafür, dass es das erfolgreichste Jahr in der Teamgeschichte war.

We're perfectly happy with the 2017 season. In addition to the first overall victory of a gentleman driver lineup at Imola, our junior, Max Edelhoff, impressively won the rookies' classification. A number of longstanding customers as well as new drivers achieved numerous podium places. This applies to the 24H Endurance Series as well as to the Nürburgring 24 Hours with second place in the Pro-Am classification. The drivers and our entire squad ensured that this has been the most successful year in the team's history.

Andreas Schmidt und Berthold Gruhn engagieren sich seit Jahren in der Spezial Tourenwagen Trophy
Andreas Schmidt and Berthold Gruhn have been active in the Spezial Tourenwagen Trophy for years

Berthold Gruhn im Audi R8 LMS der zweiten Generation
Berthold Gruhn in the second-generation Audi R8 LMS

ATTRAKTIV IM CLUBSPORT

Gut kalkulierbare Einsatzkosten und die hohe Laufleistung des seriennahen V10-Aggregats sind nur zwei Aspekte, die den Audi R8 LMS auch im Clubsport so attraktiv machen. Nachwuchsfahrer Max Edelhoff durfte sich nicht nur über den Gesamtsieg in Imola freuen, sondern gewann am Saisonende dank der Qualitäten von Auto, Team und Fahrer auch die Rookie-Wertung der 24H Endurance Series vor neun Konkurrenten. In Austin sicherte er sich zudem die Rookie-Kontinente-Wertung. Während Edelhoff international unterwegs war, stellten sich Andreas Schmidt und Berthold Gruhn dem Wettbewerb auf nationaler Ebene. Die Spezial Tourenwagen Trophy versammelt diverse moderne, aber auch historische Sport- und Tourenwagen in einem Feld. An den sieben Rennwochenenden feierte Andreas Schmidt im Audi R8 LMS ultra einen Klassensieg, drei zweite und drei dritte Plätze. Berthold Gruhn steuerte einen zweiten und einen dritten Rang bei. Zudem gewann Car Collection Motorsport bei einem Gaststart am Finalwochenende auf dem Nürburgring seine Klasse mit Peter Schmidt und Dimitri Parhofer.

ATTRACTIVE IN CLUB RACING

Well-calculable fielding costs and the high mileage achieved by the production-based V10 engine are just two of the aspects that make the Audi R8 LMS so attractive in club racing as well. Up-and-coming driver Max Edelhoff was not only able to celebrate overall victory at Imola but, thanks to the qualities of the car, team and driver, won the 24H Endurance Series rookies' classification at the end of the season trailed by nine rivals as well. Additionally, he won the Rookie Continents Championship at Austin. While Edelhoff was racing on an international scale, Andreas Schmidt and Berthold Gruhn tackled the competition on the national level. The Spezial Tourenwagen Trophy combines various modern as well as historic sports and touring cars in the same field. On seven race weekends, Andreas Schmidt in an Audi R8 LMS ultra celebrated a class victory, plus three second and three third places. Berthold Gruhn contributed a second and a third place. In addition, Car Collection Motorsport in a guest run on the final weekend at the Nürburgring won their class with Peter Schmidt and Dimitri Parhofer.

Max Edelhoff, Horst Felbermayr, Toni Forné und Dimitri Parhofer gelang in Imola der Gesamtsieg
Max Edelhoff, Horst Felbermayr, Toni Forné and Dimitri Parhofer clinched overall victory at Imola

Max Edelhoff gewann in der 24H Endurance Series die Rookie-Wertung
Max Edelhoff won the rookies' classification in the 24H Endurance Series

Andreas Schmidt vertraut auf die erste Generation des Audi R8 LMS
Andreas Schmidt relies on the first generation of the Audi R8 LMS

Gut besetzte Starterfelder – hier mit Finalsieger Aust Motorsport sowie Montaplast by Land-Motorsport in Reihe eins – prägten die DMV GTC
Well-filled fields – shown here with final winner Aust Motorsport and Montaplast by Land-Motorsport on the front row – defined the DMV GTC

WIEDERHOLUNGSTÄTER

Bereits 2016 gewann Fabian Plentz die DMV GTC und siegte in der Dunlop-60-Wertung zusammen mit Tommy Tulpe. Auch in diesem Jahr war das Team HCB-Rutronik Racing das Maß der Dinge. Plentz verteidigte seinen Titel in der DMV GTC erfolgreich. Diesmal teilte er sich einen Audi R8 LMS ultra mit dem Österreicher Egon Allgäuer. Zehn Siege gingen auf das Konto des Fahrerduos, hinzu kamen drei zweite und zwei dritte Plätze. Tommy Tulpe erreichte nach fünf Siegen den zweiten Platz im Audi R8 LMS. Ronny C'Rock gewann im Audi R8 LMS von Montaplast by Land-Motorsport vier Läufe. Evi Eizenhammer in einem weiteren Audi R8 LMS von HCB-Rutronik Racing kam auf Gesamtrang sieben und Platz eins der Klasse 10 der Pro-Am-Wertung. Rang fünf in dieser Tabelle ging an Stefan Eilentropp, Bernhard Henzel sicherte sich Platz sechs und Dimitri Parhofer Rang acht. Andy Prinz schließlich erreichte Position sechs in der Klasse 8 der Pro-Am-Wertung. Bei den Dunlop-60-Rennen setzten sich Plentz und Tulpe mit fünf Siegen in acht Rennen im Audi R8 LMS durch. Ein sechster Sieg ging ebenfalls an Audi: Carrie Schreiner und Markus Pommer gewannen das Finale für Aust Motorsport.

Der frühere Truck-Europameister Egon Allgäuer fand sich im Audi R8 LMS bestens zurecht und gewann die DMV GTC
Former European Truck Champion Egon Allgäuer perfectly got his bearings in the Audi R8 LMS and won the DMV GTC

REPEATERS

In 2016, Fabian Plentz won the DMV GTC and in the Dunlop 60 classification was victorious together with Tommy Tulpe. This year, Team HCB-Rutronik Racing was again the measure of all things. Plentz successfully defended his title in the DMV GTC, this time having shared his Audi R8 LMS ultra with Austrian Egon Allgäuer. Ten points went to the driver duo's tally, plus three second and two third places. After five victories, Tommy Tulpe achieved second place in an Audi R8 LMS. Ronny C'Rock in an Audi R8 LMS from Montaplast by Land-Motorsport won four races. Evi Eizenhammer in another Audi R8 LMS from HCB-Rutronik Racing finished seventh overall and took first place in class 10 of the Pro-Am classification. Fifth place on this table went to Stefan Eilentropp, while Bernhard Henzel secured position six and Dimitri Parhofer eight. Finally, Andy Prinz achieved position six in class 8 of the Pro-Am classification. In the Dunlop 60 races, Plentz and Tulpe with five victories in eight races prevailed in the Audi R8 LMS. A sixth win went to Audi as well: Carrie Schreiner and Markus Pommer won the finale for Aust Motorsport.

Fabian Plentz (unten links) und Tommy Tulpe (unten rechts) gewannen im Audi Nummer 2 zusammen die Dunlop-60-Serie (links), während sich Plentz und Egon Allgäuer mit der Nummer 1 in der DMV GTC durchsetzten
Fabian Plentz (bottom left) and Tommy Tulpe (bottom right) in the number 2 Audi jointly won the Dunlop 60 Series (left) while Plentz and Egon Allgäuer in car number 1 prevailed in DMV GTC

Weitere Kunden, die in der DMV GTC auf Audi vertrauten, waren Bernhard Henzel mit der Nummer 19 und Andy Prinz mit der Nummer 4
Bernhard Henzel in car number 19 and Andy Prinz in number 4 were other customers relying on Audi in the DMV GTC

TREUE AUDI-KUNDEN

Das Team Optimum Motorsport war der erste Kunde, der 2015 einen Audi R8 LMS der zweiten Generation in Empfang nahm, während Jan Brunstedt aus Schweden der Marke mit den Vier Ringen seit 2011 die Treue hält. Optimum Motorsport konzentrierte sich 2017 auf den Michelin Le Mans Cup. In der GT3-Wertung lag die britische Mannschaft von Shaun Goff nach einem zweiten und zwei dritten Plätzen in der Tabellenwertung auf Podiumskurs, als Flick Haigh aus gesundheitlichen Gründen auf die letzten beiden Rennen verzichten musste. Zusammen mit Teamkollege Joe Osborne erreichte sie am Ende Platz fünf der Fahrerwertung, während Optimum Motorsport viertbestes der 16 Teams war. Jan Brunstedt wiederum schloss das Jahr als Dritter von 21 Teilnehmern in Schweden ab. Durch zwei Nullrunden beim Finale entging ihm der Vizetitel denkbar knapp. Am zweiten Rennwochenende in Falkenberg gelang ihm der erste Sieg des Jahres, bei der dritten Veranstaltung in Karlskoga triumphierte er ein weiteres Mal im Audi R8 LMS ultra. Am Tag nach dem ersten Saisonsieg war er 68 Jahre alt geworden. Für ein Ende seiner Karriere ist er noch immer zu schnell.

Jan Brunstedt war der einzige Pilot mit einem Audi in der Schwedischen GT-Meisterschaft
Jan Brunstedt was the only campaigner driving an Audi in the Swedish GT Championship

Optimum Motorsport konzentrierte sich 2017 auf den Michelin Le Mans Cup
Optimum Motorsport in 2017 concentrated on the Michelin Le Mans Cup

Joe Osborne teilte sich das Cockpit mit Flick Haigh
Joe Osborne shared the cockpit with Flick Haigh

LOYAL AUDI CUSTOMERS

Team Optimum Motorsport was the first customer to receive a second-generation Audi R8 LMS in 2015 while Jan Brunstedt from Sweden has been loyal to the brand with the four rings since 2011. In 2017, Optimum Motorsport concentrated on the Michelin Le Mans Cup. In the GT3 classification, the UK team of Shaun Goff, following a second and two third places in the standings, was on course for a podium when Flick Haigh for health reasons was forced to pass up the last two races. Together with her teammate, Joe Osborne, the squad ultimately took fifth place in the drivers' standings whereas Optimum Motorsport was the fourth-best in the field of 16 teams. Jan Brunstedt on the other hand finished the year in position three in a field of 21 entrants in Sweden. Due to two races without points in the finale he just barely missed winning the runner-up title. On the second race weekend at Falkenberg, he managed scoring his first victory of the year and in the third event at Karlskoga, he triumphed once more in an Audi R8 LMS ultra. On the day following his first victory of the season, he turned 68, still being too fast to end his career.

„Tessitore“ gewann die FIA-Berg-Europameisterschaft
“Tessitore” won the FIA European Hill Climb Championship

Der Bergmeister der Kanarischen Inseln heißt Luis Monzón
Luis Monzón is the hill climb chcmpion of the Canary Islands

Im Eset V4-Cup war K&K Duck Racing eines von mehreren Audi-Kundenteams
In the Eset V4-Cup, K&K Duck Racing was one of several Audi customer teams

WEITERE ERFOLGE IN EUROPA

Zwei Audi-Kunden gewannen mit dem Audi R8 LMS bei Bergrennen im zentral- und südeuropäischen Raum Meisterschaftstitel. Der Österreicher mit dem Pseudonym „Tessitore“ feierte im Audi R8 LMS in der FIA-Berg-Europameisterschaft vier Siege und den Meisterschaftssieg in der GT-Klasse für Produktionswagen. 90 Teilnehmer nahmen im Laufe der Saison teil. Die Bergmeisterschaft der Kanarischen Inseln dominierte Luis Monzón. Er gewann im Audi R8 LMS ultra sechs Läufe und damit die Gesamtwertung. Im zentraleuropäischen Eset V4-Cup vertrauten verschiedene Teams auf den Audi R8 LMS. Zwei einmalige Ausflüge in Westeuropa komplettierten das Bild: Alain Ferté und Stuart Leonard teilten sich einen Audi R8 LMS des Teams WRT beim Gastrennen der Britischen GT-Meisterschaft Anfang Juli in Spa und errangen zwei zweite Plätze. Am gleichen Ort fuhr drei Wochen später Angélique Detavernier in einem Audi R8 LMS von Comtoyou Racing im Blancpain GT Sports Club am 24-Stunden-Spa-Wochenende vor großem Publikum und erreichte Platz 14.

OTHER SUCCESSES IN EUROPE

Two Audi customers won championship titles in hill climb races in the Central and Southern European region with the Audi R8 LMS. The Austrian using the pseudonym “Tessitore” in an Audi R8 LMS celebrated four victories in the FIA European Hill Climb Championship, plus the championship win in the GT class for production cars. 90 entrants participated during the course of the season. The hill climb championship on the Canary Islands was dominated by Luis Monzón, who in the Audi R8 LMS ultra won six races that earned him victory in the overall classification. In the Central European Eset V4-Cup, various teams relied on the Audi R8 LMS. Two one-time outings in Western Europe completed the picture. Alain Ferté and Stuart Leonard shared an Audi R8 LMS of Team WRT in the visit of the British GT Championship to Spa at the beginning of July and clinched two second places. At the same venue three weeks later, Angélique Detavernier raced in an Audi R8 LMS from Comtoyou Racing in the Blancpain GT Sports Club on the 24-hour Spa weekend before a large crowd, taking 14th place.

Model und Managerin Angelique Detavernier beim Heimspiel in Spa mit Comtoyou Racing
Model and manager Angelique Detavernier on home soil at Spa with Comtoyou Racing

29
Audi Sport
Team Land

DRAMATISCHER SIEG

DRAMATIC VICTORY

In einem Drehbuch wäre die Szene unrealistisch gewesen. In der Eifel aber spielte sie sich wirklich ab: Der vierte Sieg von Audi beim 24-Stunden-Rennen auf dem Nürburgring hing am seidenen Faden

In a movie script, the scene would have been unrealistic, but in the Eifel it actually happened. Audi's fourth victory in the 24-hour race at the Nürburgring was hanging by a thread

24 hours

NÜRBURGRING

DISTANZ	*4.009,724 KM*
SCHNITT	*166,784 KM/H*
STRECKENLÄNGE	*25,378 KM*
SCHNELLSTE RENNRUNDE VON AUDI	*8.22,120 MIN.*
FÜHRUNGSRUNDEN AUDI	*143*
FÜHRUNGSWECHSEL	*21*
REIFENSÄTZE DES SIEGERS	*21*
AUDI-SIEGE SEIT 2012	*4*

STARKE BILANZ IN DER EIFEL

Nach drei Klassensiegen in den Jahren 2009 bis 2011 hat Audi nun vier Gesamtsiege bei den 24 Stunden auf dem Nürburgring eingefahren. 2012 und 2014 setzte sich das Audi Sport Team Phoenix durch, 2015 das Audi Sport Team WRT und 2017 das Audi Sport Team Land.

DISTANCE	*4,009.724 KM*
AVERAGE	*166.784 KM/H*
TRACK LENGTH	*25,378 KM*
FASTEST RACE LAP BY AUDI	*8M 22.120S*
LEADING LAPS BY AUDI	*143*
LEAD CHANGES	*21*
TIRE SETS OF THE WINNER	*21*
AUDI VICTORIES SINCE 2012	*4*

STRONG TALLY IN THE EIFEL

Following three class wins from 2009 to 2011, Audi has now clinched four overall victories in the Nürburgring 24 Hours. In 2012 and 2014, Audi Sport Team Phoenix prevailed, in 2015, Audi Sport Team WRT did and in 2017, Audi Sport Team Land.

Bonk Motorsport erreichte mit dem Audi RS 3 LMS zwei TCR-Podiumsplätze
Bonk Motorsport achieved two TCR podium places with the Audi RS 3 LMS

DREIKAMPF UM DEN SIEG

Die Fans werden die 45. Ausgabe der 24 Stunden auf dem Nürburgring dank eines geradezu dramatischen Finales noch lange in Erinnerung behalten. Drei Autos hatten bis zum Schluss Siegchancen, darunter zwei Audi. Das Wetterchaos erzwang gleich mehrere Boxenstopps, und erst in der letzten Runde erkämpften sich die Teams die Reihenfolge, in der sie auch ins Ziel fuhren. Der Audi R8 LMS des Audi Sport Team Land mit Connor De Phillippi, Christopher Mies, Markus Winkelhock und Kelvin van der Linde entschied ein nervenaufreibendes Rennen für sich, in dem das Fahrerquartett lange wie der sichere Sieger aussah, in der vorletzten Rennstunde alles verloren zu haben schien und dann doch noch gewann.

THREE-WAY BATTLE FOR VICTORY

The fans will long remember the 45th running of the Nürburgring 24 Hours thanks to a downright dramatic finale. Three cars were in contention for victory up until the end, including two from Audi. The weather chaos required several pit stops and only on the last lap the teams claimed the order in which they would also cross the finish line. The Audi R8 LMS from Audi Sport Team Land with Connor De Phillippi, Christopher Mies, Markus Winkelhock and Kelvin van der Linde decided a nerve-wracking race in its favor in which the driver quartet looked like the certain winner for a long time, seemed to have lost everything in the penultimate hour of the race and ultimately won nonetheless.

Sieger-Teamchef Wolfgang Land mit seinen Fahrern Connor De Phillippi, Christopher Mies, Kelvin van der Linde, Markus Winkelhock sowie Chris Reinke, Leiter Audi Sport customer racing
Winning team principal Wolfgang Land with his drivers, Connor De Phillippi, Christopher Mies, Kelvin van der Linde, Markus Winkelhock, and Chris Reinke, Head of Audi Sport customer racing

DER LANGE WEG INS ZIEL

In der dritten Rennstunde führte das Audi Sport Team Land zum ersten Mal das Rennen an. Ab Runde 26, also seit dem Ende der vierten Rennstunde, behauptete sich der grün-weiße Montaplast-Audi dauerhaft an der Spitze, sogar während der Boxenstopps. Ein Sensorproblem in der vorletzten Rennstunde aber warf das Auto auf den dritten Platz zurück. Das Audi Sport Team WRT übernahm mit Marcel Fässler/Robin Frijns/Nico Müller/René Rast die Führung, ein BMW von Rowe Racing lag zwischen beiden Audi. In der drittletzten Runde stoppte Land und zog zunächst Slicks auf, wechselte dann aber in letzter Sekunde auf Regenreifen. Die WRT-Mannschaft stoppte in derselben Runde für Slicks. Eine falsche Wahl, einen Umlauf später erneuter Tausch auf Regenreifen. Ebenso zog BMW die Pneus mit den Drainagerillen erst in der vorletzten Rennrunde auf. Das war zu spät. So gewann Wolfgang Land mit seinem Team erstmals das 24-Stunden-Rennen.

Das Audi Sport Team WRT hatte mit Marcel Fässler, Robin Frijns, Nico Müller und René Rast bis zum Schluss beste Chancen
Audi Sport Team WRT with Marcel Fässler, Robin Frijns, Nico Müller and René Rast had perfect chances up until the end

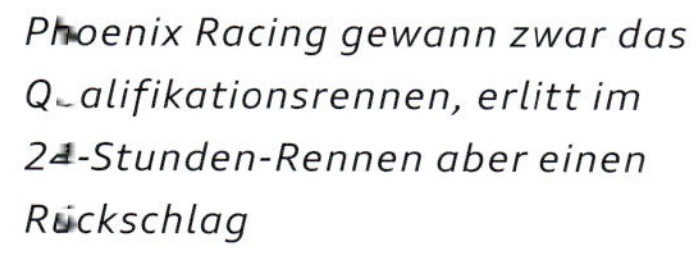

Phoenix Racing gewann zwar das Qualifikationsrennen, erlitt im 24-Stunden-Rennen aber einen Rückschlag

Although Phoenix Racing won the qualification race, the squad suffered a setback in the 24-hour race

KELVIN VAN DER LINDE

Ich bin sprachlos. Wir haben sehr lange geführt und keine Fehler gemacht. Das ganze Team hat perfekt gearbeitet. Doch dann begannen die letzten beiden Rennstunden. Als das Problem am Auto auftrat und ich die Gesichter in der Box sah, war ich eigentlich am Boden zerstört. Aber wir haben weiter alles gegeben und das hat sich ausgezahlt. Wir hatten natürlich etwas Glück, aber das gehört zum Rennsport dazu. Ein Traum ist wahr geworden.

I'm speechless. We were leading for a very long time and made no mistakes. The whole team did a perfect job. But then the last two hours of the race started. When the issue came up on the car and I saw the faces of the pit crew, I was downright devastated. But we continued to give it our all and that paid off. We obviously had a little fortune, but that's part of racing. A dream has come true.

THE LONG WAY TO THE FINISH

In the third hour of the race, Audi Sport Team Land took the lead for the first time. From lap 26 onward, in other words at the end of the fourth hour of racing, the green-white Montaplast Audi permanently maintained the lead even during the pit stops. However, a sensor issue during the race's penultimate hour caused the car to drop to third place. Audi Sport Team WRT with Marcel Fässler/Robin Frijns/Nico Müller/René Rast took the lead with a BMW from Rowe Racing in between the two Audi cars. On the third from last lap, Land pitted, initially fitting slicks but then switching to rain tires at the last moment. The WRT squad pitted for slicks on the same lap. A wrong choice resulting in another switch to rain tires one lap later. BMW, too, fitted tires with rain grooves on the race's penultimate lap. That was too late, so Wolfgang Land with his team won the 24-hour race for the first time.

ZWEI PREMIEREN

Der große Eifel-Marathon ist nicht nur ein Fest für GT3-Sportwagen. Der Audi RS 3 LMS und der Audi R8 LMS GT4 starteten zum ersten Mal bei diesem Rennen. Bonk Motorsport errang mit seinen beiden Audi RS 3 LMS auf Anhieb die TCR-Klassenplätze zwei und drei. Mit Spannung erwarteten die Fans den allerersten Renneinsatz des Audi R8 LMS GT4. Der seriennahe Sportwagen, der noch nicht homologiert war, erreichte mit Christian Abt, Rahel Frey, Patrick Huisman und Peter Terting in der SP-X-Experimentalklasse inmitten stärkerer Sportwagen den dritten Platz. Zwei Positionen dahinter kam auch der zweite GT4-Sportwagen des Audi Sport Team Phoenix mit Joonas Lappalainen, Alexander Mies, Peter Terting und Alex Yoong ins Ziel.

Zum ersten Mal stellte sich der Audi R8 LMS GT4 der Herausforderung Nordschleife

The Audi R8 LMS GT4 tackled the Nordschleife challenge for the first time

TWO PREMIERES

The big Eifel endurance race is not only a festival for GT3 sports cars. The Audi RS 3 LMS and the Audi R8 LMS GT4 competed in this race for the first time. Bonk Motorsport instantly clinched TCR class positions two and three with its two Audi RS 3 LMS cars. The fans were waiting for the first ever race of the Audi R8 LMS GT4 with bated breath. In the midst of more powerful sports cars, the production-based sports car that was not homologated yet achieved third place in the SP-X experimental class with Christian Abt, Rahel Frey, Patrick Huisman and Peter Terting. Trailing it by two positions, the second GT4 sports car from Audi Sport Team Phoenix with Joonas Lappalainen, Alexander Mies, Peter Terting and Alex Yoong saw the checkered flag as well.

Rahel Frey, Kelvin van der Linde, Pierre Kaffer, Robin Frijns, Frank Stippler, Christopher Haase, Markus Winkelhock und Christopher Mies waren 2017 die offiziellen Fahrer von Audi Sport customer racing
Rahel Frey, Kelvin van der Linde, Pierre Kaffer, Robin Frijns, Frank Stippler, Christopher Haase, Markus Winkelhock and Christopher Mies were the official drivers of Audi Sport customer racing in 2017

Car Collection Motorsport fuhr mit Klaus Koch, Lorenzo Rocco, Ronnie Saurenmann und Jan-Erik Slooten auf Platz 18 der GT3-Wertung
Car Collection Motorsport with Klaus Koch, Lorenzo Rocco, Ronnie Saurenmann and Jan-Erik Slooten came 18th in the GT3 classification

LMS Engineering schlug im privaten Audi TT RS drei Werksteams

LMS Engineering in the privateer Audi TT RS beat three factory teams

EHRGEIZIGE PRIVATIERS

Neben den von Audi Sport customer racing unterstützten Autos waren auch private Audi im Feld. Ernst Moser setzte bei Phoenix Racing auf Dennis Busch, Nicolaj Møller Madsen, Mike Rockenfeller und Frank Stippler. In Runde 14 lag ihr Audi R8 LMS erstmals unter den besten drei. Auch in der sechsten Rennstunde führten die Zeitenlisten das Auto auf dieser Position, als Møller Madsen verunfallte. Von Platz 25 arbeitete sich das Team bis ins Ziel auf die 18. Position vor. Acht Plätze dahinter sah der private Audi R8 LMS des Teams Car Collection Motorsport das Ziel. Mit einer starken Leistung glänzte das Team LMS Engineering. Es gewann mit dem Audi TT RS von Ulrich Andree/Daniela Schmid/Christian Schmitz/Stefan Wieninger die Klasse SP3T. Dabei setzte sich das Team von Andreas Lautner gegen die Werksteams der drei asiatischen Marken Hyundai, Lexus und Subaru durch.

AMBITIOUS PRIVATEERS

In addition to the cars supported by Audi Sport customer racing, the field included Audi cars entered by privateers. Ernst Moser at Phoenix Racing relied on Dennis Busch, Nicolaj Møller Madsen, Mike Rockenfeller and Frank Stippler. On lap 14, their Audi R8 LMS was running in the top three for the first time. The time sheets still listed the car in this position in the sixth hour of the race when Møller Madsen had an accident. From position 25, the team made up ground again to finish in 18th place. Eight positions behind it, the private Audi R8 LMS from Team Car Collection Motorsport saw the checkered flag. Shining with a strong performance was Team LMS Engineering. Andreas Lautner's squad won the SP3T class with the Audi TT RS of Ulrich Andree/Daniela Schmid/Christian Schmitz/Stefan Wieninger, prevailing against the factory teams of the three Asian marques Hyundai, Lexus and Subaru.

Land-Motorsport
MONTAPLAST
29
GTD

AUF ANHIEB SPITZE

INSTANTLY A FRONT RUNNER

Wolfgang Land betrat mit seinem Team in den USA Neuland. Die 24 Stunden von Daytona, die 12 Stunden von Sebring und das Petit-Le-Mans-Rennen zählen zu den drei härtesten Wettbewerben im GT-Sport. Nachdem Land den Sieg beim Auftakt nur um einen Wimpernschlag verpasst hatte, sahen die Gegner den Montaplast-Audi beim Finale nur von hinten

Wolfgang Land broke new ground with his team in the United States. The Daytona 24 Hours, the Sebring 12 Hours and the Petit Le Mans race rank among the three toughest competitions in GT racing. After Land had just barely missed victory in the opening event, rivals in the finale only saw the rear of the Montaplast Audi

SPANNENDER AUFTAKT

Die 24 Stunden von Daytona wären kein typisch amerikanisches Langstreckenrennen ohne etliche Safety-Car-Phasen. So bleiben viele Autos bis zum Ende in derselben Runde. Der Vorsprung des GTD-Siegers 2017: 0,293 Sekunden. Mit anderen Worten: Jules Gounon/ Christopher Mies/Connor De Phillippi/Jeffrey Schmidt mussten sich als Zweite nach einer Gesamtdistanz von 3.632,077 Kilometern um genau 12,304 Meter geschlagen geben. Der Audi R8 LMS von Stevenson Motorsports mit Lawson Aschenbach/Andrew Davis/ Matt Bell/Robin Liddell folgte nur fünfeinhalb Sekunden dahinter auf Platz vier. Rang sechs ging an den Audi von Alex Job Racing mit Bill Sweedler/Townsend Bell/Frank Montecalvo und Pierre Kaffer.

THRILLING OPENER

The Daytona 24 Hours would not be a typically American endurance race without several safety car periods. As a result, many cars stay on the same lap up until the end. The advantage of the 2017 GTD winner was 0.293 seconds. In other words, Jules Gounon/Christopher Mies/Connor De Phillippi/ Jeffrey Schmidt as runners-up after a total distance of 3,632.077 kilometers had to admit defeat by exactly 12.304 meters. The Audi R8 LMS from Stevenson Motorsports with Lawson Aschenbach/ Andrew Davis/Matt Bell/ Robin Liddell trailed it only five and a half seconds later in position four. Sixth place went to the Audi from Alex Job Racing with Bill Sweedler/Townsend Bell/Frank Montecalvo and Pierre Kaffer.

Teamchef Wolfgang Land setzte sich in Amerika auf Anhieb stark in Szene
Team principal Wolfgang Land instantly made a strong showing in America

Sheldon van der Linde, Connor De Phillippi und Christopher Mies beim Sieg in Road Atlanta
Sheldon van der Linde, Connor De Phillippi and Christopher Mies on clinching victory at Road Atlanta

Bereits in Daytona kämpfte Montaplast by Land-Motorsport um den Sieg
Montaplast by Land-Motorsport was in contention for victory as early as at Daytona

GROSSES FINALE

Beim 12-Stunden-Rennen in Sebring war Montaplast by Land-Motorsport wiederum bestes Audi-Team. Jules Gounon, Connor De Phillippi und Christopher Mies und fuhren auf Platz vier. Beim dritten großen Langstreckenrennen feierte das deutsche Team in Road Atlanta seinen ersten Sieg in der IMSA WeatherTech SportsCar Championship. Connor De Phillippi und Christopher Mies teilten sich das Cockpit mit dem erst 18 Jahre alten Sheldon van der Linde. Der südafrikanische Aufsteiger aus dem Audi Sport TT Cup gewann mit glänzenden Rundenzeiten sein erstes Langstreckenrennen im Audi R8 LMS. Alex Job Racing überquerte die Ziellinie auf Platz sechs mit Townsend Bell, Frank Montecalvo und Bill Sweedler.

GRAND FINALE

In the 12-hour race at Sebring, Montaplast by Land-Motorsport was again the best Audi team. Jules Gounon, Connor De Phillippi and Christopher Mies took position four. In the third major endurance race, at Road Atlanta, the German outfit celebrated its first victory in the IMSA WeatherTech SportsCar Championship. Connor De Phillippi and Christopher Mies shared the cockpit with 18-year-old Sheldon van der Linde. The South African who was promoted from the Audi Sport TT Cup won his first endurance race in the Audi R8 LMS with brilliant lap times. Alex Job Racing crossed the finish line in position six with Townsend Bell, Frank Montecalvo and Bill Sweedler.

Stevenson Motorsports konzentrierte sich in diesem Jahr auf einen einzigen Audi R8 LMS
Stevenson Motorsports concentrated on a single Audi R8 LMS this year

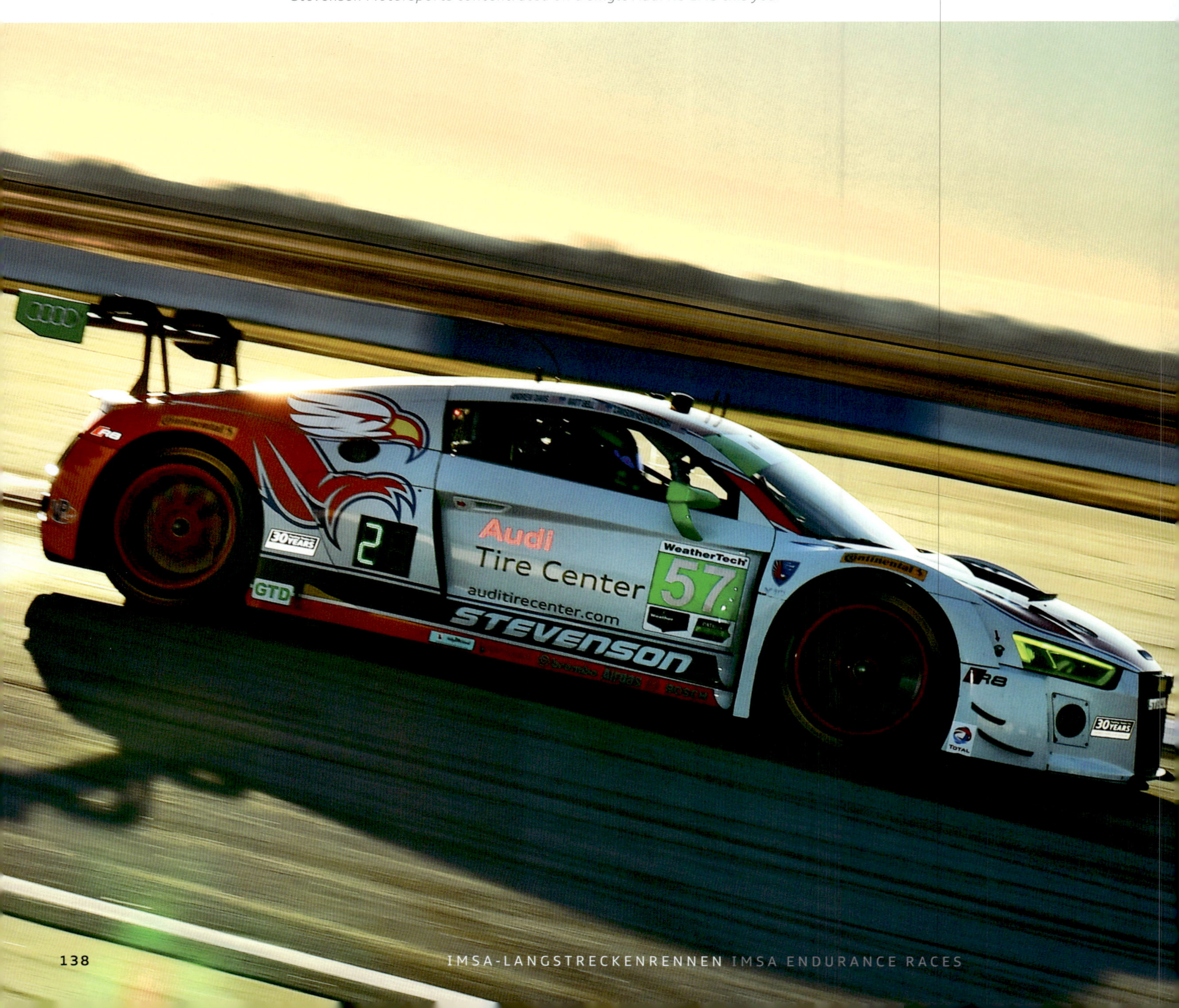

Matt Bell, Andrew Davis und Lawson Aschenbach mit Stevenson Motorsports beim Petit-Le-Mans-Rennen
Matt Bell, Andrew Davis and Lawson Aschenbach with Stevenson Motorsports at the Petit Le Mans race

SHELDON VAN DER LINDE

2017 bin ich aus dem Audi Sport TT Cup in die ADAC TCR Germany aufgestiegen. Als der GT3-Teamkollege meines Bruders Kelvin am Sachsenring krank war, sprang ich ein, rannte zwischen TCR- und GT3-Zelten hin und her, gewann dabei mein erstes Rennen im Audi RS 3 LMS und erreichte Platz vier mit dem Audi R8 LMS. Land-Motorsport beobachtete mich dabei aufmerksam und suchte für Road Atlanta einen Fahrer mit Silver-Einstufung. Kelvin half mir vor Ort mit Tipps und ehrlichen Rückmeldungen. Alles lief perfekt. Montaplast und Land-Motorsport danke ich für das Vertrauen und diese Chance. Der Sieg war ein schöner Schub in meiner Karriere.

In 2017, I was promoted from the Audi Sport TT Cup to the ADAC TCR Germany. When the teammate of my brother Kelvin was ill at the Sachsenring, I stood in for him, ran back and forth between TCR and GT3 awnings, won my first race in the Audi RS 3 LMS in the process and achieved fourth place in the Audi R8 LMS. Land-Motorsport was closely watching me in all this, looking for a Silver-rated driver for Road Atlanta. Kelvin helped me at the venue with advice and honest feedback. Everything went perfectly. I wish to thank Montaplast and Land-Motorsport for their trust and this opportunity. The victory was a nice boost for my career.

Alex Job Racing vertrat die Farben von Audi bei ausgewählten Rennen
Alex Job Racing represented Audi's colors in selected races

HARTE SAISON

A TOUGH SEASON

Die IMSA WeatherTech SportsCar Championship war auch in der Saison 2017 hart umkämpft. Sie endete für die Motorsport-Familie von Audi Sport customer racing traurig

The IMSA WeatherTech SportsCar Championship was fiercely competitive again in the 2017 season. For the motorsport family of Audi Sport customer racing, it had a sad ending

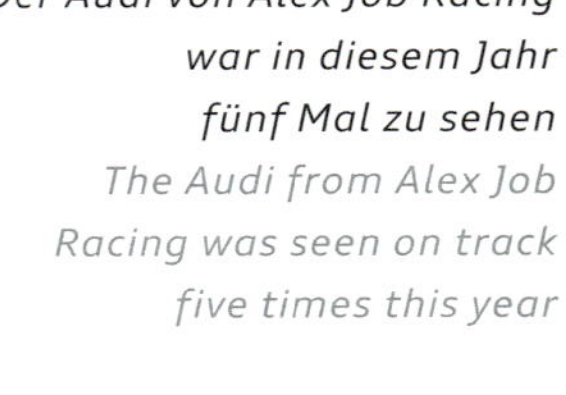

Der Audi von Alex Job Racing war in diesem Jahr fünf Mal zu sehen
The Audi from Alex Job Racing was seen on track five times this year

AUSGEWÄHLTES PROGRAMM

Alex Job Racing bestritt in der IMSA WeatherTech SportsCar Championship in der Saison 2017 ein limitiertes Programm. Fünf Mal war der Audi R8 LMS jenes Teams am Start, das 2013 den historischen ersten Klassensieg von Audi in Daytona erzielt hatte. In diesem Jahr erreichte die Mannschaft dort beim Saisonauftakt den sechsten Platz. Nach Rang 15 in Sebring, der achten Position in Lime Rock Park und dem 14. Platz in Watkins Glen endete die Saison in Road Atlanta so, wie sie begonnen hatte: mit dem sechstbesten Ergebnis. Im North American Endurance Cup, der die Läufe in Daytona, Sebring, Watkins Glen und Road Atlanta umfasst, erreichten Bill Sweedler, Frank Montecalvo und Townsend Bell den zehnten Platz.

SELECTED PROGRAM

In the 2017 season, Alex Job Racing contested a limited program in the IMSA WeatherTech SportsCar Championship. The Audi R8 LMS of the team that in 2013 had clinched Audi's historic first class win at Daytona was on the grid on five occasions. This year, the squad achieved sixth place in the season opener at Daytona. Following position 15 at Sebring, eight at Lime Rock Park and 14th place at Watkins Glen, the season ended at Road Atlanta the way it had begun: in the sixth-best result. In the North American Endurance Cup, which encompasses the rounds at Daytona, Sebring, Watkins Glen and Road Atlanta, Bill Sweedler, Frank Montecalvo and Townsend Bell achieved tenth place.

Frank Montecalvo, Bill Sweedler und Townsend Bell fuhren für das Team von Alex Job

Frank Montecalvo, Bill Sweedler and Townsend Bell drove for Alex Job's team

TRAURIGES ENDE

Jubel und Trauer lagen für das Team Stevenson Motorsports in der Saison 2017 eng beisammen. Saisonhöhepunkt war für die Mannschaft der einzige Lauf außerhalb der USA. Im benachbarten Kanada gelang Lawson Aschenbach und Andrew Davis ein Saisonsieg in der GTD-Klasse. Das Fahrerduo fuhr in Mosport Park mit drei Sekunden Vorsprung zum Sieg. Bemerkenswert: Die nächsten sieben Konkurrenten folgten innerhalb von nur 12,8 Sekunden. Am Ende lagen acht Marken unter den ersten zehn. Platz drei in Road America beim neunten Lauf war der einzige weitere Podestplatz der beiden Piloten. Zum Ablauf der Saison verkündete das Team das Ende seiner Rennsport-Aktivitäten. Kurz darauf verstarb Teamchef Johnny Stevenson.

SAD ENDING

Celebration and sorrow were not far apart from each other for Stevenson Motorsports in the 2017 season. The only round outside the United States marked the season's pinnacle event for the squad. In neighboring Canada, Lawson Aschenbach and Andrew Davis achieved victory in the GTD class, claimed by the driver duo at Mosport Park with a three-second advantage. Notably, the closest seven rivals followed within just 12.8 seconds. In the end, eight marques were in the top ten. Third place at Road America in round nine was the only other podium clinched by the two campaigners. At the end of the season, the team announced that it would cease its racing activities. Shortly afterwards, team principal Johnny Stevenson passed away.

Lawson Aschenbach und Andrew Davis feierten mit Stevenson Motorsports in Mosport den letzten Sieg

Lawson Aschenbach and Andrew Davis celebrated the last victory with Stevenson Motorsports at Mosport

TRAUER UM JOHNNY STEVENSON
MOURNING THE LOSS OF JOHNNY STEVENSON

Am 16. Oktober, neun Tage nach dem IMSA-Saisonfinale, verstarb Johnny Stevenson im Alter von 69 Jahren. Er managte eine Automobil-Handelsgruppe, die zu den 125 größten in den USA zählte. Seit 2016 vertrat er die Farben von Audi in der GTD-Klasse der IMSA WeatherTech SportsCar Championship. Im Vorjahr war er mit den Leistungen seiner Mannschaft wesentlich am Titelgewinn von Audi in der GTD-Markenwertung beteiligt. Das Beileid aller Mitarbeiter von Audi Sport customer racing gilt der gesamten Familie von Johnny Stevenson.

On October 16, nine days after the finale of the IMSA season, Johnny Stevenson passed away at the age of 69. He owned a group of automotive dealerships ranking among the top 125 in the United States. Since 2016, he represented Audi's colors in the GTD class of the IMSA WeatherTech SportsCar Championship. Last year, he had a major part in Audi's title win in the GTD manufacturers' classification with the performances of his squad. All employees of Audi Sport customer racing express their condolences to Johnny Stevenson's entire family.

Stevenson Motorsports beendete sein Motorsport-Engagement nach 15 Jahren
Stevenson Motorsports ceased its motorsport activities after 15 years

Audi Sport
PIRELLI
23
Dayson
Pegram
PIRELLI
82
R8

PRÄSENT IN VIELEN KLASSEN

PRESENT IN MANY CLASSES

Magnus Racing wechselte im Winter 2016/2017 von der IMSA in die Pirelli World Challenge und traf dort auf zwei weitere Audi-Teams. John Potter errang in der GTA-Wertung auf Anhieb die Vizemeisterschaft

Magnus Racing in winter 2016/2017 switched from IMSA to the Pirelli World Challenge where the squad met with two other Audi teams. John Potter instantly finished runner-up in the GTA classification

KLASSENERFOLGE FÜR M1 GT RACING

Drei Teams vertraten die Farben von Audi in der Pirelli World Challenge 2017. Während Magnus Racing mit zwei Rennwagen permanent dabei war, wählten McCann Racing und M1 GT Racing einzelne Läufe aus. Die Fahrermannschaften verfolgten ihre Ziele dabei in ganz unterschiedlichen Klassen. M1 GT Racing besitzt einen aktuellen Audi R8 LMS und ein Modell der ersten Generation. In Virginia erreichten James Dayson und Larry Pegram beim Saisonauftakt im Audi R8 LMS ultra des Teams Platz drei der Am-Wertung. Dayson und Mitstreiter Jason Bell fuhren in Utah beim vierten Lauf der SprintX im Audi R8 LMS zwei Mal auf Rang drei der Am-Wertung. Beim Finale in Austin sprangen für sie mit den Positionen zwei und drei erneut zwei Podiumsplätze in dieser Klasse heraus. Ihre Teamkollegen Walt Bowlin und Lars Viljoen erzielten in dieser Wertung bei derselben Veranstaltung einen vierten und einen zweiten Platz im älteren Modell.

Jason Bell und James Dayson belegten am Jahresende in der SprintX-Wertung Platz vier der Am-Klasse
Jason Bell and James Dayson finished the year in the SprintX classification in position four of the Am class

Pierre Kaffer kämpfte in der Pirelli World Challenge mit Magnus Racing um Podestplätze
Pierre Kaffer battled with Magnus Racing for podium places in the Pirelli World Challenge

Mike Skeen und Andrew Davis errangen für McCann Racing Platz zwei in Virginia (oben). Walt Bowlin/Lars Viljoen erreichten im Audi R8 LMS ultra einen zweiten und einen vierten Platz in der Am-Wertung in Austin (darunter)
Mike Skeen and Andrew Davis clinched second place in Virginia for McCann Racing (top). Walt Bowlin/Lars Viljoen in an Audi R8 LMS ultra achieved a second and a fourth place in the Am classification at Austin (bottom)

SUCCESS IN CLASS FOR M1 GT RACING

Three teams represented Audi's colors in the 2017 Pirelli World Challenge. While Magnus Racing with two cars was a permanent entrant, McCann Racing and M1 GT Racing selected individual events. The driver squads pursued their aims in totally different classes. M1 GT Racing owns a current Audi R8 LMS and a first-generation model. At the season opener in Virginia, James Dayson and Larry Pegram in the team's Audi R8 LMS ultra achieved third place in the Am classification. Dayson and his teammate, Jason Bell, piloted their Audi R8 LMS to third place twice in the Am classification in round four of the SprintX in Utah. In positions two and three, they clinched two more podium places in this class in the finale at Austin. Their teammates, Walt Bowlin and Lars Viljoen, in this classification achieved a fourth and a second place in the older model at the same event.

Zum ersten Mal setzte Magnus Racing Pierre Kaffer ein
Magnus Racing deployed Pierre Kaffer for the first time

VIZETITEL

Für John Potter war der Wechsel von Langstreckenrennen zu Sprints eine Umgewöhnung. Platz drei in der GTA-Klasse in Long Beach war ein guter Anfang. In Road America errang Potter, der Teamchef von Magnus Racing und Fahrer in Personalunion ist, zwei Mal den zweiten Platz in der Am-Wertung. Am Saisonende erreichte er den Vizetitel in der GTA-Fahrerwertung. In Lime Rock Park feierten Dane Cameron/Spencer Pumpelly für Magnus Racing einen zweiten Platz und einen Sieg. Pumpelly gelang mit Platz drei in Austin zusammen mit Pierre Kaffer ein weiteres Podestergebnis. Zu Saisonbeginn erzielte zudem McCann Racing mit Andrew Davis/Mike Skeen in Virginia mit Platz zwei ein Spitzenergebnis für Audi.

RUNNER-UP TITLE

For John Potter, switching from endurance to sprint racing meant having to readjust. Third place in the GTA class at Long Beach was a good beginning. At Road America, Potter, who is both the team principal of Magnus Racing and a driver, took second place in the Am classification twice. At the end of the season, he claimed the runner-up title in the GTA drivers' classification. At Lime Rock Park, Dane Cameron/Spencer Pumpelly celebrated a second place and a victory for Magnus Racing. Pumpelly, on clinching third place at Austin, achieved another podium finish together with Pierre Kaffer. In addition, at the beginning of the season, McCann Racing with Andrew Davis/Mike Skeen in position two scored a top result for Audi in Virginia.

Marco Seefried fuhr ausgewählte Läufe für Magnus Racing
Marco Seefried drove selected rounds for Magnus Racing

JOHN POTTER

Tabellenrang zwei in der GTA-Klasse war bei dieser harten Konkurrenz in Ordnung. Zuvor fuhr ich Langstreckenrennen in der IMSA, doch die Sprints in der Pirelli World Challenge sind anders – dort ging es in jeder Runde um das Maximum. Zum ersten Mal fuhr Pierre Kaffer das zweite Auto. Er war ein echter Gewinn für unser Team. In meinem Cockpit erhielt ich bei einigen Läufen Unterstützung von Marco Seefried, der mit uns bereits Daytona gewonnen hat.

Second place in the GTA class standings was okay in this tough competition. I previously contested endurance races in IMSA but the sprints in the Pirelli World Challenge are different – each lap being about the maximum. For the first time, Pierre Kaffer drove the second car. He was a real gain for our team. In my cockpit, I received support in some of the races from Marco Seefried who already won Daytona with us.

John Potter gewöhnte sich 2017 an den Rhythmus von Sprintrennen
John Potter got used to the rhythm of sprint races in 2017

IM ZWEITEN ANLAUF

SUCCESS IN SECOND ATTEMPT

Alessio Picariello verlor den Audi R8 LMS Cup 2016 nach einem kontroversen Finale am grünen Tisch. Eine Strafe für einen Rammstoß kostete ihn den Titel. Ein Jahr später schlug der Belgier souverän zurück und gewann den Markenpokal von Audi vorzeitig

Following a controversial finale, Alessio Picariello lost the 2016 Audi R8 LMS Cup due to an administrative decision. A penalty for hitting another car cost him the title. A year later, the Belgian fought back in commanding style, claiming an early win of Audi's one-make cup

Alessio Picariello gewann den Titel souverän
Alessio Picariello won the title in commanding style

EINE NEUE GENERATION

Zwei der jüngsten Fahrer im Feld setzten sich 2017 stark in Szene. Dem 24 Jahre alten Alessio Picariello gelangen vier Saisonsiege – mehr als jedem anderen Fahrer. Damit war er bereits in Shanghai nach dem vierten von fünf Rennwochenenden nicht mehr einholbar. Auch mit dem erfolgsabhängigen Ballastgewicht an Bord agierte der Belgier souverän und stand sieben Mal in zehn Läufen auf dem Podest. Mitchell Gilbert aus Malaysia errang in der ersten Saisonhälfte vier Mal einen Pokal. Mit seinem Sieg beim Finale in Zhejiang verbesserte sich der 23 Jahre alte Neueinsteiger vom fünften auf den zweiten Tabellenplatz. Das Team Absolute Racing betreute beide Piloten.

A NEW GENERATION

Two of the youngest drivers in the field made a strong showing in 2017. 24-year-old Alessio Picariello scored four victories this season – more than any other driver. As a result, he was out of his rivals' reach as early as at Shanghai after the fourth of five race weekends. Even with success ballast on board the Belgian acted masterfully and mounted the podium seven times in ten races. Mitchell Gilbert from Malaysia clinched a trophy on four occasions in the first half of the season. On taking victory in the finale at Zhejiang, the 23-year-old newcomer improved from fifth to second place in the standings. Team Absolute Racing supported both drivers.

Michael Schneider, Projektverantwortlicher Audi bei Absolute Racing, mit Martin Kühl, dem neuen Leiter von Audi Sport customer racing Asia, und Ingo Matter, Direktor Absolute Racing
Michael Schneider, Audi Project Manager at Absolute Racing, with Martin Kühl, the new Head of Audi Sport customer racing Asia, and Ingo Matter, Director Absolute Racing

ALESSIO PICARIELLO

In diesem Jahr bestand ein Schlüssel zum Erfolg darin, auch mit Erfolgsballast gut zu sein. Mit Gewicht waren unsere Leistungen besser als die der Konkurrenz. Meine Stärke im Rennen lag darin, unter allen Bedingungen gut mit den Reifen zu haushalten. Der Sieg in Suzuka und der Erfolg in Korea mit 9,9 Sekunden Vorsprung waren zwei der schönsten Rennen. Nach meinem Formel-Masters-Titel ist dieser Meisterschaftserfolg wichtig, um eine GT-Karriere aufzubauen. Ohne Absolute Racing, die mich in den Rennsport zurückgebracht haben, wäre dieser Titel nicht möglich gewesen.

This year one of the keys to success was being good even with success ballast. With weight our performances were better than those of the competition. My strength in the race was doing a good job of managing the tires. The victory at Suzuka and the success in Korea with a 9.9-second advantage were two of the best races. After my Formula Masters title, this championship success is important for building a GT career. Without Absolute Racing that brought me back into racing this title would not have been possible.

Mitchell Gilbert gelang eine glänzende Debütsaison mit OD Racing (oben und links)
Mitchell Gilbert achieved a brilliant debut season with OD Racing (top and left)

KEINE CHANCE FÜR FRÜHERE MEISTER

Alex Yoong hat den Audi R8 LMS Cup seit 2014 drei Mal in Folge gewonnen, Marchy Lee war 2012 der erste Titelträger. In dieser Saison waren die beiden 41 Jahre alten Routiniers allerdings chancenlos. Obwohl Yoong zwei Läufe gewann und zwei weitere Male einen Pokal holte, reichte es nur für Tabellenplatz vier. Zu oft sammelte der frühere Formel-1-Fahrer aus Malaysia nur wenige Punkte. Für Marchy Lee, der nur an drei der fünf Wochenenden antrat, blieb ein vierter Platz beim Saisonfinale das beste Ergebnis. Der 33 Jahre alte Congfu Cheng aus China war als Tabellendritter der beste der erfahrenen Piloten im Feld.

Congfu Cheng schloss die Saison als Dritter ab
Congfu Cheng finished the season in third place

Alex Yoong von Phoenix Racing Asia musste sich nach drei Titeln in Folge mit Tabellenrang vier begnügen
Alex Yoong from Phoenix Racing Asia, after three consecutive titles, had to settle for position four of the standings

Marchy Lee, hier im Gespräch mit Johannes Trost von Audi Sport customer racing, nahm an drei der fünf Veranstaltungen teil
Marchy Lee, pictured here in conversation with Johannes Trost from Audi Sport customer racing, participated in three of the five events

Der Audi R8 LMS von Audi Hong Kong
The Audi R8 LMS from Audi Hong Kong

NO CHANCE FOR FORMER CHAMPIONS

Alex Yoong has won the Audi R8 LMS Cup three times in succession since 2014. Marchy Lee in 2012 was the first title winner. This season, however, the two 41-year-old seasoned campaigners were chanceless. Although Yoong won two races and clinched a trophy in two other events, he only finished fourth in the standings, the former Formula 1 driver from Malaysia having scored only few points on too many occasions. For Marchy Lee, who only competed on three of the five weekends, a fourth place in the season finale remained the best result. 33-year-old Congfu Cheng from China in third place of the standings was the best of the experienced campaigners in the field.

Dries Vanthoor beeindruckte bei seinem Gastspiel mit WRT (rechts und rechts außen)
Dries Vanthoor impressed in his guest run with WRT (right and far right)

Auch in seiner sechsten Saison begeisterte der Audi R8 LMS Cup viele Fans
In its sixth season, the Audi R8 LMS Cup again thrilled many fans

KLASSENSIEGER UND SCHNELLE GÄSTE

Für Aufsehen sorgten mindestens drei Piloten. Chen Weian aus China setzte sich in der Am-Plus-Wertung souverän gegen Routinier Jeffrey Lee durch, obwohl er die ersten beiden Läufe verpasst hatte. Beim Finale gelang Chen sogar ein Gesamtsieg. Dries Vanthoor startete für WRT nur am Shanghai-Wochenende. Trotz eines verpassten Trainings wegen fehlenden Gepäcks und einer unfreiwilligen Reise zum Flughafen Pudong fuhr der junge Belgier zweimal auf Startplatz eins, feierte einen Gesamtsieg und einen dritten Platz. Die Am-Cup-Klassifikation schließlich entschied Bhurit Bhirombhakdi für sich. Der Rennfahrer aus Thailand gewann seine Wertung im Lauf der Saison fünf Mal.

CLASS WINNERS AND QUICK GUESTS

At least three drivers caused a sensation. Chen Weian from China masterfully won against seasoned campaigner Jeffrey Lee in the Am-Plus classification in spite of having missed the first two rounds. In the finale, Chen even achieved an overall victory. Dries Vanthoor raced for WRT only on the Shanghai weekend. In spite of a missed practice session due to lost luggage and an involuntary trip to Pudong airport, the young Belgian took pole position twice, celebrated an overall victory and a third place. Ultimately, Bhurit Bhirombhakdi decided the Am-Cup classification in his favor. The race driver from Thailand won his classification five times during the course of the season.

Bhurit Bhirombhakdi gewann den Am-Cup
Bhurit Bhirombhakdi won the Am-Cup

Chen Weian (Mitte), hier mit Shaun Thong und Mitchell Gilbert, war der erste Fahrer aus der Am-plus-Kategorie, dem ein Gesamtsieg gelang
Chen Weian (in the middle), shown here with Shaun Thong and Mitchell Gilbert, was the first driver from the Am-plus category to have scored an overall victory

SONNENAUFGANG IN ASIEN

SUNRISE IN ASIA

In Asien geht die Sonne auf: Mit der neuen Blancpain GT Series Asia erwachte der GT3-Sport in diesem Teil der Welt zu neuer Blüte. Audi Hong Kong gewann einen ersten Titel

The sun rises in Asia: The new Blancpain GT Series Asia caused GT3 racing to flourish anew. Audi Hong Kong won a first title

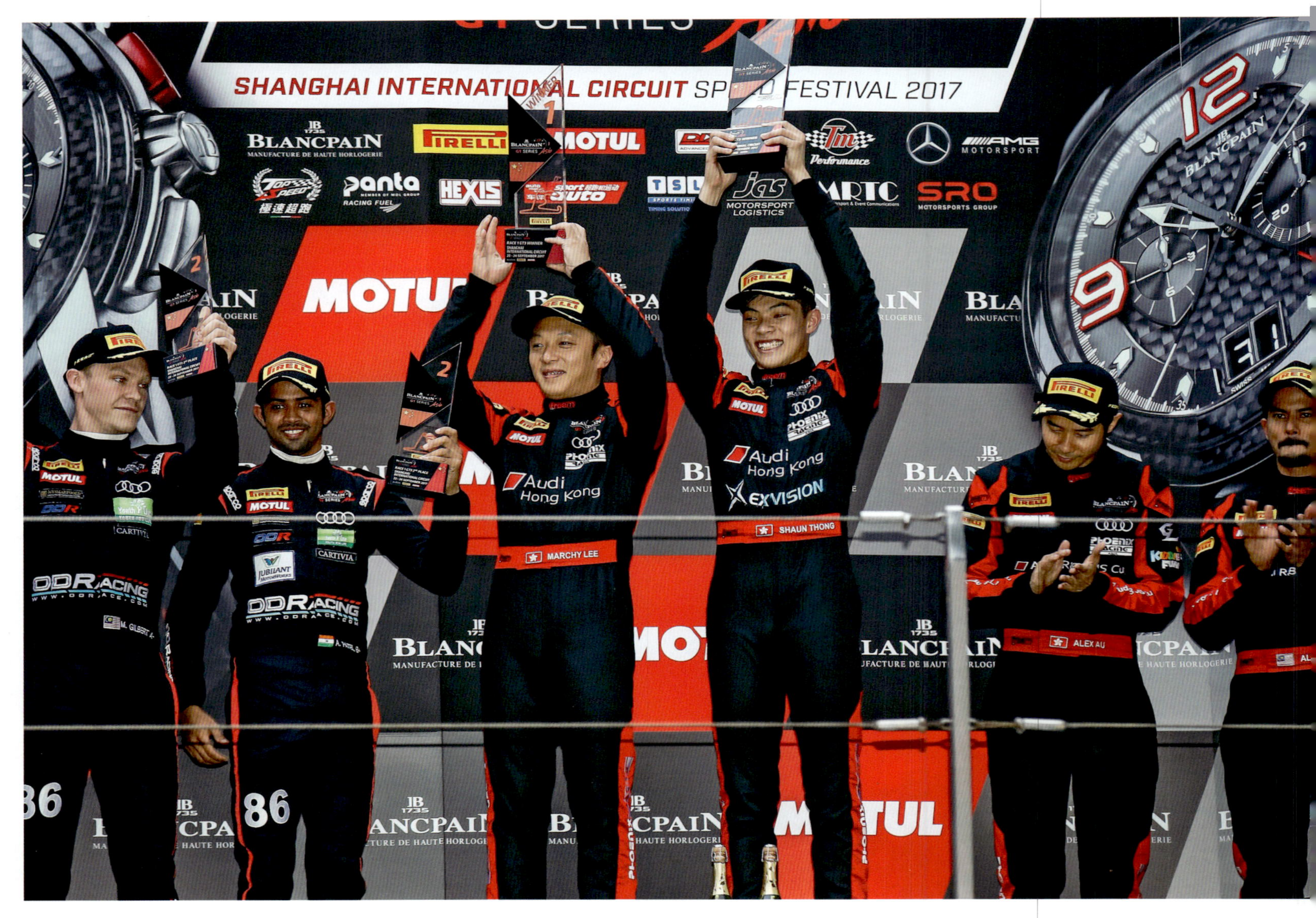

Mitchell Gilbert, Aditya Patel, Marchy Lee, Shaun Thong, Alex Au und Alex Yoong
Mitchell Gilbert, Aditya Patel, Marchy Lee, Shaun Thong, Alex Au and Alex Yoong

PERFEKTE BÜHNE

Eine professionell organisierte GT3-Rennserie von panasiatischer Reichweite gab es bislang noch nicht. Die Stéphane Ratel Organisation füllte diese Lücke zur Saison 2017 und erhielt großen Zuspruch. 59 Fahrer sammelten im Lauf der Saison Punkte in der GT3-Wertung, hinzu kamen 18 GT4-Teilnehmer. Sieben Marken waren in der GT3-Kategorie vertreten. Der Audi R8 LMS war dabei mit bis zu acht Exemplaren das beliebteste Auto. Als Einsatzteams standen mit Absolute Racing, Phoenix Racing, KCMG und WRT die gleichen erfahrenen Dienstleister wie im Audi R8 LMS Cup bereit. Bei zwölf Läufen an sechs Wochenenden in Malaysia, Thailand, Japan und China errangen die Audi-Fahrerteams insgesamt fünf Siege.

A PERFECT STAGE

A professionally organized Pan-Asian GT3 racing series had previously been non-existent. The Stéphane Ratel Organisation filled this gap starting in the 2017 season and met with huge response. 59 drivers scored points in the GT3 classification during the course of the season. In addition, the series included 18 GT4 entrants. Seven marques were represented in the GT3 category, the Audi R8 LMS with up to eight vehicles being the most popular car. The same seasoned service providers as in the Audi R8 LMS Cup – Absolute Racing, Phoenix Racing, KCMG and WRT – were ready to support the series. In twelve rounds on six weekends in Malaysia, Thailand, Japan and China, the Audi driver squads clinched five victories in total.

ERNST MOSER

Stéphane Ratel hat gewohnt professionell eine neue Serie geschaffen. Unser Ziel war es, mit lokalen Fahrern um den Titel zu fahren, während sich andere Teams Schützenhilfe aus Europa geholt haben. Bis zum Finale haben Marchy Lee und Shaun Thong um die Gesamtwertung gekämpft, als ein Gegner sie unfair rammte. Am Ende blieb der Sieg im Silver Cup. Darauf kann das ganze Team stolz sein.

Stéphane Ratel has created a new series in his usual professional way. Our goal was to compete for the title with local drivers while other teams went for support from Europe. Up until the finale, Marchy Lee and Shaun Thong were in contention for the overall classification when a rival hit them unfairly. In the end, we took victory in the Silver Cup. The whole team can be proud of this.

Beim Pflichtboxenstopp – hier das Team Milestone Racing – wechseln sich zwei Fahrer ab

At the mandatory pit stop – Team Milestone Racing pictured here – two drivers take turns

Alex Au und Alex Yoong fuhren zusammen drei Podiumsergebnisse ein (oben). Aditya Patel und Mitchell Gilbert lagen nach drei Siegen am Ende nur einen Punkt hinter dem Titelgewinner (unten)

Alex Au and Alex Yoong together clinched three podium results (top). Aditya Patel and Mitchell Gilbert, following three victories, in the end trailed the title winner by only one point (bottom)

SPANNENDE SAISON

Mitchell Gilbert aus Malaysia und Aditya Patel aus Indien begannen die Saison mit einem Sieg und einem zweiten Platz in Sepang. Dann zogen Marchy Lee/Shaun Thong mit zwei zweiten Plätzen in Thailand in der Tabelle an ihnen vorbei. In Suzuka feierte das Duo aus Hongkong im Audi R8 LMS von Phoenix Racing Asia seinen ersten Sieg. Einem dritten Platz in Fuji folgte der zweite Saisonsieg von Lee/Thong in Shanghai. Damit übernahmen die beiden Piloten von Audi Hong Kong die Tabellenführung. Durch eine rüde Attacke eines Gegners waren sie beim Finale in Zhejiang in der Gesamtwertung chancenlos, gewannen aber den Silver Cup. Mitchell Gilbert/Aditya Patel stürmten mit zwei Siegen noch zum Vizetitel mit nur einem Punkt Rückstand auf den neuen Meister.

A THRILLING SEASON

Mitchell Gilbert from Malaysia and Aditya Patel from India started the season with a victory and a second place at Sepang. Subsequently, Marchy Lee/Shaun Thong, on taking two second places in Thailand, overtook them in the standings. At Suzuka, the duo from Hong Kong in the Audi R8 LMS from Phoenix Racing Asia celebrated its first victory. A third place at Fuji was followed by the second win of the season by Lee/Thong in Shanghai. As a result, the two campaigners from Audi Hong Kong took the lead of the standings. Due to a rough attack by a rival, they were chanceless in the overall classification in the finale at Zhejiang but won the Silver Cup. Mitchell Gilbert/Aditya Patel with two victories still stormed to the runners-up title with only a one-point deficit to the new champion.

Marchy Lee/Shaun Thong gewannen in Shanghai vor Mitchell Gilbert/Aditya Patel und Alex Au/Alex Yoong

Marchy Lee/Shaun Thong won at Shanghai ahead of Mitchell Gilbert/Aditya Patel and Alex Au/Alex Yoong

Anthony Liu Xu und Davide Rizzo teilten sich den Audi R8 LMS von BBT
Anthony Liu Xu and Davide Rizzo shared the Audi R8 LMS from BBT

KCMG betreute zwei Audi R8 LMS
KCMG took care of two Audi R8 LMS cars

TAISAN SARD
ニッポンを元気に!
FUKUSHIMA
FUKUSHIMA
26
MOTUL
R8 LMS

HARTER WETTBEWERB

TOUGH COMPETITION

Die Super GT in Japan zählt zu den professionellsten und damit schwierigsten GT-Serien der Welt. Das Audi Team Hitotsuyama und das Team Taisan SARD vertraten 2017 die Farben von Audi

The Super GT in Japan ranks among the most professional and thus most difficult GT series in the world. Audi Team Hitotsuyama and Team Taisan SARD represented Audi's colors in 2017

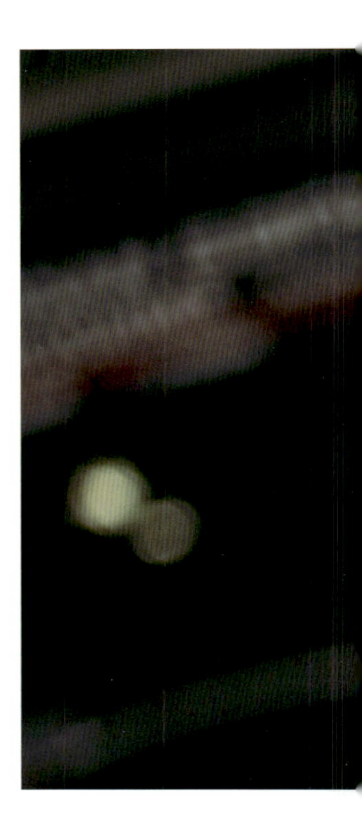

NEUE KRÄFTE

Das Team Taisan, das mit SARD kooperiert, zählt zu den Mannschaften der ersten Stunde in der 1994 gegründeten Rennserie Super GT. Vier Mal gewann es mit seinen Piloten die GT300-Fahrermeisterschaft, sieben Mal die Teamwertung. Seit 2016 setzt der Rennstall den Audi R8 LMS ein. Nun kamen frische Kräfte ins Cockpit: Der 22 Jahre alte Australier Jake Parsons zog für seine neue Aufgabe nach Japan, um sich die Arbeit mit Fahrerkollege Shinnosuke Yamada zu teilen. Der 24 Jahre alte Japaner stammt aus der Formel 4 und war 2016 erstmals in der Super GT am Start. Auch beim Audi Team Hitotsuyama ergab sich eine Änderung: Der langjährige Stammpilot Richard Lyons aus Nordirland erhielt Masataka Yanagida als neuen Teamkollegen. Beide kennen sich bereits seit 2003 aus einem anderen Programm in der Super GT.

Die beiden Audi R8 LMS bereicherten die GT300-Klasse der Super GT
The two Audi R8 LMS cars augmented the GT300 class of the Super GT

Jake Parsons fuhr seine erste Saison im Audi R8 LMS
Jake Parsons contested his first season in the Audi R8 LMS

Shinnosuke Yamada stand beim Team Taisan SARD unter Vertrag
Shinnosuke Yamada was signed by Team Taisan SARD

NEW FORCES

Team Taisan, which cooperates with SARD, is one of the first squads to have competed in the Super GT racing series that was launched in 1994. Four times it has won the GT300 drivers' championship with its campaigners and seven times the teams' classification. Since 2016, the race team has been fielding the Audi R8 LMS. Now fresh forces moved into the cockpit. 22-year-old Australian Jake Parsons relocated to Japan for his new driving duties to share the job with fellow driver Shinnosuke Yamada. The 24-year-old Japanese comes from Formula 4 and in 2016 was on the Super GT grid for the first time. There was a change with Audi Team Hitotsuyama as well. Long-standing regular driver Richard Lyons from Northern Ireland was joined by Masataka Yanagida as his new teammate. They have known each other since 2003 from another program in the Super GT.

Masataka Yanagida feierte am dritten Rennwochenende seinen 38. Geburtstag im Kreis von Teamchef Ryoji Hitotsuyama und Fahrerkollegen

Masataka Yanagida on the third race weekend celebrated his 38th birthday surrounded by team principal Ryoji Hitotsuyama and fellow drivers

AUFWIND IN THAILAND

Nach einem schwierigen Saisonbeginn war das siebte Rennwochenende in Thailand für beide Teams ein Schritt nach vorn. Das Team Taisan SARD konnte im Feld der besten zehn von 24 Teilnehmern mitmischen, bis ein Problem mit der Benzinversorgung auftrat. Das Audi Team Hitotsuyama war bereits im Qualifying Spitze. Masataka Yanagida war auf dem Kurs in Chang mehr als eine Sekunde schneller als sein bester Verfolger und eroberte die Pole-Position. Teamkollege Richard Lyons fuhr dem Feld beim Start davon. Er baute einen Vorsprung auf und übergab das Auto an seinen japanischen Teamkollegen. Auch wenn das Team nicht ins Ziel kam, hatten alle gezeigt, was an diesem Wochenende möglich gewesen wäre.

ON A TEAR IN THAILAND

Following a difficult start of the season, the seventh race weekend in Thailand marked a step forward for both teams. Team Taisan SARD was in contention in the field of the top ten of 24 entrants until a fuel supply issue emerged. Audi Team Hitotsuyama was top-class as early as in qualifying. Masataka Yanagida on the circuit at Chang was more than a second faster than his best immediate rival and clinched pole position. His teammate, Richard Lyons, broke away from the field at the start, building an advantage before turning the car over to his Japanese teammate. Even though the team did not finish, everyone showed what would have been possible that weekend.

RICHARD LYONS

Ich startete mit Masataka Yanagida als neuem Teamkollegen. Wir kennen uns schon seit 2003 und arbeiten sehr gerne zusammen. Die Teamleistung am Rennwochenende in Buriram war besonders stark. Schon im Qualifying passte die Abstimmung sehr gut. Von den drei verschiedenen Regenreifentypen von Dunlop haben wir die Variante gewählt, die auf abtrocknender Strecke am besten funktionierte. Ich konnte mir beim Start einen Vorsprung herausfahren und die Reifen schonen. Auch in der Phase der Boxenstopps behielten wir unsere Führung. Als Team haben wir die bis dahin beste Leistung gezeigt.

I raced with Masataka Yanagida as my new teammate. We've known each other since 2003 and enjoy working together. Our team performance on the race weekend at Buriram was particularly strong. The setup already fit really well in qualifying. Of the three different types of rain tires from Dunlop we chose the one that worked best on a drying track. I managed to gain an advantage at the start and take it easy on the tires. We kept out lead even during the pit stop phase. As a team we showed our best performance so far.

Das Audi Team Hitotsuyama führte das Rennen in Buriram an
Audi Team Hitotsuyama led the race at Buriram

GLÜCKSSPIEL IN MACAU

GAME OF LUCK IN MACAU

Einmal mehr ging es im FIA GT World Cup neben Können auch um viel Glück. Und im übrigen Asien war Audi in vielen Serien erfolgreich

Once again, the FIA GT World Cup was an event in which skill mattered along with plenty of luck. And in the rest of Asia, Audi was successful in many series

中 學
澳博 SJM
1
PIRELLI

Chris Reinke, Leiter Audi Sport customer racing, im Gespräch mit Stephan Winkelmann, Geschäftsführer der Audi Sport GmbH (oben). Ein Unfall brachte Markus Pommer in Macau um ein gutes Ergebnis (unten)

Chris Reinke, Head of Audi Sport customer racing, in conversation with Stephan Winkelmann, CEO of Audi Sport GmbH (top). An accident deprived Markus Pommer of a good result in Macau (bottom)

STARKER ROOKIE

Robin Frijns gelang beim FIA GT World Cup ein überzeugendes Debüt. Von Startplatz 17 verbesserte sich der Niederländer im Qualifikationsrennen auf Platz vier, nachdem ein Unfall zwölf Teilnehmer aus dem Rennen gerissen hatte, darunter Nico Müller aus dem Audi Sport Team WRT, Lucas di Grassi und Fabian Plentz von HCB-Rutronik Racing sowie Markus Pommer von Aust Motorsport. Tags darauf blieb Frijns mit Slicks auf abtrocknender Strecke im World Cup erneut fehlerlos, vermied die Kämpfe und Rückschläge seiner Konkurrenten um ihn herum und errang so Platz zwei. Seine Klasse bewies er außerdem mit der schnellsten Rennrunde am Samstag und der zweitschnellsten am Sonntag. Zum Sieg fehlten ihm und dem Audi Sport Team WRT am Ende nur 0,618 Sekunden.

STRONG ROOKIE

Robin Frijns made an impressive debut in the FIA GT World Cup. Having started from 17th on the grid, the Dutchman improved to fourth place in the qualification race after an accident had taken twelve participants out of the race, including Nico Müller from Audi Sport Team WRT, Lucas di Grassi and Fabian Plentz from HCB-Rutronik Racing, and Markus Pommer from Aust Motorsport. A day later, Frijns, running on slicks on a drying track, again made no mistakes in the World Cup, avoided the battles and setbacks of the competitors surrounding him, so achieving second place. In addition, he demonstrated his class by setting the fastest race lap on Saturday and the second-fastest one on Sunday. In the end, he and Audi Sport Team WRT fell short of victory with a deficit of only 0.618 seconds.

Robin Frijns errang in Macau den zweiten Platz
Robin Frijns clinched second place in Macau

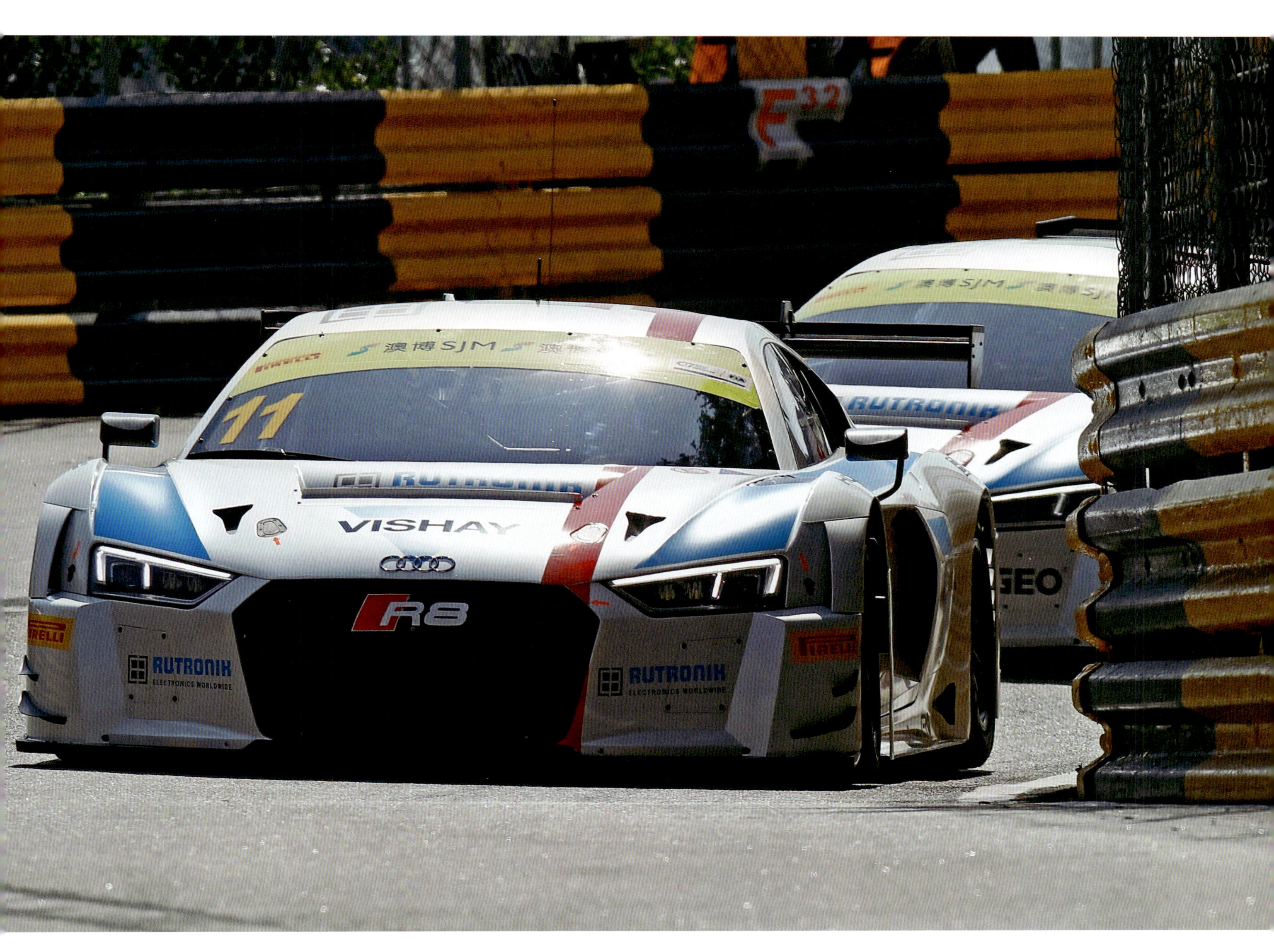

Lucas di Grassi und Fabian Plentz waren für HCB-Rutronik Racing in Macau
Lucas di Grassi and Fabian Plentz were in Macau for HCB-Rutronik Racing

B-Quik Racing war in der Thailand Super Series mit bis zu drei Audi R8 LMS für Shaun Varney, Henk Kiks und Daniel Bilski am Start
B-Quik Racing in the Thailand Super Series was on the grid with up to three Audi R8 LMS cars for Shaun Varney, Henk Kiks and Daniel Bilski

B-Quik-Racing-Teamchef Henk Kiks (hintere Reihe links) und Daniel Bilski (hintere Reihe Mitte) mit Teammanager Paspak Kijnopsri (vordere Reihe Mitte) nach dem Titelgewinn (oben links). Henk Kiks setzt seit 2014 auf Audi (rechts oben). Das Tianshi Racing Team beim Saisonauftakt 2017/18 der Asian Le Mans Series (unten links). Bhurit Bhirombhakdi und Kantasak Kusiri beim ersten Lauf zum Asian Le Mans Sprint Cup (unten rechts)
B-Quik-Racing team principal Henk Kiks (pictured left, rear row) and Daniel Bilski (pictured in the middle, rear row) with team manager Paspak Kijnopsri (pictured in the middle, front row) following the title win (top left). Henk Kiks has been relying on Audi since 2014 (top right). The Tianshi Racing team at the 2017/18 season opener of the Asian Le Mans Series (bottom left). Bhurit Bhirombhakdi and Kantasak Kusiri at round one of the Asian Le Mans Sprint Cup (bottom right)

THAI-BOXEN

Während Macau der alljährliche Höhepunkt im November ist, haben die Teams in vielen anderen asiatischen Serien ihre Saison bereits hinter sich. Seit 2014 setzt das B-Quik Racing Team in der Thailand Super Series auf Audi und gewann nun erstmals einen Titel. Teamchef und Fahrer Henk Kiks und der Australier Daniel Bilski gewannen mit B-Quik Racing die Teamwertung in der Klasse Super Car GTM Plus. In der Asian Le Mans Series beschloss das Team Audi Korea die Saison 2016/17 im Januar mit einem Klassensieg von Kyong Ouk You/Marchy Lee/Alex Yoong auf dem Kurs von Sepang. Das Tianshi Racing Team begann die neue Saison 2017/18 in Zhuhai mit Klassenrang drei von Liu Peng/Chen Weian/Massimiliano Wiser. In der Asian Le Mans Sprint Series erzielten Bhurit Bhirombhakdi/Kantasak Kusiri mit Singha Plan B Motorsport beim Auftakt in Sepang einen Sieg und einen zweiten Platz in ihrer Klasse. Nach Redaktionsschluss der Vorjahresausgabe feierte Audi noch zwei Erfolge bei den 12 Stunden von Sepang. Robin Frijns/Christopher Haase/Laurens Vanthoor waren die Gesamtsieger, Vanthoor und Audi zudem Meister in der Intercontinental GT Challenge. Die GTC-Wertung in Sepang ging an B-Quik Racing mit Daniel Bilski/Henk Kiks/Peter Kox.

THAI BOXING

While Macau is the annual pinnacle event in November, the teams in many other Asian series have already finished their seasons. Since 2014, the B-Quik Racing team has been relying on Audi in the Thailand Super Series, now having won a title for the first time. Team principal and driver Henk Kiks and Australian Daniel Bilski won the teams' classification in the Super Car GTM Plus class with B-Quik Racing. In the Asian Le Mans Series, Team Audi Korea finished the 2016/17 season in January with a class victory by Kyong Ouk You/Marchy Lee/Alex Yoong on the circuit at Sepang. Team Tianshi Racing started the new 2017/18 season at Zhuhai in position three in class clinched by Liu Peng/Chen Weian/Massimiliano Wiser. In the Asian Le Mans Sprint Series, Bhurit Bhirombhakdi/Kantasak Kusiri with Singha Plan B Motorsport scored a victory and a second place in their class in the opener at Sepang. Following the editorial deadline of last year's edition, Audi still celebrated two successes in the Sepang 12 Hours. Robin Frijns/Christopher Haase/Laurens Vanthoor were the overall winners, plus Vanthoor and Audi champions in the Intercontinental GT Challenge. The GTC classification at Sepang went to B-Quik Racing with Daniel Bilski/Henk Kiks/Peter Kox.

HENK KIKS

Das Finale in Thailand war mit seinen drei Rennen ein Thriller. Ein wichtiger Gegner hatte ein Motorproblem, stattdessen aber holte mit dem Team Vattana Motorsport ein anderer Konkurrent mächtig auf. Ich musste das letzte Rennen aus der Boxengasse starten, und das bei starkem Regen. Daniel war mit zwei dritten Plätzen und einem Klassensieg in Buriram extrem stark, ich steuerte weitere Punkte bei. So hat es am Ende gereicht. Alle Audi R8 LMS liefen das ganze Jahr über perfekt. Danke an Audi Sport customer racing für die Hilfe bei der Abstimmung, das Coaching und alle weiteren Ratschläge. Es ist ungeheuer motivierend, einen guten Hersteller hinter sich zu haben. Das war unsere bislang beste Motorsport-Saison.

The finale in Thailand with its three races was a thriller. An important rival had an engine problem but instead another competitor – Team Vattana Motorsport – massively made up ground. I had to start the last race from the pit lane, in heavy rain. Daniel with two third places and a class win at Buriram was extremely strong and I contributed additional points, so in the end, it was enough. All Audi R8 LMS cars were running perfectly the whole year. Thank you to Audi Sport customer racing for the help with the setup, the coaching and all the other advice. It's incredibly motivating to have the backing of a good manufacturer. That has been our best motorsport season to date.

Das Audi Sport Team Phoenix gewann die 12 Stunden von Sepang 2016 (unten rechts) und Audi damit die Intercontinental GT Challenge (unten links). Laurens Vanthoor, Robin Frijns, Markus Winkelhock, Christopher Haase, Pierre Kaffer, Ernst Moser, René Rast, Chris Reinke, Henk Kiks, Daniel Bilski, Peter Kox (ganz unten)

Audi Sport Team Phoenix won the Sepang 12 Hours in 2016 (top right) and, as a result, Audi the Intercontinental GT Challenge (top left). Laurens Vanthoor, Robin Frijns, Markus Winkelhock, Christopher Haase, Pierre Kaffer, Ernst Moser, René Rast, Chris Reinke, Henk Kiks, Daniel Bilski, Peter Kox (bottom)

Ein großes Publikum in Shanghai verfolgte Kings Racing, hier Xu Jia im Audi Nummer 7, auf dem Weg zum Titelgewinn in der GT China
A large crowd at Shanghai watched Kings Racing, pictured here is Xu Jia in the number 7 Audi, on the way to winning the title in the GT China

Alex Au, Marchy Lee, Eric Loh, Melvin Moh, Martin Rump und Wang Liang beim Dreifachsieg in der GT China in Zhuhai (links). Xu Jia, rechts neben Dries Vanthoor, gewann den Titel in der GT China (rechts)
Alex Au, Marchy Lee, Eric Loh, Melvin Moh, Martin Rump and Wang Liang on clinching a one-two-three result in the GT China at Zhuhai (pictured left). Xu Jia, pictured right alongside Dries Vanthoor, won the title in the GT China (right)

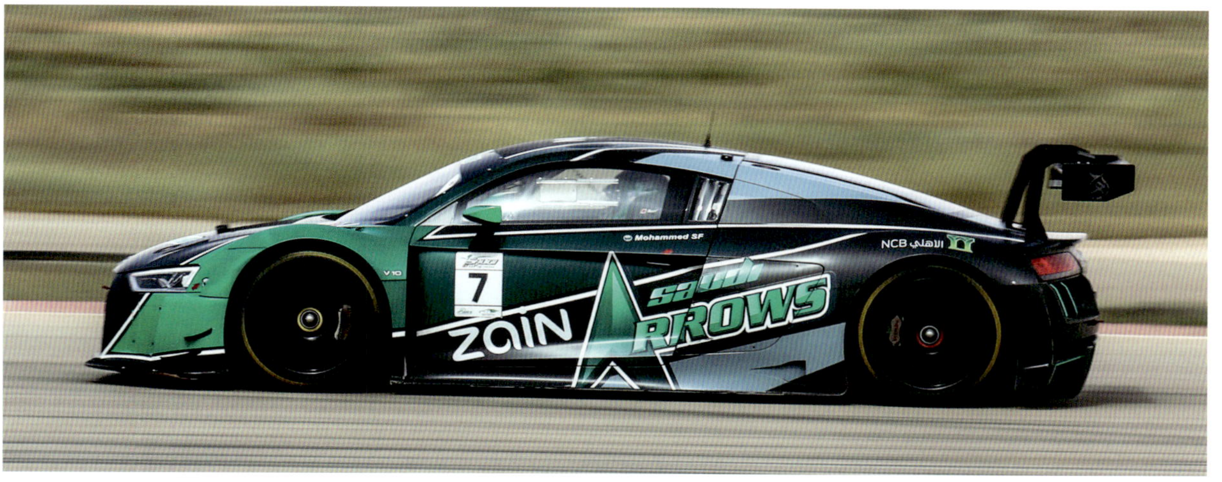

Mohammed Bin Saud gewann erstmals in einem Audi die Saudi GT Championship (oben und links)

Mohammed Bin Saud won the Saudi GT Championship for the first time in an Audi (above and left)

(S)AUDI ARABIEN

Eine Premiere feierte die Marke in Saudi-Arabien. Erstmals bestritt Mohammed Bin Saud die Saudi GT Championship in einem Audi R8 LMS. Austragungsort der sechs Meisterschaftsläufe war der Reem Circuit westlich von Riad. Mit Unterstützung des Einsatzteams WRT gewann Mohammed Bin Saud das erste, das dritte, das fünfte und das sechste Rennen und damit auch den Titel in der Saison 2016/17. Bei den 24 Stunden von Dubai errang er zudem den sechsten Platz. Einen weiteren Meisterschaftssieg verbuchte ein Kunde am östlichen Ende des asiatischen Kontinents. Xu Jia gewann die China GT Championship. Der Chinese, der Teamchef von Kings Racing und Fahrer ist, errang im Audi R8 LMS fünf Siege in zwölf Läufen. Zu seinen wechselnden Teamkollegen zählten Alex Yoong aus Malaysia, der Brite Jake Dennis und der Belgier Dries Vanthoor, die jeweils auch an einzelnen Siegen beteiligt waren. Das China GT Masters, das Pan Delta Super Racing Festival und das Circuit-Hero-Rennen in Zhuhai boten den asiatischen Audi-Kundenteams im Clubsport weitere Bühnen.

(S)AUDI ARABIA

In Saudi Arabia, the brand celebrated a premiere. For the first time, Mohammed Bin Saud contested the Saudi GT Championship in an Audi R8 LMS. Reem Circuit west of Riyadh was the venue of the six championship rounds. With support by the fielding team, WRT, Mohammed Bin Saud won the first, the third, the fifth and the sixth race and thus the title as well in the 2016/17 season. In the Dubai 24 Hours, he additionally clinched sixth place. Another championship win was scored by a customer at the eastern end of the Asian continent. Xu Jia won the China GT Championship. The Chinese, who is the team principal and a driver of Kings Racing, clinched five victories in twelve rounds in the Audi R8 LMS. His changing teammates included Alex Yoong from Malaysia, Briton Jake Dennis and Belgian Dries Vanthoor who were involved in individual victories as well. The China GT Masters, the Pan Delta Super Racing Festival and the Circuit Hero race at Zhuhai offered Audi's Asian customer teams additional stages in club racing.

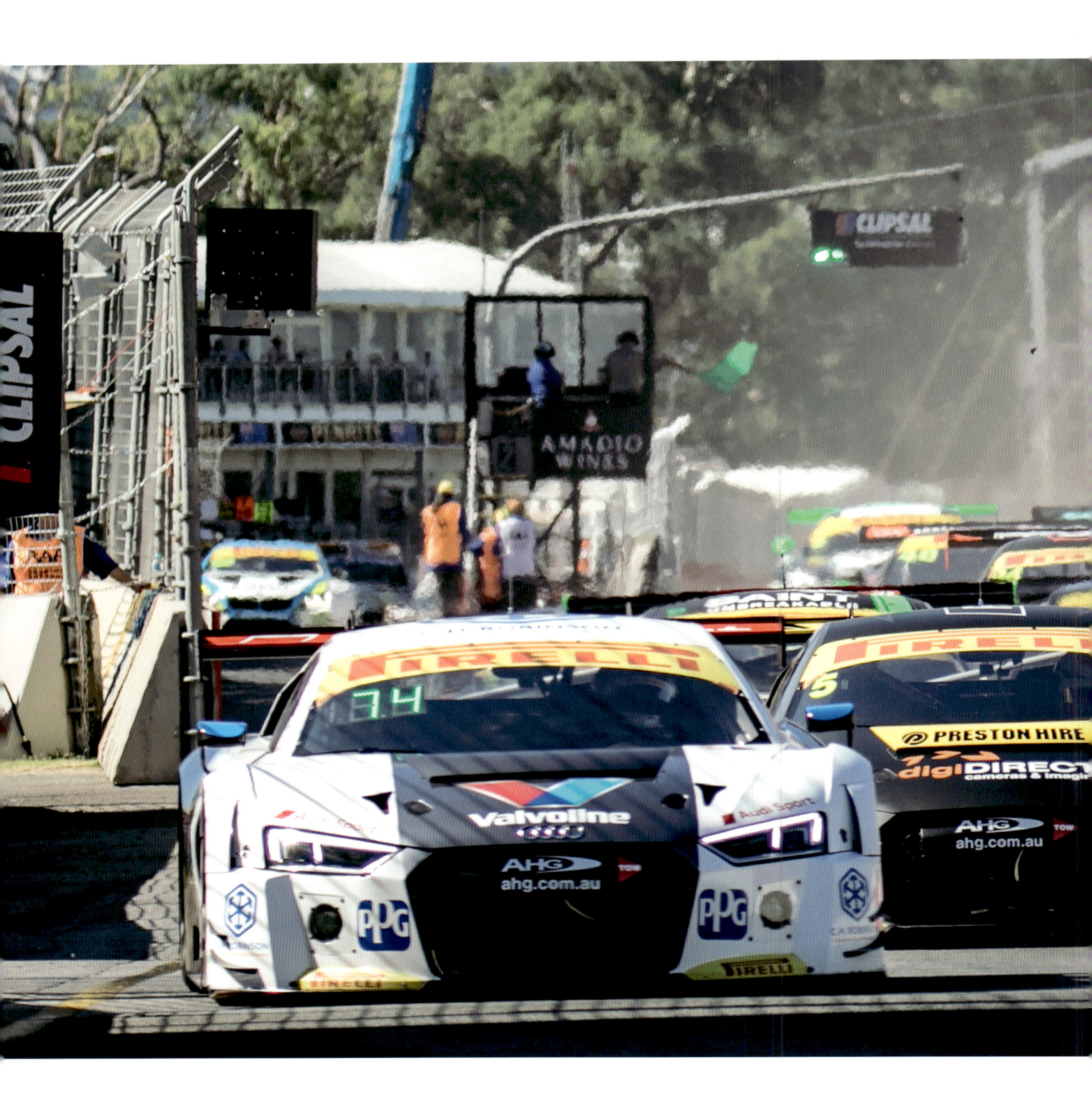
CLIPSAL
CLIPSAL
AMADIO
WINES
PIRELLI
74
Valvoline
AHG
ahg.com.au
PPG
PPG
PIRELLI
PIRELLI
5
PRESTON HIRE
digiDIRECT
AHG
ahg.com.au

VOLLER ERFOLG

RESOUNDING SUCCESS

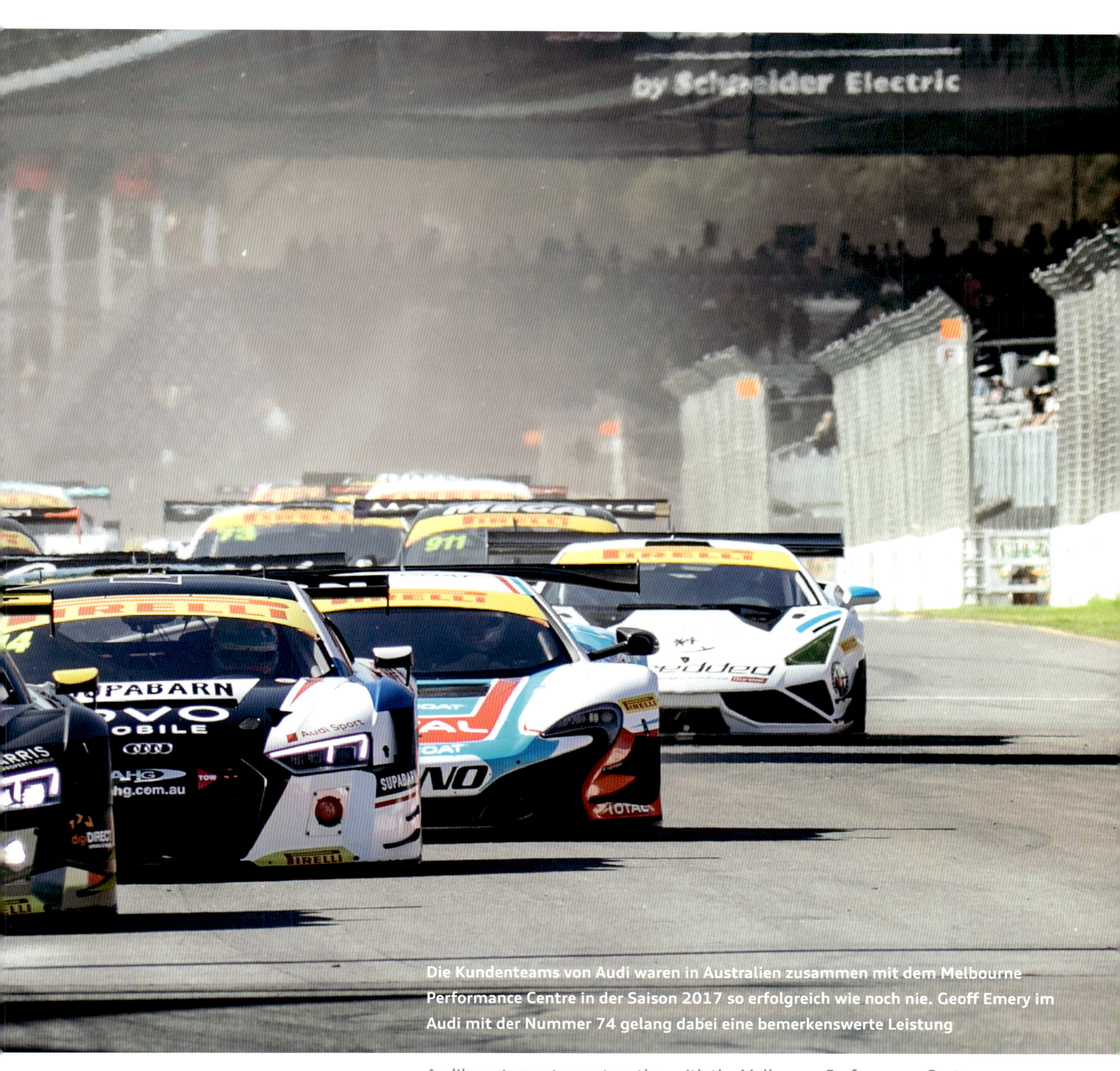

Die Kundenteams von Audi waren in Australien zusammen mit dem Melbourne Performance Centre in der Saison 2017 so erfolgreich wie noch nie. Geoff Emery im Audi mit der Nummer 74 gelang dabei eine bemerkenswerte Leistung

Audi's customer teams together with the Melbourne Performance Centre were as successful as never before in Australia in the 2017 season, Geoff Emery in the number 74 Audi having achieved a remarkable feat

GEOFF EMERY

Nach einem Unfall vor einem Jahr wollte ich ursprünglich in diesem Jahr gar keine Rennen fahren. Noch im Dezember entfernten mir die Ärzte Schrauben aus meiner Wirbelsäule. Im Februar testete ich eine Woche vor Saisonstart, hatte aber noch Schmerzen. Mein Teamkollege Kelvin van der Linde war ein exzellenter Mentor. Das erste Rennwochenende wollte ich einfach nur überstehen. Bereits bei der zweiten Veranstaltung sammelten wir die meisten Punkte, und am Ende reichte es zum Titelgewinn. Was für ein Jahr!

Following an accident a year ago, I originally didn't want to race at all. In December, doctors still removed some screws from my spine. In February, I did some testing one week prior to the season, but was still in pain. My teammate, Kelvin van der Linde, was an excellent mentor. I just wanted to survive the first race weekend. Right at the second event, we scored the most points and in the end, we managed to win the title. What a year!

Ash Walsh fuhr als zweitbester Audi-Pilot auf Platz drei der Meisterschaft (oben). Geoff Emery (im Overall neben Kelvin van der Linde) gewann die Australische GT-Meisterschaft (rechts)

Ash Walsh as the second-best Audi campaigner finished the championship in third place (above). Geoff Emery (in a racing suit, pictured alongside Kelvin van der Linde) won the Australian GT Championship (pictured right)

James Koundouris und Ash Walsh im Audi R8 LMS
James Koundouris and Ash Walsh in the Audi R8 LMS

GLÄNZENDES COMEBACK

Nach einem schweren Unfall im Mai 2016 verpasste Geoff Emery den Rest der Saison. Die schwierige Rückkehr ins Cockpit bewältigte er glänzend. Sein südafrikanischer Teamkollege Kelvin van der Linde unterstützte ihn dabei perfekt. Nach einem schwierigen Auftakt verbuchte van der Linde am zweiten Rennwochenende in Melbourne zwei von vier möglichen Laufsiegen. So sammelte das Fahrerteam des Audi R8 LMS mit der Nummer 74 die höchste Punktzahl aller Teilnehmer. Dennoch musste Emery als Tabellenvierter noch einen Rückstand von 116 Punkten aufholen. Nach einem dritten und einem zweiten Platz in den nächsten Rennen kam der Australier als Zweiter zum Finale. Ein Sieg, ein zweiter und ein fünfter Platz in Sandown reichten schließlich zum Titelgewinn.

BRILLIANT COMEBACK

After a serious accident in May 2016, Geoff Emery missed the rest of the season, subsequently mastering his difficult return to the cockpit brilliantly. His South African teammate, Kelvin van der Linde, perfectly supported him in this. Following a difficult opener, van der Linde clinched two of four possible race wins on the second race weekend at Melbourne. As a result, the driver squad of the number 74 Audi R8 LMS scored the largest number of points in the field. Still, Emery, in fourth place of the standings, had to make up a deficit of 116 points. Following a third and a second place in the next races, the Australian arrived at the finale in second place. Finally, a victory, plus a second and a fifth place at Sandown were enough for the title win.

Matthew Stoupas gewann die Victorian State Circuit Racing Championships
Matthew Stoupas won the Victorian State Circuit Racing Championships

Steven McLaughlan ist der Meister in der Australian GT Trophy
Steven McLaughlan is the Australian GT Trophy Champion

Die beiden Neuseeländer Tim Miles und Jaxon Evans erreichten den Vizetitel in der Australian Endurance Championship
The two New Zealanders Tim Miles and Jaxon Evans were runners-up in the Australian Endurance Championship

WEITERE SPITZENERGEBNISSE

Unter dem Dach der Australian GT sind neben der GT-Meisterschaft zwei weitere Serien vereint. In der Australian Endurance Championship setzten sich Tim Miles und Jaxon Evans gut in Szene. Die beiden Neuseeländer gewannen mit einem Audi R8 LMS des Teams Valvoline den Auftakt in Phillip Island und den zweiten Lauf in Sydney. Nach einem zweiten Platz in Hampton Downs und einem Ausfall beim Finale erreichten sie den Vizetitel in der Langstreckenserie. In der Australian GT Trophy für ältere Rennwagen fuhr Steven McLaughlan von Erfolg zu Erfolg. Nach insgesamt sechs Rennsiegen in Sandown, Winton, Phillip Island und Wakefield gewann er die Serie mit einem Vorsprung von 189 Punkten auf Rod Salmon in einem weiteren Audi R8 LMS ultra. Die ausschließlich im Bundesstaat Victoria ausgetragenen State Circuit Racing Championships gewann Matthew Stoupas nach neun Siegen in einem Audi R8 LMS ultra.

Troy Russell und Lee Burley betreuen mit dem Melbourne Performance Centre die meisten Audi-Kunden in Australien und Neuseeland
Troy Russell and Lee Burley with the Melbourne Performance Centre support most Audi customers in Australia and New Zealand

OTHER TOP RESULTS

In addition to the GT Championship, the umbrella of the Australian GT combines two other series. In the Australian Endurance Championship, Tim Miles and Jaxon Evans made a good showing. The two New Zealanders in an Audi R8 LMS from Team Valvoline won the opener at Phillip Island and round two at Sydney. Following a second place at Hampton Downs and a retirement in the finale, they finished runners-up in the endurance racing series. In the Australian GT Trophy for older race cars, Steven McLaughlan drove from success to success. Following a total of six race victories at Sandown, Winton, Phillip Island and Wakefield, he won the series with a 189-point advantage over Rod Salmon in another Audi R8 LMS ultra. The State Circuit Racing Championships held exclusively in the state of Victoria were won by Matthew Stoupas after nine victories in an Audi R8 LMS ultra.

Tim Miles und Jaxon Evans gewannen mit dem Team Valvoline zwei Langstreckenrennen
Tim Miles and Jaxon Evans won two endurance races with Team Valvoline

NEUE BESEN KEHREN GUT

A NEW BROOM SWEEPS CLEAN

Im März trat ein neues Kundenteam aus Neuseeland mit dem dort erstmals eingesetzten R8 LMS der zweiten Generation ins Rampenlicht. Es steuerte den ersten Titel zur umfassenden Saisonbilanz von Audi Sport customer racing bei

In March, a new customer team from New Zealand came into the limelight with a second-generation R8 LMS fielded there for the first time. It contributed the first title to an extensive season tally of Audi Sport customer racing

SIMON EVANS

Der Audi R8 LMS war für mich neu und verlangt als GT-Sportwagen mit seiner guten Aerodynamik und Fahrhilfen wie ABS und Traktionskontrolle einen runden Fahrstil. Das ist ganz anders als bei den mir bekannten V8-Tourenwagen, kommt mir aber sehr entgegen. Das Jahr war spannend, ebenso die Titelentscheidung in Pukekohe. Das ist eine schnelle, aber wellige Strecke. Der Veranstalter sagte das Qualifying wegen starken Regens ab und verschob das Rennen um einen Tag. Unsere Titelgegner hatten dort zwei Tage getestet, wir fuhren ohne Training los. Audi Sport customer racing Australia beriet uns perfekt bei der Abstimmung. Alles passte, und so haben wir das Rennen und den Titel gewonnen.

The Audi R8 LMS was new for me and as a GT sports car with its good aerodynamics and driver assistance such as ABS and traction control requires a smooth driving style. This is completely different from the V8 touring cars I'm familiar with, but suits me really well. The year was exciting, just like the title decision at Pukekohe. That's a fast but bumpy track. The organizer cancelled qualifying due to heavy rain and postponed the race by a day. Our rivals for the title had tested there for two days while we went ahead and started without practice. Audi Sport customer racing Australia gave us perfect advice for

Simon Evans und Gene Rollinson, Sieger der North Island Endurance Series
Simon Evans and Gene Rollinson, winners of the North Island Endurance Series

Das Team Smeg setzte den neuen Audi R8 LMS erstmals in Neuseeland ein
Team Smeg fielded the new Audi R8 LMS for the first time in New Zealand

EIN TEAM, ZWEI TITEL

Die Nord- und die Südinsel Neuseelands tragen jeweils ihre eigenen Langstreckenmeisterschaften aus. Im März trafen sich die Besten beider Serien zu einem gemeinsamen Wettstreit in Ruapuna. Das Team Smeg Racing, das in dieser Saison zum ersten Mal die zweite Generation des Audi R8 LMS einsetzte, gewann mit einer Runde Vorsprung das Rennen und damit den Drei-Stunden-Langstreckentitel. Anschließend setzten die frisch gekürten Meister Simon Evans und Gene Rollinson ihre Erfolgsserie in der North Island Endurance Championship fort. Beim Auftakt in Taupo gelang ihnen im Mai der nächste Sieg, im zweiten Rennen mussten sie sich um 6,9 Sekunden geschlagen geben. Das Finale in Pukekohe gewannen sie mit zwölf Sekunden Vorsprung und entschieden damit auch die Meisterschaft für sich.

ONE TEAM, TWO TITLES

The North and South Islands of New Zealand each hold their own endurance racing championships. In March, the best contenders from both series met for a joint competition at Ruapuna. Team Smeg Racing that fielded the second generation of the Audi R8 LMS for the first time this season won the race with a one-lap advantage and thus the Three-Hour Endurance title. Subsequently, the brand new champions, Simon Evans and Gene Rollinson, continued their string of success in the North Island Endurance Championship. In the opener at Taupo in May, they achieved their next victory while in the second race they had to admit defeat by 6.9 seconds. With a twelve-second advantage they won the finale at Pukekohe and, as a result, decided the championship in their favor as well.

ZWEITER AUDI FÜR TRADITIONSTEAM

Bereits im dritten Jahr in Folge vertraute das Team International Motorsport auf Audi. 2015 hatte es auf der Südinsel und 2016 auf der Nordinsel jeweils einen Titel mit der ersten Generation des Audi R8 LMS gewonnen. In diesem Jahr hatte das Team aus Auckland erstmals auch einen neuen R8 LMS im Einsatz. Nach einem dritten Platz mit dem bewährten Modell auf der Nordinsel in Taupo erlebte die Mannschaft ihren größten Erfolg im September auf der Südinsel. Andrew Bagnall/Matt Halliday gewannen den zweiten Lauf der Drei-Stunden-Serie im Süden im neuen Audi R8 LMS. Platz zwei ging an ihre Teamkollegen Neil Foster/ Jonny Reid. Ein schöner Erfolg für das Traditionsunternehmen von Lyall Williamson, der sein Team 1960 gegründet und einst sogar mit Formel-1-Weltmeister Denny Hulme gearbeitet hat.

International Motorsport bereitete je einen Audi R8 LMS der zweiten (vorn) und der ersten Generation vor (dahinter)
International Motorsport prepared one Audi R8 LMS of the second (pictured in front) and one of the first generation (pictured behind it)

Das Team von Lyall Williamson (rechts am Heckflügel) mit den Fahrern Neil Foster, Matt Halliday und Andrew Bagnall
Lyall Williamson's team (pictured right at the rear wing) with drivers Neil Foster, Matt Halliday and Andrew Bagnall

SECOND AUDI FOR TRADITION-STEEPED TEAM

Already for the third year in succession, Team International Motorsport relied on Audi. In 2015, the squad had won a title with the first generation of the Audi R8 LMS on the South Island and one on the North Island in 2016. This year, the team from Auckland fielded a new R8 LMS for the first time as well. Following a third place with the proven model on the North Island at Taupo, the squad experienced its greatest success on the South Island in September. Andrew Bagnall/ Matt Halliday won round two of the Three-Hour Series in the south in the new Audi R8 LMS. Second place went to their teammates, Neil Foster/Jonny Reid: a sweet success for the tradition-steeped company of Lyall Williamson who formed his

PARTNER PARTNERS

Akrapovič genießt breite Anerkennung als innovatives Unternehmen im Bereich der Materialtechnologie. Die Marke steht für höchste Ansprüche an das Design, für eine kontinuierliche Leistungssteigerung und für die Kreation eines unverkennbar tiefen und satten Auspuffsounds. Ein kompetentes Team aus mehr als 800 Mitarbeitern entwirft und fertigt alle Produkte passgenau für Motorräder und Automobile.

Akrapovič enjoys wide recognition as an innovative company in the field of material technology. The brand represents the highest standards of design, continuous performance increases and the creation of an unmistakably deep and rich exhaust sound. A competent team of more than 800 employees designs and manufactures all products tailor-made for motorcycles and automobiles.

Castrol ist der global führende Hersteller, Distributor und Händler von hochwertigen Schmierölen, -fetten und verwandten Services. Seine Kunden kommen aus den Bereichen Kraftfahrzeugtechnik, Industrie, See- und Luftfahrt, Ölförderung und -produktion. Das Unternehmen hat seinen Hauptsitz im Vereinigten Königreich und ist zudem in mehr als 40 Ländern direkt vertreten. Castrol hat weltweit 7.000 Mitarbeiter.

Castrol is the world's leading manufacturer, distributor and trader of high-quality lubricating oils, greases and related services. Its customers come from the fields of automotive engineering, industry, maritime and aerospace transport, and oil extraction and production. The company is headquartered in the United Kingdom and is also directly represented in more than 40 countries. Castrol has 7,000 employees worldwide.

Eibach genießt weltweit den Ruf als führender Hersteller von hochwertigen Federungs- und Fahrwerkssystemen sowie technischen Spezialfedern für anspruchsvolle Anwendungen. Das Einsatzspektrum umfasst nahezu alle hochwertigen Bereiche der Industrie- und Automobiltechnik. Seit Jahrzehnten ist Eibach darüber hinaus ein wichtiger Partner im weltweiten Hochleistungsmotorsport.

Eibach enjoys a reputation worldwide as a leading manufacturer of high-quality suspension and chassis systems as well as technical specialty springs for demanding uses. The range of applications covers almost all high-quality areas of industrial and automotive engineering. For decades, Eibach has also been an important partner in the world of high-performance motorsport.

Der Präzisionsteilehersteller Hör Technologie engagiert sich seit Jahrzehnten im Motorsport, der Luft- und Raumfahrt, der Motorradindustrie und im Automotive-Sektor. Das Know-how umfasst die Entwicklung, Konstruktion, Fertigung, Wärmebehandlung und Qualitätskontrolle. Vom Prototyp bis zur Serie bietet Hör Technologie maßgeschneiderte Kundenlösungen in der Getriebetechnik und der Nockenwellentechnik.

The precision parts manufacturer Hör Technologie has been involved in motorsport, aerospace and motorcycle industry, and the automotive sector for decades. The know-how covers development, design, manufacture, heat treatment and quality control. From the prototype to production, Hör Technologie offers tailor-made customer solutions in transmission technology and camshaft technology.

Präzision – bis ins kleinste Detail. Dafür steht Krontec Maschinenbau GmbH seit über 25 Jahren. Mit rund 90 hoch qualifizierten Mitarbeitern liefert Krontec Hydraulik-und Pneumatiksysteme für den Rennsport. Zum Produktportfolio gehören Rohr- und Schlauchsysteme in Leichtbauweise, pneumatische Schnellhebeanlagen, hydraulische Schnelltrennkupplungen oder auch Schnellbetankungssysteme.

Precision – down to the smallest detail. This is what Krontec Maschinenbau GmbH has represented for over 25 years. With around 90 highly qualified employees, Krontec supplies hydraulic and pneumatic systems for motor racing. The product portfolio includes pipe and hose systems in lightweight construction, pneumatic air jack systems, hydraulic quick-disconnect couplings as well as fast-refueling systems.

Montaplast steht für mehr als 50 Jahre Erfahrung bei Kunststoff-Präzisionsteilen und -Systemen. Zunächst war das Unternehmen im Bereich Haushaltsgeräte tätig, um später als verlässlicher Partner der Automobilindustrie weltweit aufzutreten. Neben den Produktionswerken in Deutschland, USA, Indien und China ist das Unternehmen auch in Mexiko, Brasilien, Südafrika, Japan und Thailand durch Vertriebsniederlassungen etabliert.

Montaplast represents more than 50 years of experience in plastic precision parts and systems. Initially, the company was active in household appliances and later became a reliable partner in the automotive industry worldwide. In addition to production plants in Germany, USA, India and China, the company is also established in Mexico, Brazil, South Africa, Japan and Thailand through its sales offices.

LANGSTRECKENRENNEN ENDURANCE RACES

24H NÜRBURGRING (D), 27-28/05/2017

RENNERGEBNIS RACE RESULT

FAHRER DRIVERS				
1*	(1)	Connor De Phillippi/Christopher Mies/Markus Winkelhock/Kelvin van der Linde (USA/D/D/ZA)	Audi Sport Team Land	Audi R8 LMS GT3
3	(3)	Nico Müller/Marcel Fässler/Robin Frijns/René Rast (CH/CH/NL/D)	Audi Sport Team WRT	Audi R8 LMS GT3
16	(18)	Frank Stippler/Mike Rockenfeller/Dennis Busch/Nicolaj Møller Madsen (D/D/D/DK)	Phoenix Racing	Audi R8 LMS GT3
18	(26)	Ronnie Saurenmann/Lorenzo Rocco/Klaus Koch/Jan-Erik Slooten (CH/I/D/D)	Car Collection Motorsport	Audi R8 LMS GT3
3	(31)	Christian Abt/Rahel Frey/Patrick Huisman/Peter Terting (D/CH/NL/D)	Audi Sport Team Phoenix	Audi R8 LMS GT4
2	(48)	Hermann Bock/Rainer Partl/Max Partl (D/D/D)	Bonk Motorsport	Audi RS 3 LMS
3	(52)	Michael Bonk/Volker Piepmeyer/Axel Burghardt/Andreas Möntmann (D/D/D/D)	Bonk Motorsport	Audi RS 3 LMS
5	(66)	Joonas Lappalainen/Alexander Mies/Peter Terting/Alex Yoong (FIN/D/D/MAL)	Audi Sport Team Phoenix	Audi R8 LMS GT4
-	-	Connor De Phillippi/Christopher Mies/Christopher Haase/Pierre Kaffer (USA/D/D/D)	Audi Sport Team Land	Audi R8 LMS GT3
-	-	Ulrich Andree/Mike Jäger/Matthias Wasel/Pierre Humbert (D/D/D/D)	LMS Engineering	Audi RS 3 LMS
-	-	Frank Stippler/René Rast/Frédéric Vervisch/Nico Müller (D/D/B/CH)	Audi Sport Team WRT	Audi R8 LMS GT3

12H IMOLA (I), 30/06-01/07/2017

RENNERGEBNIS RACE RESULT

FAHRER DRIVERS				
1	(1)	Dimitri Parhofer/Max Edelhoff/Horst Felbermayr Jr./Toni Forné (D/D/A/E)	Car Collection Motorsport	Audi R8 LMS GT3
2	(7)	Dr. Johannes Kirchhoff/Gustav Edelhoff/Elmar Grimm/Ingo Vogler (D/D/D/D)	Car Collection Motorsport	Audi R8 LMS GT3
5	(33)	Erik Holstein/Jason Coupal/James Kaye (IRL/USA/GB)	Cadspeed Racing	Audi RS 3 LMS
-		Jesus Fuster/Miguel Abello/Jaime Fuster/Mirko van Oostrum (E/E/E/NL)	Speed Factory Racing	Audi RS 3 LMS

24H SPA (B), 29-30/07/2017

RENNERGEBNIS RACE RESULT

FAHRER DRIVERS			
1	Christopher Haase/Jules Gounon/Markus Winkelhock (D/F/D)	Audi Sport Team Saintéloc	Audi R8 LMS GT3
5	Connor De Phillippi/Christopher Mies/Frédéric Vervisch (USA/D/B)	Audi Sport Team WRT	Audi R8 LMS GT3
6	Antonio García/Nico Müller/René Rast (E/CH/D)	Audi Sport Team WRT	Audi R8 LMS GT3
9	Pierre Kaffer/Frank Stippler/Kelvin van der Linde (D/D/ZA)	Audi Sport Team I.S.R.	Audi R8 LMS GT3
11	Marcel Fässler/André Lotterer/Dries Vanthoor (CH/D/B)	Audi Sport Team WRT	Audi R8 LMS GT3
27	Christian Kelders/Marc Rostan/Fred Bouvy (B/F/B)	Saintéloc Racing	Audi R8 LMS GT3
-	Josh Caygill/Richard Lyons/Niki Mayr-Melnhof/Jon Venter (GB/GB/A/AUS)	Belgian Audi Club Team WRT	Audi R8 LMS GT3
-	Nathanaël Berthon/Stéphane Richelmi/Benoît Tréluyer (F/MC/F)	Belgian Audi Club Team WRT	Audi R8 LMS GT3
-	Filipe Albuquerque/Filip Salaquarda/Clemens Schmid (P/CZ/A)	I.S.R.	Audi R8 LMS GT3
-	Jake Dennis/Jamie Green/Stuart Leonard (GB/GB/GB)	Belgian Audi Club Team WRT	Audi R8 LMS GT3

PETIT LE MANS (USA), 07/10/2017

RENNERGEBNIS RACE RESULT

FAHRER DRIVERS				
1	(16)	Christopher Mies/Connor De Phillippi/Sheldon van der Linde (D/USA/ZA)	Montaplast by Land-Motorsport	Audi R8 LMS GT3
6	(22)	Frank Montecalvo/Bill Sweedler/Townsend Bell (USA/USA/USA)	Alex Job Racing	Audi R8 LMS GT3
13	(32)	Lawson Aschenbach/Andrew Davis/Matt Bell (USA/USA/USA)	Stevenson Motorsports	Audi R8 LMS GT3

8H LAGUNA SECA (USA), 15/10/2017

RENNERGEBNIS RACE RESULT

FAHRER DRIVERS				
1	(1)	Pierre Kaffer/Kelvin van der Linde/Markus Winkelhock (D/ZA/D)	Audi Sport Team Magnus	Audi R8 LMS GT3
2	(2)	Connor de Phillippi/Christopher Mies/Christopher Haase (USA/D/D)	Audi Sport Team Land	Audi R8 LMS GT3
5	(6)	Stuart Leonard/Jake Dennis/Robin Frijns (GB/GB/NL)	Belgian Audi Club Team WRT	Audi R8 LMS GT3

25H THUNDERHILL (USA), 02-03/12/2017

RENNERGEBNIS RACE RESULT

FAHRER DRIVERS			
1	Tom Haacker/Charly Hayes/Darren Law/Nate Stacy (USA/USA/USA/USA)	Flying Lizard Motorsports	Audi R8 LMS GT3

* Die erste Zahl bezeichnet jeweils den Klassenrang, die Zahl in Klammern die Gesamtposition The first number indicates the position in class, the number in brackets refers to the overall position

TCR

24H TOURING CAR ENDURANCE SERIES

ENDSTAND FINAL POSITIONS

FAHRER DRIVERS				PT
12	Zach Arnold/Roberto Ferri/John Filippi/ (USA/I/F)	Pit Lane Competizioni	Audi RS 3 LMS	56
16	Alberto Vescovi (I)	Pit Lane Competizioni	Audi RS 3 LMS	48
29	Mark Lemmer (GB)	Cadspeed Racing	Audi RS 3 LMS	28
-	Enrico Bettera (I)	Pit Lane Competizioni	Audi RS 3 LMS	28
-	James Kaye/Peter Cate/James Cottingham (GB/GB/GB)	Cadspeed Racing	Audi RS 3 LMS	18
-	Hermann Bock/Max Partl/Philip Ellis (D/D/GB)	Bonk Motorsport	Audi RS 3 LMS	16
-	Stephane Perrin/Vincent Radermecker/Rafael Galiana/Marc Guillot/Jean-Marc Thevenot (F/B/F/F/F)	AC Motorsport	Audi RS 3 LMS	6
-	Michael Bonk/Volker Piepmeyer/Axel Burghardt (D/D/D)	Bonk Motorsport	Audi RS 3 LMS	0
-	Jesus Fuster/Miguel Abello/Jaime Fuster/Mirko van Oostrum/Michael Vergers (E/E/E/NL/GB)	Speed Factory Racing	Audi RS 3 LMS	0
-	Ivan Demis Benvenutti (I)	Pit Lane Competizioni	Audi RS 3 LMS	0

TEAMS			PT
9	Pit Lane Competizioni	Audi RS 3 LMS	56
-	Cadspeed Racing	Audi RS 3 LMS	18
-	Bonk Motorsport	Audi RS 3 LMS	16
-	AC Motorsport	Audi RS 3 LMS	6
-	Speed Factory Racing	Audi RS 3 LMS	0
-	Bonk Motorsport	Audi RS 3 LMS	0

ADAC TCR GERMANY
ENDSTAND FINAL POSITIONS

FAHRER DRIVERS				PT
3	Sheldon van der Linde (ZA)	AC 1927 Mayen e.V. im ADAC	Audi RS 3 LMS	315
5	Niels Langeveld (NL)	Racing One	Audi RS 3 LMS	276
8	Antti Buri (FIN)	LMS Racing	Audi RS 3 LMS	202
11	Max Hofer (A)	AC 1927 Mayen e.V. im ADAC	Audi RS 3 LMS	177
13	Sandro Kaibach (D)	Aust Motorsport	Audi RS 3 LMS	168
15	Tim Zimmermann (D)	Target Competition GER	Audi RS 3 LMS	141
19	Tom Lautenschlager (D)	Target Competition GER	Audi RS 3 LMS	95
21	Niko Kankkunen (FIN)	LMS Racing	Audi RS 3 LMS	59
25	Thomas Kramwinkel (D)	GermanFLAVOURS Racing	Audi RS 3 LMS	35
27	Simon Reicher (A)	Certainty Racing Team	Audi RS 3 LMS	28
30	Gosia Rdest (PL)	Target Competition SWE-POL	Audi RS 3 LMS	26
32	Robin Brezina (D)	Aust Motorsport	Audi RS 3 LMS	17
33	Maurits Sandberg (NL)	Racing One 2	Audi RS 3 LMS	16
34	Dillon Koster (NL)	Certainty Racing Team	Audi RS 3 LMS	16
36	Jaap van Lagen (NL)	Bas Koeten Racing 1/Certainty Racing Team	Audi RS 3 LMS	10
37	Toni Wolf (D)	Aust Motorsport	Audi RS 3 LMS	6
38	Loris Hezemans (NL)	Aust Motorsport	Audi RS 3 LMS	3
38	Simon Larsson (S)	Target Competition SWE-POL	Audi RS 3 LMS	3
41	Max Hesse (D)	Aust Motorsport	Audi RS 3 LMS	0
41	Michael Verhagen (NL)	Bas Koeten Racing 1	Audi RS 3 LMS	0
41	Floris Dullaart (NL)	Racing One 2	Audi RS 3 LMS	0
41	Sven Markert (D)	GermanFLAVOURS Racing	Audi RS 3 LMS	0

TEAMS			PT
2	AC 1927 Mayen e.V. im ADAC	Audi RS 3 LMS	378
5	Racing One	Audi RS 3 LMS	306
8	LMS Racing	Audi RS 3 LMS	269
10	Target Competition GER	Audi RS 3 LMS	218
11	Aust Motorsport	Audi RS 3 LMS	209
17	Certainty Racing Team	Audi RS 3 LMS	76
18	GermanFLAVOURS Racing	Audi RS 3 LMS	70
20	Target Competition SWE-POL	Audi RS 3 LMS	55
21	Racing One 2	Audi RS 3 LMS	47
24	Bas Koeten Racing 1	Audi RS 3 LMS	0

FAHRER DRIVERS JUNIORS				PT
2	Simon Reicher (A)	Certainty Racing Team	Audi RS 3 LMS	67
4	Robin Brezina (D)	Aust Motorsport	Audi RS 3 LMS	32
5	Max Hesse (D)	Aust Motorsport	Audi RS 3 LMS	28
6	Toni Wolf (D)	Aust Motorsport	Audi RS 3 LMS	14

FIA EUROPEAN TOURING CAR CUP
ENDSTAND FINAL POSITIONS

FAHRER DRIVERS				PT
7	Plamen Kralev (BG)	Kraf Racing	Audi RS 3 LMS	25
15	Rudolf Pesovic (SRB)	ASK GM Racing	Audi RS 3 LMS	5

PIRELLI WORLD CHALLENGE SPRINT TC
ENDSTAND FINAL POSITIONS

FAHRER DRIVERS				PT
1	Paul Holton (USA)	C360R	Audi RS 3 LMS	235
8	Jason Coupal (USA)	BERG Racing	Audi RS 3 LMS	131
10	Anthony Geraci (USA)	S.A.C. Racing	Audi RS 3 LMS	96
25	Travis Washay (USA)	Indian Summer Racing	Audi RS 3 LMS	30
49	John Allen (USA)	BERG Racing	Audi RS 3 LMS	0

TEAMS			PT
1	C360R	Audi RS 3 LMS	227
7	BERG Racing	Audi RS 3 LMS	139
9	S.A.C. Racing	Audi RS 3 LMS	95
17	Indian Summer Racing	Audi RS 3 LMS	30

MARKEN MANUFACTURERS			PT
2	Audi	Audi RS 3 LMS	83

SUPER TAIKYU SERIES
ENDSTAND FINAL POSITIONS

TEAMS			PT
3	Birth Racing Project (BRP)	Audi RS 3 LMS	84.5
4	Audi Team DreamDrive	Audi RS 3 LMS	73

TCR ASIA SERIES
ENDSTAND FINAL POSITIONS

FAHRER DRIVERS				PT
6	Jasper Thong (HK)	Audi Hong Kong	Audi RS 3 LMS	94
10	Shaun Thong (HK)	Audi Hong Kong	Audi RS 3 LMS	40
12	Tong Siu Kau (HK)	Phoenix Racing Asia	Audi RS 3 LMS	12
13	Alex Fong (HK)	Audi Hong Kong	Audi RS 3 LMS	2
14	Huang Chu Han (CN)	Tianshi Racing Team	Audi RS 3 LMS	0
14	Chen Wei An (CN)	Tianshi Racing Team	Audi RS 3 LMS	0

FAHRER DRIVERS CUP				PT
2	Jasper Thong (HK)	Audi Hong Kong	Audi RS 3 LMS	166
7	Tong Siu Kau (HK)	Phoenix Racing Asia	Audi RS 3 LMS	30
8	Alex Fong (HK)	Audi Hong Kong	Audi RS 3 LMS	10

TEAMS			PT
5	Audi Hong Kong	Audi RS 3 LMS	136
7	Phoenix Racing Asia	Audi RS 3 LMS	12
8	Tianshi Racing Team	Audi RS 3 LMS	0

MARKEN MANUFACTURERS			PT
4	Audi	Audi RS 3 LMS	160

TCR BENELUX TOURING CAR CHAMPIONSHIP
ENDSTAND FINAL POSITIONS

FAHRER DRIVERS				PT
7	Mika Morien (NL)	Bas Koeten Racing	Audi RS 3 LMS	231
8	Willem Meijer (NL)	Bas Koeten Racing	Audi RS 3 LMS	209
12	Stefano Comini (CH)	Comtoyou Racing	Audi RS 3 LMS	138
13	Paul Sieljes (NL)	Bas Koeten Racing	Audi RS 3 LMS	128
14	Stan van Oord (NL)	Bas Koeten Racing	Audi RS 3 LMS	120
15	Lorenzo Donniacuo (B)	Bas Koeten Racing	Audi RS 3 LMS	117
16	Sheldon van der Linde (ZA)	Comtoyou Racing	Audi RS 3 LMS	105
17	Rik Breukers (NL)	Bas Koeten Racing	Audi RS 3 LMS	74
19	Jaap van Lagen/Simon Reicher (NL/A)	Certainty Racing Team	Audi RS 3 LMS	67
25	Alexis van de Poele (B)	Bas Koeten Racing	Audi RS 3 LMS	47
26	Meindert van Buuren (NL)	Bas Koeten Racing	Audi RS 3 LMS	44
27	Frédéric Vervisch (B)	Comtoyou Racing	Audi RS 3 LMS	33
30	Dillon Koster/Bernhard van Oranje (NL/NL)	Certainty Racing Team	Audi RS 3 LMS	20

JUNIOR				PT
4	Mika Morien (NL)	Bas Koeten Racing	Audi RS 3 LMS	147
6	Willem Meijer (NL)	Bas Koeten Racing	Audi RS 3 LMS	143
7	Stan van Oord (NL)	Bas Koeten Racing	Audi RS 3 LMS	62
8	Sheldon van der Linde (ZA)	Comtoyou Racing	Audi RS 3 LMS	55
9	Rik Breukers (NL)	Bas Koeten Racing	Audi RS 3 LMS	48

TEAMS				PT
3		Bas Koeten Racing	Audi RS 3 LMS	83
6		Comtoyou Racing	Audi RS 3 LMS	15
6		Certainty Racing Team	Audi RS 3 LMS	15

MARKEN MANUFACTURERS				PT
3	Audi		Audi RS 3 LMS	382

TCR EUROPE TROPHY
ENDSTAND FINAL POSITIONS

FAHRER DRIVERS				PT
7	Antii Buri (FIN)	LMS Racing	Audi RS 3 LMS	17
11	Plamen Kralev (BG)	Kraf Racing	Audi RS 3 LMS	5
18	Ermanno Dionisio (I)	TCR Academy	Audi RS 3 LMS	1
-	Giovanni Berton (I)	TCR Academy	Audi RS 3 LMS	0

TEAMS				PT
6		LMS Racing	Audi RS 3 LMS	14
9		Kraf Racing	Audi RS 3 LMS	2

TCR IBÉRICO TOURING CAR SERIES
ENDSTAND FINAL POSITIONS

FAHRER DRIVERS				PT
2	Patrick Cunha/Rafael Lobato (P/P)	Sporting Clube de Braga	Audi RS 3 LMS	145

TCR INTERNATIONAL SERIES
ENDSTAND FINAL POSITIONS

FAHRER DRIVERS				PT
3	Stefano Comini (CH)	Comtoyou Racing	Audi RS 3 LMS	196
10	Frédéric Vervisch (B)	Comtoyou Racing	Audi RS 3 LMS	84
27	Zhendong Zhang (CN)	ZZZ Team	Audi RS 3 LMS	10
35	Enrico Bettera (I)	Pit Lane Competizioni	Audi RS 3 LMS	0
35	Milovan Vesnić (SRB)	ASK Vesnić	Audi RS 3 LMS	0
35	Tengyi Jiang (CN)	ZZZ Team	Audi RS 3 LMS	0

TEAMS				PT
4		Comtoyou Racing	Audi RS 3 LMS	289
13		ZZZ Team	Audi RS 3 LMS	10
18		Pit Lane Competizioni	Audi RS 3 LMS	0
18		ASK Vesnić	Audi RS 3 LMS	0

MARKEN MANUFACTURERS				PT
4	Audi		Audi RS 3 LMS	321

TCR ITALY TOURING CAR CHAMPIONSHIP
ENDSTAND FINAL POSITIONS

FAHRER DRIVERS				PT
4	Massimiliano Mugelli (I)	Pit Lane Competizioni	Audi RS 3 LMS	97
5	Plamen Kralev (BG)	Kraf Racing	Audi RS 3 LMS	63
8	Giacomo Altoè (I)	Target Competition	Audi RS 3 LMS	45
17	Simon Reicher (A)	Certainty Racing Team	Audi RS 3 LMS	16
19	Enrico Bettera (I)	Pit Lane Competizioni	Audi RS 3 LMS	12
36	Carlotta Fedeli (I)	Pit Lane Competizioni	Audi RS 3 LMS	0

MARKEN MANUFACTURERS				PT
3	Audi		Audi RS 3 LMS	145

TCR MIDDLE EAST
ENDSTAND FINAL POSITIONS

FAHRER DRIVERS				PT
8	James Kaye (GB)	Cadspeed Racing	Audi RS 3 LMS	22

TEAMS				PT
4		Cadspeed Racing	Audi RS 3 LMS	28

TCR PORTUGAL TOURING CAR CHAMPIONSHIP
ENDSTAND FINAL POSITIONS

FAHRER DRIVERS				PT
3	Patrick Cunha/Rafael Lobato (P/P)	Sporting Clube de Braga	Audi RS 3 LMS	206

TCR RUSSIA TOURING CAR CHAMPIONSHIP
ENDSTAND FINAL POSITIONS

FAHRER DRIVERS

				PT
1	Dmitry Bragin (RUS)	STK Taif Motorsport	Audi RS 3 LMS/Seat Leon TCR	241
6	Irek Minnakhmetov (RUS)	STK Chingiskhan	Audi RS 3 LMS	140
12	Marat Sharapov (RUS)	STK Taif Motorsport	Audi RS 3 LMS	74
14	Timur Shigabutdinov (RUS)	STK Taif Motorsport	Audi RS 3 LMS	58

TEAMS

			PT
3	STK Taif Motorsport	Audi RS 3 LMS	315
-	STK Chingiskhan	Audi RS 3 LMS	0

FAHRER DRIVERS SMP RSKG TROPHY

				PT
1	Irek Minnakhmetov (RUS)	STK Chingiskhan	Audi RS 3 LMS	228
5	Marat Sharapov (RUS)	STK Taif Motorsport	Audi RS 3 LMS	135
6	Timur Shigabutdinov (RUS)	STK Taif Motorsport	Audi RS 3 LMS	119

TCR SCANDINAVIA TOURING CAR CHAMPIONSHIP
ENDSTAND FINAL POSITIONS

FAHRER DRIVERS

				PT
7	Tobias Brink (S)	Brink Motorsport	Audi RS 3 LMS	121
8	Joonas Lappalainen (FIN)	Kart In Club Driving Academy	Audi RS 3 LMS	100
10	Micke Ohlsson (S)	Brink Motorsport	Audi RS 3 LMS	61
12	Reuben Kressner (S)	Brovallen Design	Audi RS 3 LMS	60
19	Antti Buri (FIN)	LMS Racing	Audi RS 3 LMS	8
20	Mikaela Åhlin-Kottulinsky (S)	PWR Racing - Junior Team	Audi RS 3 LMS	6
21	Niko Kankkunen (FIN)	LMS Racing	Audi RS 3 LMS	6
22	John Bryant-Meisner (S)	PWR Racing - Junior Team	Audi RS 3 LMS	2
25	Joakim Darbom (S)	Brovallen Design	Audi RS 3 LMS	1

TEAMS

			PT
3	Brink Motorsport	Audi RS 3 LMS	222
5	Kart In Club Driving Academy	Audi RS 3 LMS	115
11	PWR Racing - Junior Team	Audi RS 3 LMS	20
14	LMS Racing	Audi RS 3 LMS	10

GT INTERNATIONAL

24H ENDURANCE SERIES
ENDSTAND FINAL POSITIONS

FAHRER DRIVERS

				PT
5	Max Edelhoff (D)	Car Collection Motorsport	Audi R8 LMS GT3	101
7	Gustav Edelhoff/Elmar Grimm/Ingo Vogler (D/D/D)	Car Collection Motorsport	Audi R8 LMS GT3	99
19	Dr. Johannes Kirchhoff (D)	Car Collection Motorsport	Audi R8 LMS GT3	77
24	Toni Forné (E)	Car Collection Motorsport	Audi R8 LMS GT3	66
24	Horst Felbermayr Jr. (A)	Car Collection Motorsport	Audi R8 LMS GT3	66
25	James Kaye (GB)	Cadspeed Racing	Audi RS 3 LMS	65
32	Rik Breukers (NL)	Car Collection Motorsport	Audi RS 3 LMS	55
43	Hermann Bock/Max Partl (D/D)	Bonk Motorsport	Audi RS 3 LMS	43
44	David Drinkwater (GB)	Cadspeed Racing	Audi RS 3 LMS	42
44	Paul White (GB)	Cadspeed Racing	Audi RS 3 LMS	42
44	Dirk Vorländer (D)	Car Collection Motorsport	Audi RS 3 LMS	42
44	Ricky Coomber (GB)	Cadspeed Racing	Audi RS 3 LMS	42
45	Erik Holstein (IRL)	Cadspeed Racing	Audi RS 3 LMS	41
50	Rahel Frey (CH)	Car Collection Motorsport	Audi R8 LMS GT3	36
50	Jason Coupal (USA)	Cadspeed Racing	Audi RS 3 LMS	36
54	Peter Schmidt (D)	Car Collection Motorsport	Audi R8 LMS GT3	32
59	Adrian Amstutz (CH)	Car Collection Motorsport	Audi R8 LMS GT3	26
59	JM Littman (GB)	Car Collection Motorsport	Audi RS 3 LMS	26
60	Dimitri Parhofer (D)	Car Collection Motorsport	Audi R8 LMS GT3	25
63	Heinz Schmersal/Markus von Oeynhausen (D/D)	Raeder Motorsport	Audi R8 LMS GT3	22
67	Monika Parhofer (D)	Car Collection Motorsport	Audi RS 3 LMS	16
70	Jesus Fuster/Miguel Abello/Mirko van Oostrum/Jaime Fuster (E/E/NL/E)	Speed Factory Racing	Audi RS 3 LMS	11
73	Dirg Parhofer (D)	Car Collection Motorsport	Audi R8 LMS GT3	6
74	Rémi Terrail (F)	Car Collection Motorsport	Audi R8 LMS GT3	0
*	Henry Littig/Klaus Koch (D/D)	Car Collection Motorsport	Audi R8 LMS GT3	32
*	Finlay Hutchison/Julian Griffin (GB/GB)	Cadspeed Racing	Audi RS 3 LMS	29
*	Patrick Kujala/Martin Kodric/Connor De Phillippi (FIN/HR/USA)	Car Collection Motorsport	Audi R8 LMS GT3	26
*	Christian Kranenberg (D)	Car Collection Motorsport	Audi RS 3 LMS	26
*	Joe Osborne/Flick Haigh/Ryan Ratcliffe/Christopher Haase (GB/GB/GB/D)	Optimum Motorsport	Audi R8 LMS GT3	24
*	Mohammed Bin Saud Al Saud/Mohammed Bin Faisal Al Saud/Marcel Fässler/Michael Vergers (KSA/KSA/CH/NL)	Belgian Audi Club Team WRT	Audi R8 LMS GT3	20
*	Markus Oestreich (D)	Raeder Motorsport	Audi R8 LMS GT3	14
*	Stuart Leonard/Robin Frijns/Christopher Mies/Ruben Maes (GB/NL/D/B)	Belgian Audi Club Team WRT	Audi R8 LMS GT3	16
*	Christian Schmitz/Siegfried Kuzdas (D/A)	Car Collection Motorsport	Audi RS 3 LMS	16
*	Johannes Siegler/Kelvin van der Linde (D/ZA)	Car Collection Motorsport	Audi R8 LMS GT3	6
*	Enzo Ide (B)	Belgian Audi Club Team WRT	Audi R8 LMS GT3	0
*	Daniel Diaz Varela (E)	Car Collection Motorsport	Audi R8 LMS GT3	0
*	Isaac Tutumlu Lopez (E)	Car Collection Motorsport	Audi R8 LMS GT3	0
*	Thomas Gannon (GB)	Cadspeed Racing	Audi RS 3 LMS	0
*	Jim Eriody (USA)	Cadspeed Racing	Audi RS 3 LMS	0

* Fahrer erfüllten nicht die Mindestanzahl von zwei Rennteilnahmen Drivers did not participate in a minimum of 2 races

FAHRER DRIVERS A6

				PT
3	Max Edelhoff (D)	Car Collection Motorsport	Audi R8 LMS GT3	101
4	Gustav Edelhoff/Elmar Grimm/Ingo Vogler (D/D/D)	Car Collection Motorsport	Audi R8 LMS GT3	99
11	Dr. Johannes Kirchhoff (D)	Car Collection Motorsport	Audi R8 LMS GT3	77
14	Horst Felbermayr Jr. (A)	Car Collection Motorsport	Audi R8 LMS GT3	66
14	Toni Forné (E)	Car Collection Motorsport	Audi R8 LMS GT3	66
25	Rahel Frey (CH)	Car Collection Motorsport	Audi R8 LMS GT3	36
27	Peter Schmidt (D)	Car Collection Motorsport	Audi R8 LMS GT3	32
30	Adrian Amstutz (CH)	Car Collection Motorsport	Audi R8 LMS GT3	26
31	Dimitri Parhofer (D)	Car Collection Motorsport	Audi R8 LMS GT3	25
36	Dirg Parhofer (D)	Car Collection Motorsport	Audi R8 LMS GT3	6

TEAMS A6

			PT
3	Car Collection Motorsport (#34)	Audi R8 LMS GT3	99
5	Car Collection Motorsport (#32)	Audi R8 LMS GT3	92
16	Car Collection Motorsport (#33)	Audi R8 LMS GT3	6

FAHRER DRIVERS TCR

				PT
4	James Kaye (GB)	Cadspeed Racing	Audi RS 3 LMS	65
9	Dirk Vorländer (D)	Car Collection Motorsport	Audi RS 3 LMS	42
10	Erik Holstein (IRL)	Cadspeed Racing	Audi RS 3 LMS	41
13	Jason Coupal (USA)	Cadspeed Racing	Audi RS 3 LMS	36
15	David Drinkwater/Ricky Coomber (GB/GB)	Cadspeed Racing	Audi RS 3 LMS	24
16	Monika Parhofer (D)	Car Collection Motorsport	Audi RS 3 LMS	16
17	Jesus Fuster/Miguel Abello/Mirko van Oostrum/Jaime Fuster (E/E/NL/E)	Speed Factory Racing	Audi RS 3 LMS	11

TEAMS TCR

				PT
3		Cadspeed Racing	Audi RS 3 LMS	65
6		Car Collection Motorsport	Audi RS 3 LMS	42
8		Speed Factory Racing	Audi RS 3 LMS	11

ROOKIES

				PT
1	Max Edelhoff (D)	Car Collection Motorsport	Audi R8 LMS GT3	101
2	Rik Breukers (NL)	Car Collection Motorsport	Audi RS 3 LMS	55
4	Jason Coupal (USA)	Cadspeed Racing	Audi RS 3 LMS	36
11	Jaime Fuster (E)	Speed Factory Racing	Audi RS 3 LMS	11

CONTINENTS CHAMPIONSHIP ROOKIES

				PT
1	Max Edelhoff (D)	Car Collection Motorsport	Audi R8 LMS GT3	90
3	Rik Breukers (NL)	Car Collection Motorsport	Audi RS 3 LMS	51
6	Jason Coupal (USA)	Cadspeed Racing	Audi RS 3 LMS	36
7	Ryan Ratcliffe (GB)	Optimum Motorsport	Audi R8 LMS GT3	24

INTERCONTINENTAL GT CHALLENGE
ENDSTAND FINAL POSITIONS

FAHRER DRIVERS

				PT
1	Markus Winkelhock (D)	Jamec Pem Racing/Audi Sport Team Saintéloc/ Audi Sport Team Magnus	Audi R8 LMS GT3	50
2	Christopher Haase (D)	Jamec Pem Racing/Audi Sport Team Saintéloc/ Audi Sport Team Land	Audi R8 LMS GT3	44
3	Christopher Mies (D)	Jamec Pem Racing/Audi Sport Team WRT/ Audi Sport Team Land	Audi R8 LMS GT3	29
4	Connor De Phillippi (USA)	Audi Sport Team WRT/Audi Sport Team Land	Audi R8 LMS GT3	28
5	Kelvin van der Linde/Pierre Kaffer (ZA/D)	Audi Sport Team I.S.R./Audi Sport Team Magnus	Audi R8 LMS GT3	27
6	Jules Gounon (F)	Audi Sport Team Saintéloc	Audi R8 LMS GT3	25
11	Frédéric Vervisch (B)	Audi Sport Team WRT	Audi R8 LMS GT3	10
12	Ash Samadi/Matt Halliday (AUS/NZ)	Team ASR	Audi R8 LMS GT3	8
12	Nico Müller/Antonio Garcia/René Rast (CH/E/D)	Audi Sport Team WRT	Audi R8 LMS GT3	8
12	Robin Frijns (NL)	Jamec Pem Racing/Belgian Audi Club Team WRT	Audi R8 LMS GT3	8
12	Stuart Leonard/Jake Dennis (GB/GB)	Belgian Audi Club Team WRT	Audi R8 LMS GT3	8
15	Frank Stippler (D)	Jamec Pem Racing/Audi Sport Team I.S.R.	Audi R8 LMS GT3	2
16	Garth Tander (AUS)	Jamec Pem Racing	Audi R8 LMS GT3	1
17	Josh Caygill/Richard Lyons/Niki Mayr-Melnhof/Jon Venter (GB/GB/A/AUS)	Belgian Audi Club Team WRT	Audi R8 LMS GT3	0
17	Nathanaël Berthon/Stéphane Richelmi/Benoît Tréluyer (F/MC/F)	Belgian Audi Club Team WRT	Audi R8 LMS GT3	0
17	Jamie Green (GB)	Belgian Audi Club Team WRT	Audi R8 LMS GT3	0
17	Marcel Fässler/André Lotterer/Dries Vanthoor (CH/D/B)	Audi Sport Team WRT	Audi R8 LMS GT3	0
17	Fred Bouvy/Christian Kelders/Marc Rostan (B/B/F)	Saintéloc Racing	Audi R8 LMS GT3	0
17	Filipe Albuquerque/Filip Salaquarda/Clemens Schmid (P/CZ/A)	I.S.R.	Audi R8 LMS GT3	0

MARKEN MANUFACTURERS GT3

				PT
1	Audi		Audi R8 LMS GT3	87

EUROPA EUROPE

ADAC GT MASTERS
ENDSTAND FINAL POSITIONS

FAHRER DRIVERS

				PT
3	Christopher Mies/Connor De Phillippi (D/USA)	Montaplast by Land-Motorsport	Audi R8 LMS GT3	120
5	Kelvin van der Linde (ZA)	Aust Motorsport	Audi R8 LMS GT3	107
9	Jeffrey Schmidt/Christopher Haase (CH/D)	Montaplast by Land-Motorsport	Audi R8 LMS GT3	91
10	Markus Pommer (D)	Aust Motorsport	Audi R8 LMS GT3	87
21	Patric Niederhauser/Dennis Marschall (CH/D)	Aust Motorsport	Audi R8 LMS GT3	34
26	Mike David Ortmann (D)	BWT Mücke Motorsport	Audi R8 LMS GT3	22
27	Sheldon van der Linde (ZA)	Aust Motorsport	Audi R8 LMS GT3	20
28	Filip Salaquarda (CZ)	BWT Mücke Motorsport	Audi R8 LMS GT3	20
31	Frank Stippler (D)	BWT Mücke Motorsport	Audi R8 LMS GT3	16
33	Markus Winkelhock (D)	BWT Mücke Motorsport	Audi R8 LMS GT3	14
34	Jamie Green/Alessio Picariello (GB/B)	BWT Mücke Motorsport	Audi R8 LMS GT3	10
36	Philip Geipel/Rahel Frey (D/CH)	YACO Racing	Audi R8 LMS GT3	3
38	Christopher Höher/Elia Erhart (A/D)	Audi Sport racing academy	Audi R8 LMS GT3	0
38	Ricardo Feller (CH)	Audi Sport racing academy	Audi R8 LMS GT3	0
38	Mikaela Åhlin-Kottulinsky (S)	Audi Sport racing academy	Audi R8 LMS GT3	0
38	Pierre Kaffer (D)	Audi Sport racing academy	Audi R8 LMS GT3	0
38	Marc Busch/Dennis Busch (D/D)	Twin Busch Motorsport	Audi R8 LMS GT3	0

TEAMS

				PT
2		Montaplast by Land-Motorsport	Audi R8 LMS GT3	167
3		BWT Mücke Motorsport	Audi R8 LMS GT3	152
4		Aust Motorsport	Audi R8 LMS GT3	129
15		Yaco Racing	Audi R8 LMS GT3	10
17		Audi Sport racing academy	Audi R8 LMS GT3	1
18		Twin Busch Motorsport	Audi R8 LMS GT3	0

JUNIORS

				PT
2	Jeffrey Schmidt (CH)	Montaplast by Land-Motorsport	Audi R8 LMS GT3	175
6	Dennis Marschall (D)	Aust Motorsport	Audi R8 LMS GT3	107
7	Mike David Ortmann (D)	BWT Mücke Motorsport	Audi R8 LMS GT3	104
12	Ricardo Feller (CH)	Audi Sport racing academy	Audi R8 LMS GT3	46.5
13	Mikaela Åhlin-Kottulinsky (S)	Audi Sport racing academy	Audi R8 LMS GT3	40.5
14	Christopher Höher (A)	Audi Sport racing academy	Audi R8 LMS GT3	35
15	Sheldon van der Linde (ZA)	Aust Motorsport	Audi R8 LMS GT3	33
16	Alessio Picariello (B)	BWT Mücke Motorsport	Audi R8 LMS GT3	21

AUDI SPORT TT CUP
ENDSTAND FINAL POSITIONS

FAHRER DRIVERS			PT
1	Philip Ellis (GB)	Audi TT cup	259
2	Mikel Azcona (E)	Audi TT cup	235
3	Tommaso Mosca (I)	Audi TT cup	196
4	Milan Dontje (NL)	Audi TT cup	193
5	Drew Ridge (AUS)	Audi TT cup	153
6	Gosia Rdest (PL)	Audi TT cup	149
7	Keagan Masters (ZA)	Audi TT cup	148
8	Yannik Brandt (CH)	Audi TT cup	141
9	Fabian Vettel (D)	Audi TT cup	122
10	Simon Wirth (D)	Audi TT cup	105
11	Fabienne Wohlwend (FL)	Audi TT cup	97
12	Kevin Arnold (D)	Audi TT cup	71
13	Vivien Keszthelyi (H)	Audi TT cup	65
14	Mike Beckhusen (D)	Audi TT cup	51
15	Josh Caygill (GB)	Audi TT cup	40
16	Finlay Hutchison (GB)	Audi TT cup	37
17	Jack Manchester (GB)	Audi TT cup	30

AUDI TT CUP RACE OF LEGENDS HOCKENHEIM (D), 15/10/2017
RENNERGEBNIS RACE RESULT

FAHRER DRIVERS		
1	Frank Stippler (D)	Audi TT cup
2	Lucas di Grassi (BR)	Audi TT cup
3	Marcel Fässler (CH)	Audi TT cup
4	Emanuele Pirro (I)	Audi TT cup
5	Dindo Capello (I)	Audi TT cup
6	Jean-Marc Gounon (F)	Audi TT cup
7	Vanina Ickx (B)	Audi TT cup
8	Hans-Joachim Stuck (D)	Audi TT cup
9	Lucas Luhr (D)	Audi TT cup
10	Marco Werner (D)	Audi TT cup
-	Christian Abt (D)	Audi TT cup
-	Rahel Frey (CH)	Audi TT cup
-	Stéphane Ortelli (MC)	Audi TT cup
-	Frank Biela (D)	Audi TT cup
-	Tom Kristensen (DK)	Audi TT cup
-	Filipe Albuquerque (P)	Audi TT cup

BLANCPAIN GT SERIES
ENDSTAND FINAL POSITIONS

FAHRER DRIVERS				PT
4	Robin Frijns/Stuart Leonard (NL/GB)	Team WRT/Belgian Audi Club Team WRT	Audi R8 LMS GT3	110
6	Markus Winkelhock (D)	Belgian Audi Club Team WRT	Audi R8 LMS GT3	104
8	Will Stevens (GB)	Belgian Audi Club Team WRT	Audi R8 LMS GT3	74
10	Marcel Fässler/Dries Vanthoor (CH/B)	Belgian Audi Club Team WRT	Audi R8 LMS GT3	62
13	Jake Dennis (GB)	Team WRT/Belgian Audi Club Team WRT	Audi R8 LMS GT3	55
16	Christopher Haase (D)	Saintéloc Junior Team/Audi Sport Team Saintéloc	Audi R8 LMS GT3	46
22	Pieter Schothorst (NL)	TeamWRT/Audi Sport Team WRT	Audi R8 LMS GT3	31
23	Filip Salaquarda (CZ)	I.S.R.	Audi R8 LMS GT3	31
24	Nico Müller/Antonio Garcia/René Rast (CH/E/D)	Audi Sport Team WRT	Audi R8 LMS GT3	29
25	Jules Gounon (F)	Audi Sport Team Saintéloc	Audi R8 LMS GT3	28
27	Clemens Schmid (A)	I.S.R.	Audi R8 LMS GT3	27
32	Christopher Mies (D)	Belgian Audi Club Team WRT/ Audi Sport Team WRT	Audi R8 LMS GT3	22
33	Frédéric Vervisch (B)	Audi Sport Team WRT	Audi R8 LMS GT3	20
35	Connor De Phillippi (USA)	Audi Sport Team WRT	Audi R8 LMS GT3	16
37	Romain Monti (F)	Saintéloc Junior Team	Audi R8 LMS GT3	16
43	Frank Stippler (D)	I.S.R/Audi Sport Team I.S.R.	Audi R8 LMS GT3	9
48	Filipe Albuquerque (P)	I.S.R.	Audi R8 LMS GT3	6
52	Pierre Kaffer/Kelvin van der Linde (D/ZA)	Audi Sport Team I.S.R.	Audi R8 LMS GT3	5
54	Kevin Ceccon (I)	I.S.R.	Audi R8 LMS GT3	4
56	Enzo Ide (B)	Belgian Audi Club Team WRT	Audi R8 LMS GT3	2
57	Benoît Tréluyer/Nathanaël Berthon/Stéphane Richelmi (F/F/MC)	Belgian Audi Club Team WRT	Audi R8 LMS GT3	2
57	Peter Terting (D)	Audi Sport Team Saintéloc	Audi R8 LMS GT3	2

TEAMS			PT
3	Belgian Audi Club Team WRT	Audi R8 LMS GT3	154
6	Team WRT	Audi R8 LMS GT3	127
10	I.S.R.	Audi R8 LMS GT3	37
11	Saintéloc Junior Team	Audi R8 LMS GT3	35

FAHRER DRIVERS PRO AM CUP				PT
44	Josh Caygill/Jon Venter (GB/A)	Team WRT/Belgian Audi Club Team WRT	Audi R8 LMS GT3	4
46	Richard Lyons/Niki Mayr-Melnhof (GB/A)	Belgian Audi Club Team WRT	Audi R8 LMS GT3	2
47	Hugo de Sadeleer (CH)	Belgian Audi Club Team WRT	Audi R8 LMS GT3	2

TEAMS PRO AM CUP			PT
15	Team WRT	Audi R8 LMS GT3	11
17	Saintéloc Junior Team	Audi R8 LMS GT3	2

FAHRER DRIVERS AM CUP				PT
10	Marc Rostan (F)	Saintéloc Junior Team	Audi R8 LMS GT3	44
14	Fred Bouvy/Christian Kelders (B/B)	Saintéloc Junior Team	Audi R8 LMS GT3	26

TEAMS AM CUP			PT
5	Saintéloc Junior Team	Audi R8 LMS GT3	26

BLANCPAIN GT SERIES ENDURANCE CUP
ENDSTAND FINAL POSITIONS

FAHRER DRIVERS				PT
8	Markus Winkelhock/Christopher Haase (D/D)	Audi Sport Team Saintéloc	Audi R8 LMS GT3	30
9	René Rast/Nico Müller/Antonio García (D/CH/E)	Audi Sport Team WRT	Audi R8 LMS GT3	29
10	Jake Dennis/Stuart Leonard (GB/GB)	Team WRT/Belgian Audi Club Team WRT	Audi R8 LMS GT3	28
10	Robin Frijns (NL)	Team WRT	Audi R8 LMS GT3	28
11	Jules Gounon (F)	Audi Sport Team Saintéloc	Audi R8 LMS GT3	28
15	Christopher Mies/Frédéric Vervisch (D/B)	Audi Sport Team WRT	Audi R8 LMS GT3	20
17	Connor De Phillippi (USA)	Audi Sport Team WRT	Audi R8 LMS GT3	16
21	Filip Salaquarda (CZ)	I.S.R.	Audi R8 LMS GT3	10

22	Frank Stippler (D)	I.S.R./Audi Sport Team I.S.R.	Audi R8 LMS GT3	9
24	Filipe Albuquerque/Clemens Schmid (P/A)	I.S.R.	Audi R8 LMS GT3	6
26	Pierre Kaffer/Kelvin van der Linde (D/ZA)	Audi Sport Team I.S.R.	Audi R8 LMS GT3	5
27	Kevin Ceccon (I)	I.S.R.	Audi R8 LMS GT3	4
27	Pieter Schothorst (NL)	Audi Sport Team WRT	Audi R8 LMS GT3	4
28	Benoît Tréluyer/Stéphane Richelmi/Nathanaël Berthon (F/MC/F)	Belgian Audi Club Team WRT	Audi R8 LMS GT3	2
31	Peter Terting (D)	Audi Sport Team Saintéloc	Audi R8 LMS GT3	0
31	Marcel Fässler/Dries Vanthoor (CH/B)	Belgian Audi Club Team WRT/ Audi Sport Team WRT	Audi R8 LMS GT3	0
31	André Lotterer (D)	Audi Sport Team WRT	Audi R8 LMS GT3	0
31	Will Stevens (GB)	Belgian Audi Club Team WRT	Audi R8 LMS GT3	0
31	Jon Venter/Josh Caygill (AUS/GB)	Team WRT/Belgian Audi Club Team WRT	Audi R8 LMS GT3	0
31	Niki Mayr-Melnhof (A)	Team WRT	Audi R8 LMS GT3	0
31	Richard Lyons (GB)	Team WRT	Audi R8 LMS GT3	0
31	Hugo de Sadeleer (CH)	Belgian Audi Club Team WRT	Audi R8 LMS GT3	0
31	Clement Mateu (F)	Team WRT	Audi R8 LMS GT3	0
31	Stuart Leonard/Jake Dennis (GB/GB)	Team WRT/Belgian Audi Club Team WRT	Audi R8 LMS GT3	0
31	Jamie Green (GB)	Team WRT/Audi Sport Team I.S.R./ Belgian Audi Club Team WRT	Audi R8 LMS GT3	0
31	Marc Rostan (F)	Saintéloc Junior Team	Audi R8 LMS GT3	0
31	Christian Kelders (B)	Saintéloc Junior Team	Audi R8 LMS GT3	0
31	Grégory Guilvert (F)	Saintéloc Junior Team	Audi R8 LMS GT3	0
31	Simon Gachet/Romain Monti (F/F)	Saintéloc Junior Team	Audi R8 LMS GT3	0
31	Fred Bouvy (B)	Saintéloc Junior Team	Audi R8 LMS GT3	0

TEAMS				PT
7		Belgian Audi Club Team WRT	Audi R8 LMS GT3	48
8		Team WRT	Audi R8 LMS GT3	30
13		I.S.R.	Audi R8 LMS GT3	14
17		Saintéloc Junior Team	Audi R8 LMS GT3	4

FAHRER DRIVERS PRO AM CUP				PT
38	Jon Venter/Josh Caygill (AUS/GB)	Team WRT/Belgian Audi Club Team WRT	Audi R8 LMS GT3	4
40	Niki Mayr-Melnhof/Richard Lyons (A/GB)	Belgian Audi Club Team WRT	Audi R8 LMS GT3	2
41	Hugo de Sadeleer (CH)	Belgian Audi Club Team WRT	Audi R8 LMS GT3	2

TEAMS PRO AM CUP				PT
14		Team WRT	Audi R8 LMS GT3	11
16		Saintéloc Junior Team	Audi R8 LMS GT3	2

FAHRER DRIVERS AM CUP				PT
8	Marc Rostan (F)	Saintéloc Junior Team	Audi R8 LMS GT3	44
12	Fred Bouvy (B)	Saintéloc Junior Team	Audi R8 LMS GT3	26
12	Christian Kelders (B)	Saintéloc Junior Team	Audi R8 LMS GT3	26

TEAMS AM CUP				PT
5		Saintéloc Junior Team	Audi R8 LMS GT3	26

BLANCPAIN GT SERIES SPRINT CUP
ENDSTAND FINAL POSITIONS

FAHRER DRIVERS				PT
1	Robin Frijns/Stuart Leonard (NL/GB)	Team WRT	Audi R8 LMS GT3	82
2	Markus Winkelhock/Will Stevens (D/GB)	Belgian Audi Club Team WRT	Audi R8 LMS GT3	74
5	Dries Vanthoor/Marcel Fässler (B/CH)	Belgian Audi Club Team WRT	Audi R8 LMS GT3	62
9	Pieter Schothorst/Jake Dennis (NL/GB)	Team WRT	Audi R8 LMS GT3	27
13	Clemens Schmid/Filip Salaquarda (A/CZ)	I.S.R.	Audi R8 LMS GT3	21
16	Romain Monti/Christopher Haase (F/D)	Saintéloc Junior Team	Audi R8 LMS GT3	17
26	Enzo Ide (B)	Belgian Audi Club Team WRT	Audi R8 LMS GT3	3
27	Christopher Mies (D)	Belgian Audi Club Team WRT	Audi R8 LMS GT3	3
32	Frank Stippler/Kevin Ceccon (D/I)	I.S.R.	Audi R8 LMS GT3	0
32	Jamie Green (GB)	Team WRT	Audi R8 LMS GT3	0
32	Simon Gachet/Peter Terting (F/D)	Saintéloc Junior Team	Audi R8 LMS GT3	0
32	Frédéric Vervisch (B)	Belgian Audi Club Team WRT	Audi R8 LMS GT3	0

TEAMS				PT
1		Belgian Audi Club Team WRT	Audi R8 LMS GT3	106
2		Team WRT	Audi R8 LMS GT3	97
8		Saintéloc Junior Team	Audi R8 LMS GT3	31
10		I.S.R.	Audi R8 LMS GT3	23

CAMPEONATO DISA DE CANARIAS DE MONTAÑA
ENDSTAND FINAL POSITIONS

FAHRER DRIVERS				PT
1	Luis Monzón Artiles (E)	Auto-Laca Competición	Audi R8 LMS GT3	210

CLUBS				PT
1		Auto-Laca Competición	Audi R8 LMS GT3	423

CAMPIONATO ITALIANO GRAN TURISMO
ENDSTAND FINAL POSITIONS

FAHRER DRIVERS SUPER GT3 PRO				PT
8	Benoît Tréluyer/Vittorio Ghirelli (F/I)	Audi Sport Italia	Audi R8 LMS GT3	114

MARKE MANUFACTURERS SUPER GT3 PRO				PT
3	Audi	Audi Sport Italia	Audi R8 LMS GT3	91

FAHRER DRIVERS GT3				PT
10	Luca Magnoni/Luca Rangoni (I/I)	Audi Sport Italia	Audi R8 LMS GT3	70
12	Davide Di Benedetto/Michele Merendino (I/I)	Audi Sport Italia	Audi R8 LMS GT3	40

MARKE MANUFACTURERS GT3				PT
4	Audi	Audi Sport Italia	Audi R8 LMS GT3	75

DMV GTC / DUNLOP 60
ENDSTAND FINAL POSITIONS

FAHRER DRIVERS				PT
1	Fabian Plentz/Egon Allgäuer (D/A)	HCB-Rutronik Racing	Audi R8 LMS GT3	319
2	Tommy Tulpe (D)	HCB-Rutronik Racing	Audi R8 LMS GT3	278
7	Evi Eizenhammer (D)	HCB-Rutronik Racing	Audi R8 LMS GT3	180

9	Stefan Eilentropp/Ronny C. Rock (D/D)	Land-Motorsport	Audi R8 LMS GT3	169
25	Bernhard Henzel (D)	Racing Engineers	Audi R8 LMS GT3	43
26	Andy Prinz (D)	HCB-Rutronik Racing	Audi R8 LMS GT3	30
29	Markus Pommer (D)	Aust Motorsport	Audi R8 LMS GT3	0
29	Carrie Schreiner (D)	Aust Motorsport	Audi R8 LMS GT3	0
29	Armin Schröder (D)	HCB-Rutronik Racing	Audi R8 LMS GT3	0
29	Kevin Arnold (D)	HCB-Rutronik Racing	Audi RS 3 LMS	0
29	Peter Schmidt/Dimitri Parhofer (D/D)	Car Collection Motorsport	Audi R8 LMS GT3	0

FAHRER DRIVERS DUNLOP 60

				PT
1	Fabian Plentz/Tommy Tulpe (D/D)	HCB-Rutronik Racing	Audi R8 LMS GT3	158
6	Egon Allgäuer (A)	HCB-Rutronik Racing	Audi R8 LMS GT3	80.75
9	Fabian Plentz (D)	HCB-Rutronik Racing	Audi R8 LMS GT3	68.75
24	Kevin Arnold (D)	HCB-Rutronik Racing	Audi RS 3 LMS	31.25
25	Bernhard Henzel (D)	Racing Engineers	Audi R8 LMS GT3	30
29	Carrie Schreiner/Markus Pommer (D/D)	Aust Motorsport	Audi R8 LMS GT3	25
36	Rahel Frey (CH)	Racing Engineers	Audi R8 LMS GT3	18
47	Evi Eizenhammer/Sebastian Amossé (D/D)	HCB-Rutronik Racing	Audi R8 LMS GT3	15
55	Rahel Frey (CH)	HCB-Rutronik Racing	Audi RS 3 LMS	12.50
61	Peter Schmidt/Dimitri Parhofer (D/D)	Car Collection Motorsport	Audi R8 LMS GT3	10
67	Armin Schröder (D)	HCB-Rutronik Racing	Audi R8 LMS GT3	4

FIA EUROPEAN HILL CLIMB CHAMPIONSHIP
ENDSTAND FINAL POSITIONS

FAHRER DRIVERS CATEGORY 1

				PT
1	"Tessitore" (A)	Tessitore Racing	Audi R8 LMS GT3	185

MICHELIN LE MANS CUP
ENDSTAND FINAL POSITIONS

FAHRER DRIVERS GT3

				PT
5	Flick Haigh/Joe Osborne (GB/GB)	Optimum Motorsport	Audi R8 LMS GT3	49.5

TEAMS GT3

			PT
4	Optimum Motorsport	Audi R8 LMS GT3	49.5

SWEDISH GT CHAMPIONSHIP
ENDSTAND FINAL POSITIONS

FAHRER DRIVERS

				PT
3	Jan Brunstedt (S)	JB Motorsport	Audi R8 LMS GT3	117

SPEZIAL TOURENWAGEN TROPHY
ENDSTAND FINAL POSITIONS

FAHRER DRIVERS

				PT
8	Berthold Gruhn (D)	*	Audi R8 LMS GT3	203
10	Andreas Schmidt (D)	*	Audi R8 LMS GT3	193
59	Dimitri Parhofer/Peter Schmidt (D/D)	Car Collection Motorsport	Audi R8 LMS GT3	0

*Teilnehmer ohne offizielle Team-Registrierung Entrant without official team registration

VLN LANGSTRECKENMEISTERSCHAFT NÜRBURGRING
ENDSTAND FINAL POSITIONS

SPEED TROPHÄE

			PT
2	Montaplast by Land-Motorsport (#28)	Audi R8 LMS GT3	100
3	Phoenix Racing (#15)	Audi R8 LMS GT3	58
13	Audi Sport Team WRT (#49)	Audi R8 LMS GT3	25
17	Phoenix Racing (#5)	Audi R8 LMS GT3	16
20	Audi Sport Team WRT (#50)	Audi R8 LMS GT3	12

AMERIKA AMERICA

IMSA WEATHERTECH SPORTSCAR CHAMPIONSHIP
ENDSTAND FINAL POSITIONS

FAHRER DRIVERS GTD

				PT
7	Andrew Davis/Lawson Aschenbach (USA/USA)	Stevenson Motorsports	Audi R8 LMS GT3	283
25	Bill Sweedler/Townsend Bell (USA/USA)	Alex Job Racing	Audi R8 LMS GT3	106
28	Connor De Phillippi/Christopher Mies (USA/D)	Montaplast by Land-Motorsport	Audi R8 LMS GT3	96
32	Frank Montecalvo (USA)	Alex Job Racing	Audi R8 LMS GT3	83
36	Matt Bell (USA)	Stevenson Motorsports	Audi R8 LMS GT3	70
40	Jules Gounon (F)	Montaplast by Land-Motorsport	Audi R8 LMS GT3	60
52	Sheldon van der Linde (ZA)	Montaplast by Land-Motorsport	Audi R8 LMS GT3	36
55	Jeffrey Schmidt (CH)	Montaplast by Land-Motorsport	Audi R8 LMS GT3	32
58	Robin Liddell (GB)	Stevenson Motorsports	Audi R8 LMS GT3	28
60	Pierre Kaffer (CH)	Alex Job Racing	Audi R8 LMS GT3	25

TEAMS GTD

			PT
6	Stevenson Motorsports	Audi R8 LMS GT3	283
16	Alex Job Racing	Audi R8 LMS GT3	106
17	Montaplast by Land-Motorsport	Audi R8 LMS GT3	96

MARKEN MANUFACTURERS GTD

		PT
5	Audi	334

NORTH AMERICAN ENDURANCE CUP
ENDSTAND FINAL POSITIONS

FAHRER DRIVERS GTD

				PT
5	Connor De Phillippi/Christopher Mies (USA/D)	Montaplast by Land-Motorsport	Audi R8 LMS GT3	30
11	Andrew Davis/Lawson Aschenbach (USA/USA)	Stevenson Motorsports	Audi R8 LMS GT3	25
12	Bill Sweedler/Frank Montecalvo/Townsend Bell (USA/USA/USA)	Alex Job Racing	Audi R8 LMS GT3	25
17	Matt Bell (USA)	Stevenson Motorsports	Audi R8 LMS GT3	21
19	Jules Gounon (F)	Montaplast by Land-Motorsport	Audi R8 LMS GT3	19
24	Jeffrey Schmidt (CH)	Montaplast by Land-Motorsport	Audi R8 LMS GT3	12
26	Sheldon van der Linde (ZA)	Montaplast by Land-Motorsport	Audi R8 LMS GT3	11

30	Pierre Kaffer (D)	Alex Job Racing	Audi R8 LMS GT3	9
30	Robin Liddell (GB)	Stevenson Motorsports	Audi R8 LMS GT3	9

TEAMS GTD

				PT
10		Stevenson Motorsports	Audi R8 LMS GT3	25
11		Alex Job Racing	Audi R8 LMS GT3	25
17		Montaplast by Land-Motorsport	Audi R8 LMS GT3	19

MARKEN MANUFACTURERS GTD

				PT
3	Audi		Audi R8 LMS GT3	38

PIRELLI WORLD CHALLENGE SPRINT GT/SPRINTX

ENDSTAND FINAL POSITIONS

FAHRER DRIVERS GT OVERALL

				PT
11	Pierre Kaffer (D)	Magnus Racing	Audi R8 LMS GT3	174
16	Spencer Pumpelly (USA)	Magnus Racing	Audi R8 LMS GT3	151
27	John Potter (USA)	Magnus Racing	Audi R8 LMS GT3	100
37	Dane Cameron (USA)	Magnus Racing	Audi R8 LMS GT3	48
44	Andrew Davis/Mike Skeen (USA/USA)	McCann Racing	Audi R8 LMS GT3	38
47	Marco Seefried (A)	Magnus Racing	Audi R8 LMS GT3	35
54	Michael McCann (USA)	McCann Racing	Audi R8 LMS GT3	21
62	Andrew Davis (USA)	Magnus Racing	Audi R8 LMS GT3	13
65	Mike Skeen (USA)	McCann Racing	Audi R8 LMS GT3	11
69	James Dayson/Jason Bell (USA/USA)	M1 GT Racing	Audi R8 LMS GT3	7
71	Walt Bowlin/Lars Viljoen (USA/GB)	M1 GT Racing	Audi R8 LMS GT3	6
74	James Dayson/David Ostella (USA/USA)	M1 GT Racing	Audi R8 LMS GT3	4
81	Larry Pegram (USA)	M1 GT Racing	Audi R8 LMS GT3	0

MARKEN MANUFACTURERS GT OVERALL

				PT
6	Audi		Audi R8 LMS GT3	64

FAHRER DRIVERS SPRINT GT

				PT
11	Pierre Kaffer (D)	Magnus Racing	Audi R8 LMS GT3	81
17	John Potter (USA)	Magnus Racing	Audi R8 LMS GT3	52
27	Spencer Pumpelly (USA)	Magnus Racing	Audi R8 LMS GT3	10
28	Michael McCann (USA)	McCann Racing	Audi R8 LMS GT3	10

FAHRER DRIVERS SPRINT GTA

				PT
2	John Potter (USA)	Magnus Racing	Audi R8 LMS GT3	171
8	Michael McCann (USA)	McCann Racing	Audi R8 LMS GT3	62

TEAMS SPRINT GT

				PT
8		Magnus Racing	Audi R8 LMS GT3	96
19		McCann Racing	Audi R8 LMS GT3	10

FAHRER DRIVERS SPRINTX GT OVERALL

				PT
6	Spencer Pumpelly (USA)	Magnus Racing	Audi R8 LMS GT3	141
14	Pierre Kaffer (D)	Magnus Racing	Audi R8 LMS GT3	93
22	Dane Cameron (USA)	Magnus Racing	Audi R8 LMS GT3	48
24	John Potter (USA)	Magnus Racing	Audi R8 LMS GT3	48
27	Andrew Davis/Mike Skeen (USA/USA)	McCann Racing	Audi R8 LMS GT3	38
30	Marco Seefried (A)	Magnus Racing	Audi R8 LMS GT3	35
40	Andrew Davis (USA)	Magnus Racing	Audi R8 LMS GT3	13
44	Michael McCann/Mike Skeen (USA/USA)	McCann Racing	Audi R8 LMS GT3	11
46	James Dayson/Jason Bell (USA/USA)	M1 GT Racing	Audi R8 LMS GT3	7
48	Walt Bowlin/Lars Viljoen (USA/GB)	M1 GT Racing	Audi R8 LMS GT3	6
49	James Dayson/David Ostella (USA/USA)	M1 GT Racing	Audi R8 LMS GT3	4
54	Larry Pegram (USA)	M1 GT Racing	Audi R8 LMS GT3	0

FAHRER DRIVERS SPRINTX GT PRO AM

				PT
5	John Potter (USA)	Magnus Racing	Audi R8 LMS GT3	156
8	Marco Seefried (A)	Magnus Racing	Audi R8 LMS GT3	122
13	Michael McCann/Mike Skeen (USA/USA)	McCann Racing	Audi R8 LMS GT3	36
15	Andrew Davis (USA)	Magnus Racing	Audi R8 LMS GT3	34
20	James Dayson/David Ostella (USA/USA)	M1 GT Racing	Audi R8 LMS GT3	25

FAHRER DRIVERS SPRINTX GT AM AM

				PT
3	James Dayson (USA)	M1 GT Racing	Audi R8 LMS GT3	128
5	Jason Bell (USA)	M1 GT Racing	Audi R8 LMS GT3	86
8	Walt Bowlin/Lars Viljoen (USA/GB)	M1 GT Racing	Audi R8 LMS GT3	42
9	Larry Pegram (USA)	M1 GT Racing	Audi R8 LMS GT3	42

TEAMS SPRINTX GT

				PT
6		Magnus Racing	Audi R8 LMS GT3	149
12		McCann Racing	Audi R8 LMS GT3	48
19		M1 GT Racing	Audi R8 LMS GT3	13

ASIEN ASIA

AUDI R8 LMS CUP

ENDSTAND FINAL POSITIONS

FAHRER DRIVERS

				PT
1	Alessio Picariello (B)	MGT by Absolute	Audi R8 LMS GT3	178
2	Mitch Gilbert (MAL)	OD Racing Team	Audi R8 LMS GT3	134
3	Congfu Cheng (CN)	FAW-VW Audi Racing Team	Audi R8 LMS GT3	127
4	Alex Yoong (MAL)	Audi R8 LMS Cup	Audi R8 LMS GT3	121
5	Shaun Thong (HK)	Audi TEDA Racing Team	Audi R8 LMS GT3	109
6	Martin Rump (EST)	Champion Racing Team	Audi R8 LMS GT3	76
7	Chen Weian (CN)	Tianshi Racing Team	Audi R8 LMS GT3	67
8	Marchy Lee (HK)	Audi Hong Kong Team	Audi R8 LMS GT3	50
9	Dries Vanthoor (B)	Castrol Racing Team	Audi R8 LMS GT3	42
10	Stéphane Richelmi (MC)	Castrol Racing Team	Audi R8 LMS GT3	25
11	Kyong-Ouk You (ROK)	Team Audi Korea	Audi R8 LMS GT3	25
12	Akash Nandy (MAL)	KCMG	Audi R8 LMS GT3	12
13	Jing Zu Sun (CN)	Milestone Racing	Audi R8 LMS GT3	11
14	Anthony Liu (CN)	Absolute Racing	Audi R8 LMS GT3	10
15	Jeffrey Lee (RC)	Team Audi Volkswagen Taiwan	Audi R8 LMS GT3	10
16	Bhurit Bhirombhakdi (THA)	Singha Plan-B Motorsport	Audi R8 LMS GT3	7
17	Sanghwi Yoon (ROK)	KCMG	Audi R8 LMS GT3	2
18	Xin Jiang (CN)	KCMG	Audi R8 LMS GT3	1
19	Andrew Kim (ROK)	Audi Hong Kong Team	Audi R8 LMS GT3	0
20	Keong Wee Lim (MAL)	Audi Hong Kong Team	Audi R8 LMS GT3	0

FAHRER DRIVERS AM+ CUP

				PT
1	Chen Weian (CN)	Tianshi Racing Team	Audi R8 LMS GT3	193
2	Jeffrey Lee (RC)	Team Audi Volkswagen Taiwan	Audi R8 LMS GT3	144
3	Anthony Liu (CN)	Absolute Racing	Audi R8 LMS GT3	69
4	Xin Jiang (CN)	KCMG	Audi R8 LMS GT3	27
5	Andrew Kim (RC)	Audi Hong Kong Team	Audi R8 LMS GT3	15

FAHRER DRIVERS AM CUP

				PT
1	Bhurit Bhirombhakdi (THA)	Singha Plan-B Motorsport	Audi R8 LMS GT3	162
2	Jing Zu Sun (CN)	Milestone Racing	Audi R8 LMS GT3	127
3	Sanghwi Yoon (ROK)	KCMG	Audi R8 LMS GT3	47
4	Keong Wee Lim (MAL)	Audi Hong Kong Team	Audi R8 LMS GT3	16

TEAMS

			PT
1	MGT by Absolute	Audi R8 LMS GT3	178
2	OD Racing Team	Audi R8 LMS GT3	134
3	FAW-VW Audi Racing Team	Audi R8 LMS GT3	127
4	Audi R8 LMS Cup	Audi R8 LMS GT3	121
5	Audi TEDA Racing Team	Audi R8 LMS GT3	109
6	Champion Racing Team	Audi R8 LMS GT3	76
7	Tianshi Racing Team	Audi R8 LMS GT3	67
8	Castrol Racing Team	Audi R8 LMS GT3	67
9	Audi Hong Kong Team	Audi R8 LMS GT3	50
10	Team Audi Korea	Audi R8 LMS GT3	25
11	KCMG	Audi R8 LMS GT3	13
12	Milestone Racing	Audi R8 LMS GT3	11
13	Absolute Racing	Audi R8 LMS GT3	10
14	Team Audi Volkswagen Taiwan	Audi R8 LMS GT3	10
15	Singha Plan-B Motorsport	Audi R8 LMS GT3	7

ASIAN LE MANS SPRINT CUP
ENDSTAND FINAL POSITIONS

FAHRER DRIVERS GT

				PT
3	Bhurit Bhirombhakdi/Kantasak Kusiri (THA/THA)	Singha Plan-B Motorsport	Audi R8 LMS GT3	44

TEAMS GT

			PT
3	Singha Plan-B Motorsport	Audi R8 LMS GT3	44

BLANCPAIN GT SERIES ASIA
ENDSTAND FINAL POSITIONS

FAHRER DRIVERS

				PT
2	Mitchell Gilbert/Aditya Patel (MAL/IND)	OD Racing Team	Audi R8 LMS GT3	160
3	Marchy Lee/Shaun Thong (HK/HK)	Audi Hong Kong	Audi R8 LMS GT3	158
9	Alex Au/Alex Yoong (HK/MAL)	Team Audi R8 LMS Cup	Audi R8 LMS GT3	60
11	Jeffrey Lee (RC)	Team WRT/J-Fly by Absolute Racing	Audi R8 LMS GT3	50
12	Alessio Picariello (B)	J-Fly by Absolute Racing	Audi R8 LMS GT3	46
16	Anthony Liu Xu/Davide Rizzo (CN/I)	BBT	Audi R8 LMS GT3	33
19	Sanghwi Rick Yoon/Martin Rump (HK/EST)	KCMG by Champion Racing	Audi R8 LMS GT3	29
25	Jingzu Sun/Congfu Cheng (CN/CN)	Milestone Racing	Audi R8 LMS GT3	15
30	Will Stevens (GB)	Team WRT	Audi R8 LMS GT3	4
34	Naoto Takeda/Takuya Shirasaka (J/J)	KCMG	Audi R8 LMS GT3	0
34	Bhurit Bhirombhakdi/Kantasak Kusiri (THA/THA)	Singha Plan-B Motorsport Team	Audi R8 LMS GT3	0
34	Lim Keong Wee/Melvin Moh (MAL/MAL)	Phoenix Racing Asia	Audi R8 LMS GT3	0

FAHRER DRIVERS PRO/AM

				PT
2	Alex Au/Alex Yoong (HK/MAL)	Team Audi R8 LMS Cup	Audi R8 LMS GT3	147
3	Jeffrey Lee (RC)	Team WRT/J-Fly by Absolute Racing	Audi R8 LMS GT3	146
5	Alessio Picariello (B)	J-Fly by Absolute Racing	Audi R8 LMS GT3	121
7	Jingzu Sun/Congfu Cheng (CN/CN)	Milestone Racing	Audi R8 LMS GT3	103
9	Sanghwi Rick Yoon/Martin Rump (HK/EST)	KCMG by Champion Racing	Audi R8 LMS GT3	61
10	Anthony Liu Xu/Davide Rizzo (CN/I)	BBT	Audi R8 LMS GT3	55
15	Bhurit Bhirombhakdi/Kantasak Kusiri (THA/THA)	Singha Plan-B Motorsport Team	Audi R8 LMS GT3	27
16	Will Stevens (GB)	Team WRT	Audi R8 LMS GT3	25

FAHRER DRIVERS SILVER CUP

				PT
1	Marchy Lee/Shaun Thong (HK/HK)	Audi Hong Kong	Audi R8 LMS GT3	206
2	Mitchell Gilbert/Aditya Patel (MAL/IND)	OD Racing Team	Audi R8 LMS GT3	188

FAHRER DRIVERS AM CUP

				PT
4	Naoto Takeda/Takuya Shirasaka (J/J)	KCMG	Audi R8 LMS GT3	131

TEAMS

			PT
2	OD Racing Team	Audi R8 LMS GT3	160
3	Audi Hong Kong	Audi R8 LMS GT3	158
8	Team Audi R8 LMS Cup	Audi R8 LMS GT3	60
9	J-Fly by Absolute Racing	Audi R8 LMS GT3	46
10	BBT	Audi R8 LMS GT3	33
11	KCMG by Champion Racing	Audi R8 LMS GT3	29
14	Milestone Racing	Audi R8 LMS GT3	15
18	Team WRT	Audi R8 LMS GT3	4
21	KCMG	Audi R8 LMS GT3	0
21	Singha Plan-B Motorsport Team	Audi R8 LMS GT3	0
21	Phoenix Racing Asia	Audi R8 LMS GT3	0

CHINA GT CHAMPIONSHIP
ENDSTAND FINAL POSITIONS

FAHRER DRIVERS GT3

				PT
1	Xu Jia (CN)	Kings Linky Racing	Audi R8 LMS GT3	189
3	Wang Liang (CN)	Kings Linky Racing	Audi R8 LMS GT3	162
4	Martin Rump (EST)	Kings Linky Racing	Audi R8 LMS GT3	160
6	Marchy Lee/Alex Au (HK/HK)	Audi Hong Kong	Audi R8 LMS GT3	86
7	Melvin Moh (MAL)	Audi Hong Kong	Audi R8 LMS GT3	71
12	Lim Keong Wee (MAL)	Audi Hong Kong	Audi R8 LMS GT3	40
13	Dries Vanthoor (B)	Kings Linky Racing	Audi R8 LMS GT3	40
13	Jake Dennis (GB)	Kings Linky Racing	Audi R8 LMS GT3	40
17	Alex Yoong (MAL)	Kings Linky Racing	Audi R8 LMS GT3	37
18	Eric Lo (HK)	Audi Hong Kong	Audi R8 LMS GT3	31
22	Terry Huang Chuhan/Massimiliano Wiser (CN/I)	Tianshi Racing Team	Audi R8 LMS GT3	20
23	Yang Yuan (CN)	Kings Linky Racing	Audi R8 LMS GT3	18
28	Han Huilin (CN)	Kings Linky Racing	Audi R8 LMS GT3	0
28	Zhang Zhiqiang (CN)	Kings Linky Racing	Audi R8 LMS GT3	0
-	Congfu Cheng/Anthony Liu (CN/CN)	BBT	Audi R8 LMS GT3	0

TEAMS GT3

			PT
1	Kings Linky Racing	Audi R8 LMS GT3	382
4	Audi Hong Kong	Audi R8 LMS GT3	157
7	Tianshi Racing Team	Audi R8 LMS GT3	20
-	BBT	Audi R8 LMS GT3	0

FAHRER DRIVERS GTC

				PT
2	Bian Hao/Will Bamber (CN/NZ)	JRM Force China	Audi R8 LMS GT3	162.5
7	Pu Shu/Liang Kaifeng (CN/CN)	Tianshi Racing Team	Audi R8 LMS GT3	42
8	Kimi Qin Tianqi (CN)	Spirit Z-Racing	Audi R8 LMS GT3	40
9	Chen Weian/Jiao Peng (CN/CN)	Tianshi Racing Team	Audi R8 LMS GT3	37
13	Sun Zheng/Sunny Risheng Wang (CN/CN)	Spirit Z-Racing	Audi R8 LMS GT3	28
23	Chen Junhua/Li Yueqin (CN/CN)	Top Speed	Audi R8 LMS GT3	10
31	Xie Ruilin (CN)	Spirit Z-Racing	Audi R8 LMS GT3	0
31	Chang Jiong (CN)	Tianshi Racing Team	Audi R8 LMS GT3	0
31	Matteo Cressoni (I)	Tianshi Racing Team	Audi R8 LMS GT3	0
31	Huang Yiqing (CN)	Tianshi Racing Team	Audi R8 LMS GT3	0
31	Zhang Jian/Li Huiwei (CN/CN)	300+	Audi R8 LMS GT3	0
31	Yuan Tingting (CN)	LEO 109/300+	Audi R8 LMS GT3	0

TEAMS GTC

			PT
4	JRM Force China	Audi R8 LMS GT3	109
6	Tianshi Racing Team	Audi R8 LMS GT3	81
7	Spirit Z-Racing	Audi R8 LMS GT3	70
11	Top Speed	Audi R8 LMS GT3	10
12	300+	Audi R8 LMS GT3	0
12	LEO 109	Audi R8 LMS GT3	0

SAUDI GT CHAMPIONSHIP
ENDSTAND FINAL POSITIONS

FAHRER DRIVERS

				PT
1	Mohammed Bin Saud (KSA)	Saudi Arrows Racing Team	Audi R8 LMS GT3	151

SUPER GT
ENDSTAND FINAL POSITIONS

FAHRER DRIVERS GT300

				PT
20	Richard Lyons/Masataka Yanagida (GB/J)	Audi Team Hitotsuyama	Audi R8 LMS GT3	5
24	Jake Parsons/Shinnosuke Yamada (AUS/J)	Team TAISAN SARD	Audi R8 LMS GT3	0
24	Christian Klien (A)	Team TAISAN SARD	Audi R8 LMS GT3	0

TEAMS GT300

			PT
19	Audi Team Hitotsuyama	Audi R8 LMS GT3	21
24	Team TAISAN SARD	Audi R8 LMS GT3	11

THAILAND SUPER SERIES
ENDSTAND FINAL POSITIONS

FAHRER DRIVERS GTM PLUS

				PT
3	Daniel Bilski (AUS)	B-Quik Racing Team	Audi R8 LMS GT3	114
5	Henk Kiks (NL)	B-Quik Racing Team	Audi R8 LMS GT3	80
8	Shaun Varney (NZ)	B-Quik Racing Team	Audi R8 LMS GT3	30

TEAMS GTM PLUS

			PT
1	B-Quik Racing Team	Audi R8 LMS GT3	194

PAZIFIK PACIFIC

AUSTRALIAN ENDURANCE CHAMPIONSHIP
ENDSTAND FINAL POSITIONS

FAHRER DRIVERS

				PT
2	Tim Miles/Jaxon Evans (NZ/NZ)	Valvoline Jamec Pem Racing	Audi R8 LMS GT3	598
10	Geoff Emery (AUS)	Valvoline Jamec Pem Racing	Audi R8 LMS GT3	317
15	Daniel Gaunt (NZ)	KFC	Audi R8 LMS GT3	233
16	Kelvin van der Linde (ZA)	Valvoline Jamec Pem Racing	Audi R8 LMS GT3	188
17	Andrew Bagnall/Matt Halliday (NZ/NZ)	International Motorsport	Audi R8 LMS GT3	187
18	Dylan O'Keeffe (AUS)	KFC	Audi R8 LMS GT3	183
18	Jonny Reid (NZ)	International Motorsport	Audi R8 LMS GT3	183
25	Garth Tander (AUS)	Valvoline Jamec Pem Racing	Audi R8 LMS GT3	129
29	Jon Udy/Matt Whittaker (NZ/NZ)	International Motorsport	Audi R8 LMS GT3	102
30	Neil Foster (NZ)	International Motorsport	Audi R8 LMS GT3	95
31	Matthew Stoupas (AUS)	KFC	Audi R8 LMS GT3	72
33	Ash Samadi/Chris Pither (AUS/NZ)	Ah Apartments	Audi R8 LMS GT3	58
36	Grant Denyer/Greg Taylor (AUS/AUS)	GT Motorsport	Audi R8 LMS GT3	0

AUSTRALIAN GT CHAMPIONSHIP
ENDSTAND FINAL POSITIONS

FAHRER DRIVERS

				PT
1	Geoff Emery (AUS)	Valvoline Jamec Pem Racing	Audi R8 LMS GT3	680
3	Ash Walsh (AUS)	Supabarn Supermarkets	Audi R8 LMS GT3	585
9	James Koundouris (AUS)	Supabarn Supermarkets	Audi R8 LMS GT3	319
12	Duvashen Padayachee (AUS)	Supabarn Supermarkets	Audi R8 LMS GT3	266
15	Ash Samadi (AUS)	Ah Apartments	Audi R8 LMS GT3	216
19	Marc Cini (AUS)	Hallmarc Constructions	Audi R8 LMS GT3	136
21	Steven McLaughlan (AUS)	Valvoline Jamec Pem Racing	Audi R8 LMS GT3	124
24	Gary Higgon/Daniel Gaunt (AUS/NZ)	KFC	Audi R8 LMS GT3	95
28	Dean Fiore (AUS)	Hallmarc Constructions	Audi R8 LMS GT3	64
29	Tim Miles (NZ)	Valvoline Jamec Pem Racing	Audi R8 LMS GT3	63
33	Nick Kelly (AUS)	Industrie Clothing	Audi R8 LMS GT3	32
35	Greg Taylor/Nathan Antunes (AUS/AUS)	GT Motorsport	Audi R8 LMS GT3	26
39	Kelvin van der Linde (ZA)	Valvoline Jamec Pem Racing	Audi R8 LMS GT3	0

FAHRER DRIVERS GOLD DRIVER CUP

				PT
5	Ash Samadi (AUS)	Ah Apartments	Audi R8 LMS GT3	386
8	Tim Miles (NZ)	Valvoline Jamec Pem Racing	Audi R8 LMS GT3	174
9	Marc Cini (AUS)	Hallmarc Constructions	Audi R8 LMS GT3	154
10	Nick Kelly (AUS)	Industrie Clothing	Audi R8 LMS GT3	122
16	Greg Taylor (AUS)	GT Motorsport	Audi R8 LMS GT3	8

AUSTRALIAN GT TROPHY SERIES
ENDSTAND FINAL POSITIONS

FAHRER DRIVERS				PT
1	Steven McLaughlan (AUS)	Audi Sport Customer Racing	Audi R8 LMS GT3	893
2	Rod Salmon (AUS)	Audi Sport Customer Racing	Audi R8 LMS GT3	704
5	Rick Mensa (AUS)	CCC Polished Concrete	Audi R8 LMS GT3	422
7	Rob Smith (AUS)	Audi Sport Customer Racing	Audi R8 LMS GT3	377
8	Travers Beynon (AUS)	Travers Beynon Racing	Audi R8 LMS GT3	327
9	Rio Nugara (AUS)	Audi Sport Customer Racing	Audi R8 LMS GT3	318
11	Con Whitlock (AUS)	Whitlock Bull Bars	Audi R8 LMS GT3	211
12	Matthew Stoupas (AUS)	KFC	Audi R8 LMS GT3	181
13	Jake Fouracre (AUS)	Audi Sport Customer Racing	Audi R8 LMS GT3	83
15	Gary Higgon (AUS)	KFC	Audi R8 LMS GT3	67

NEW ZEALAND ENDURANCE RACING CHAMPIONSHIP
ENDSTAND FINAL POSITIONS

FAHRER DRIVERS THREE HOUR				PT
1	Simon Evans/Gene Rollinson (NZ/NZ)	SMEG Racing	Audi R8 LMS GT3	75
4	Neil Foster/Jonny Reid (NZ/NZ)	International Motorsport	Audi R8 LMS GT3	62

NORTH ISLAND ENDURANCE SERIES
ENDSTAND FINAL POSITIONS

FAHRER DRIVERS THREE HOUR				PT
1	Simon Evans/Gene Rollinson (NZ/NZ)	SMEG Racing	Audi R8 LMS GT3	310
12	Neil Foster/Jonny Reid (NZ/NZ)	International Motorsport	Audi R8 LMS GT3	185

FAHRER DRIVERS THREE HOUR CLASS GT-A				PT
1	Simon Evans/Gene Rollinson (NZ/NZ)	SMEG Racing	Audi R8 LMS GT3	310
3	Neil Foster/Jonny Reid (NZ/NZ)	International Motorsport	Audi R8 LMS GT3	185

SOUTH ISLAND ENDURANCE SERIES
ENDSTAND FINAL POSITIONS

FAHRER DRIVERS THREE HOUR				PT
26	Andrew Bagnall/Matt Halliday (NZ/NZ)	International Motorsport	Audi R8 LMS GT3	95
28	Neil Foster/Jonny Reid (NZ/NZ)	International Motorsport	Audi R8 LMS GT3	90

FAHRER DRIVERS THREE HOUR CLASS D & E				PT
7	Andrew Bagnall/Matt Halliday (NZ/NZ)	International Motorsport	Audi R8 LMS GT3	95
8	Neil Foster/Jonny Reid (NZ/NZ)	International Motorsport	Audi R8 LMS GT3	90

VICTORIAN STATE CIRCUIT RACING CHAMPIONSHIPS
ENDSTAND FINAL POSITIONS

FAHRER DRIVERS				PT
1	Matthew Stoupas (AUS)	KFC	Audi R8 LMS GT3	468
3	Ross Lilley (AUS)	Koala Furniture	Audi R8 LMS GT3	252
6	Gary Higgon (AUS)	KFC	Audi R8 LMS GT3	219
8	Richard Mensa (AUS)	CCC Polished Concrete	Audi R8 LMS GT3	190
15	Ryan How (AUS)	GT Motorsport	Audi R8 LMS GT3	74
21	Con Whitlock (AUS)	Whitlock Bull Bars	Audi R8 LMS GT3	47

ADDENDA 2016

12H SEPANG (MAL), 10/12/2016
RENNERGEBNIS RACE RESULT

FAHRER DRIVERS				
1	(1)	Laurens Vanthoor/Christopher Haase/Robin Frijns (B/D/NL)	Audi Sport Team Phoenix	Audi R8 LMS GT3
3	(3)	René Rast/Markus Winkelhock/Pierre Kaffer (D/D/D)	Audi Sport Team Phoenix	Audi R8 LMS GT3
1	(12)	Daniel Bilski/Henk Kiks/Peter Kox (AUS/NL/NL)	B-Quik Racing Team	Audi R8 LMS GT3

25H THUNDERHILL 2016 (USA), 3-4/12/2016
RENNERGEBNIS RACE RESULT

FAHRER DRIVERS			
1	Darren Law/Mike Hedlund/Johannes van Overbeek/Dion von Moltke (USA/USA/USA/USA)	Flying Lizard Motorsports	Audi R8 LMS GT3

ASIAN LE MANS SERIES 2016/2017
ENDSTAND FINAL POSITIONS

FAHRER DRIVERS				PT
6	Marchy Lee/Kyoung-Ouk You/Alex Yoong (HK/ROK/MAL)	Team Audi Korea	Audi R8 LMS GT3	35
12	Go Max/Toru Tanaka/Tetsuya Tanaka (J/J/J)	KCMG	Audi R8 LMS GT3	13
14	Congfu Cheng/Steven Lin/Alessio Picariello (CN/CN/B)	Absolute Racing	Audi R8 LMS GT3	10
21	Peng Liu/Massimilano Wiser/Christopher Haase (CN/I/D)	Tianshi Racing Team	Audi R8 LMS GT3	0

TEAMS			PT
5	Team Audi Korea	Audi R8 LMS GT3	35
10	KCMG	Audi R8 LMS GT3	13
11	Absolute Racing	Audi R8 LMS GT3	10
16	Tianshi Racing Team	Audi R8 LMS GT3	0

INTERCONTINENTAL GT CHALLENGE
ENDSTAND FINAL POSITIONS

FAHRER DRIVERS				PT
1	Laurens Vanthoor (B)	Phoenix Racing/Audi Sport Team WRT/Audi Sport Team Phoenix	Audi R8 LMS GT3	58
2	René Rast (D)	Jamec Pem Racing/Audi Sport Team WRT/Audi Sport Team Phoenix	Audi R8 LMS GT3	44
5	Markus Winkelhock (D)	Phoenix Racing/Audi Sport Team Phoenix	Audi R8 LMS GT3	33
7	Christopher Haase/Robin Frijns (D/NL)	Audi Sport Team Phoenix	Audi R8 LMS GT3	25
9	Nico Müller (CH)	Audi Sport Team WRT	Audi R8 LMS GT3	18
11	Alex Davison (AUS)	Phoenix Racing	Audi R8 LMS GT3	15
14	Steven McLaughlan/Garth Tander (AUS/AUS)	Jamec Pem Racing	Audi R8 LMS GT3	8
16	Dries Vanthoor/Will Stevens/Frédéric Vervisch (B/GB/B)	Belgian Audi Club Team WRT	Audi R8 LMS GT3	4

18	Christopher Mies/Frank Stippler (D/D)	Audi Sport Team Phoenix	Audi R8 LMS GT3	0
18	Pierre Kaffer	Audi Sport Team Phoenix	Audi R8 LMS GT3	0

MARKE MANUFACTURER

			PT
1	Audi	Audi R8 LMS GT3	86

THAILAND SUPER SERIES (2016/2017)

ENDSTAND FINAL POSITIONS

FAHRER DRIVERS

				PT
4	Daniel Bilski (AUS)	B-Quik Racing Team	Audi R8 LMS GT3	82
7	Henk Kiks (NL)	B-Quik Racing Team	Audi R8 LMS GT3	56

TEAMS

			PT
4	B-Quik Racing Team	Audi R8 LMS GT3	78

STATISTIK STATISTICS 2009–2017

FAHRERTITEL GESAMTWERTUNG / OVERALL DRIVERS' TITLES

2009

ADAC GT Masters	Christian Abt (D)	Audi R8 LMS GT3
Belgien / Belgium	Jean-François Hemroulle/Tim Verbergt (B/B)	Audi R8 LMS GT3
FIA GT3 (Europa / Europe)	Christopher Haase/Christopher Mies (D/D)	Audi R8 LMS GT3

2010

DMSB-GT-Meisterschaft / DMSB GT Championship	Luca Ludwig (D)	Audi R8 LMS GT3
Belgien / Belgium	Greg Franchi/Anthony Kumpen (B/B)	Audi R8 LMS GT3
Portugal	César Campaniço/João Figueiredo (P/P)	Audi R8 LMS GT3
Spanien / Spain	César Campaniço/João Figueiredo (P/P)	Audi R8 LMS GT3

2011

Australien / Australia	Mark Eddy (AUS)	Audi R8 LMS GT3
Blancpain Endurance Series	Greg Franchi (B)	Audi R8 LMS GT3
Italien / Italy	Marco Bonanomi (I)	Audi R8 LMS GT3
Super Taikyu Series	Tomonobu Fujii/Akihiro Tsuzuki/ Michael Kim (J/J/USA)	Audi R8 LMS GT3
Taça Portugal	César Campaniço/João Figueiredo (P/P)	Audi R8 LMS GT3
Spanien / Spain	César Campaniço/João Figueiredo (P/P)	Audi R8 LMS GT3

2012

Blancpain Endurance Series	Christopher Haase/Christopher Mies/ Stéphane Ortelli (D/D/MC)	Audi R8 LMS GT3
Portugal	César Campaniço/Carlos Vieira (P/P)	Audi R8 LMS GT3
Taça Portugal	César Campaniço/Carlos Vieira (P/P)	Audi R8 LMS GT3
Iberian Supercars Trophy	César Campaniço/Carlos Vieira (P/P)	Audi R8 LMS GT3
Spanien / Spain	Mikko Eskelinen (FIN)	Audi R8 LMS GT3

2013

Belgien / Belgium	Anthony Kumpen/Bert Longin/ Maarten Makelberge (B/B/B)	Audi R8 LMS GT3
FIA GT Series	Stéphane Ortelli/Laurens Vanthoor (MC/B)	Audi R8 LMS GT3
GT Sprint International	Thomas Schöffler (D)	Audi R8 LMS GT3
Portugal	César Campaniço (P)	Audi R8 LMS GT3
Schweden / Sweden	Jan Brunstedt (S)	Audi R8 LMS GT3

2014

ADAC GT Masters	Kelvin van der Linde/René Rast (ZA/D)	Audi R8 LMS GT3
Blancpain Endurance Series	Laurens Vanthoor (B)	Audi R8 LMS GT3
Blancpain GT Series	Laurens Vanthoor (B)	Audi R8 LMS GT3

2015

Australien / Australia	Christopher Mies (D)	Audi R8 LMS GT3
Blancpain GT Series	Robin Frijns (NL)	Audi R8 LMS GT3

2016

ADAC GT Masters	Christopher Mies/Connor De Phillippi (D/USA)	Audi R8 LMS GT3
Blancpain GT Series Sprint Cup	Enzo Ide (B)	Audi R8 LMS GT3
DMV GTC	Fabian Plentz (D)	Audi R8 LMS GT3
DMV GTC Dunlop 60	Fabian Plentz/Tommy Tulpe (D/D)	Audi R8 LMS GT3
Dunlop Endurance Championship	Phil Hanson/Nigel Moore (GB/GB)	Audi R8 LMS GT3
FIA GT World Cup Drivers	Laurens Vanthoor (B)	Audi R8 LMS GT3
Intercontinental GT Challenge	Laurens Vanthoor (B)	Audi R8 LMS GT3
North Island Endurance Series Three Hour	Neil Foster/Jonny Reid (NZ/NZ)	Audi R8 LMS GT3
Victorian State Circuit Racing Championships Sports Cars	Steven McLaughlan (AUS)	Audi R8 LMS GT3

2017

Australien / Australia	Geoff Emery (AUS)	Audi R8 LMS GT3
Blancpain GT Series Sprint Cup	Robin Frijns/Stuart Leonard (NL/GB)	Audi R8 LMS GT3
Canarian Hill Climb Championship	Luis Monzón (E)	Audi R8 LMS GT3
China GT Championship	Xu Jia (CN)	Audi R8 LMS GT3
DMV GTC	Fabian Plentz/Egon Allgäuer (D/A)	Audi R8 LMS GT3
DMV GTC Dunlop 60	Fabian Plentz/Tommy Tulpe (D/D)	Audi R8 LMS GT3
FIA European Hillclimb Championship	"Tessitore" (A)	Audi R8 LMS GT3
Intercontinental GT Challenge	Markus Winkelhock (D)	Audi R8 LMS GT3
North Island Endurance Series Three Hour	Simon Evans/Gene Rollinson (NZ/NZ)	Audi R8 LMS GT3
Pirelli World Challenge TC	Paul Holton (USA)	Audi RS 3 LMS
Saudi GT	Mohammed Bin Saud (KSA)	Audi R8 LMS GT3
TCR Russia	Dmitry Bragin (RUS)	Audi RS 3 LMS/Seat Leon
Three Hour Endurance Championship	Simon Evans/Gene Rollinson (NZ/NZ)	Audi R8 LMS GT3
Victorian State Circuit Racing Championships Sports Cars	Matthew Stoupas (AUS)	Audi R8 LMS GT3

WEITERE TITEL / ADDITIONAL TITLES

2010

ADAC GT Masters Teams	Abt Sportsline	Audi R8 LMS GT3
Belgien / Belgium Teams	W Racing Team	Audi R8 LMS GT3

2011

Blancpain Endurance Series Teams	Belgian Audi Club Team WRT	Audi R8 LMS GT3

2012

Blancpain Endurance Series Gentlemen Trophy	Robert Hissom/Pierre Hirschi (GB/CH)	Audi R8 LMS GT3
Blancpain Endurance Series Teams	Belgian Audi Club Team WRT	Audi R8 LMS GT3
Blancpain Endurance Series Gentlemen Trophy Teams	Saintéloc Racing	Audi R8 LMS GT3

2013

ADAC GT Masters Teams	Prosperia C. Abt Racing	Audi R8 LMS GT3
FIA GT Series Pro-Cup Teams	Belgian Audi Club Team WRT	Audi R8 LMS GT3
Großbritannien / Great Britain Gentleman Driver Trophy	Mark Patterson (USA)	Audi R8 LMS GT3
GT Asia Teams	Team R8 LMS ultra	Audi R8 LMS GT3
Schweden / Sweden Teams	JB Motorsport	Audi R8 LMS GT3

2014

ADAC GT Masters Teams	Prosperia C. Abt Racing	Audi R8 LMS GT3
Australien / Australia GT Trophy	Rod Salmon (AUS)	Audi R8 LMS GT3
Blancpain Endurance Series Teams	Belgian Audi Club Team WRT	Audi R8 LMS GT3
Blancpain GT Series Teams	Belgian Audi Club Team WRT	Audi R8 LMS GT3
Blancpain Sprint Series Teams	Belgian Audi Club Team WRT	Audi R8 LMS GT3
Blancpain Sprint Series Pro Am Cup	Marc Basseng/Alessandro Latif (D/GB)	Audi R8 LMS GT3
Blancpain Sprint Series Pro Am Cup Teams	Phoenix Racing	Audi R8 LMS GT3
Blancpain Sprint Series Silver Cup	Vincent Abril/Mateusz Lisowski (F/PL)	Audi R8 LMS GT3
Blancpain Sprint Series Silver Cup Teams	Belgian Audi Club Team WRT	Audi R8 LMS GT3
Challenge Endurance GT / Tourisme V de V GTV2	Franck Thybaud (F)	Audi R8 LMS GT3
GT Asia GTM	Jacky Yeung (HK)	Audi R8 LMS GT3
Italien / Italy Teams	Audi Sport Italia	Audi R8 LMS GT3

2015

ADAC GT Masters Gentlemen Cup	Andreas Weishaupt (D)	Audi R8 LMS GT3
Australien / Australia GT Trophy	Barton Mawer/Greg Taylor (AUS/AUS)	Audi R8 LMS GT3
Blancpain Endurance Series Pro-Cup Teams	Belgian Audi Club Team WRT	Audi R8 LMS GT3
Blancpain GT Series Teams	Belgian Audi Club Team WRT	Audi R8 LMS GT3
Blancpain Sprint Series Cup Teams	Belgian Audi Club Team WRT	Audi R8 LMS GT3

Blancpain Endurance Series Am Cup	Ian Loggie/Julian Westwood (GB/GB)	Audi R8 LMS GT3
Challenge Endurance GT / Tourisme V de V, Prestige	Eric van de Vyver/Tiziano Carugati (F/CH)	Audi R8 LMS GT3
GT Asia GTM	Jerry Wang (HK)	Audi R8 LMS GT3
Italien / Italy Teams	Audi Sport Italia	Audi R8 LMS GT3
Junior Challenge FFSA GT	Valentin Simonet (F)	Audi R8 LMS GT3
One Hour Asko South Island Endurance Series	Neil Foster (NZ)	Audi R8 LMS GT3

2016

ADAC GT Masters Junior	Connor De Phillippi (USA)	Audi R8 LMS GT3
ADAC GT Masters Teams	Montaplast by Land-Motorsport	Audi R8 LMS GT3
Australian GT Trophy Series	Rob Smith (AUS)	Audi R8 LMS GT3
Blancpain GT Series Sprint Cup Teams	Belgian Audi Club Team WRT	Audi R8 LMS GT3
British GT3 Silver Drivers	Will Moore/Ryan Ratcliffe (GB/GB)	Audi R8 LMS GT3
FIA GT World Cup Manufacturers	Audi	Audi R8 LMS GT3
GT Asia Series Pro-Am-Cup	Shaun Thong (HK)	Audi R8 LMS GT3
IMSA WeatherTech SportsCar Championship GT Daytona Car Manufacturers	Audi	Audi R8 LMS GT3
Intercontinental GT Challenge Manufacturers	Audi	Audi R8 LMS GT3
International Endurance Series Rookies	Max Edelhoff (D)	Audi R8 LMS GT3
Pan Delta Circuit Hero One GT	Huang Hsi-Chan (RC)	Audi R8 LMS GT3
SprintX Pro Drivers	Dion von Moltke (USA)	Audi R8 LMS GT3
Tequila Patrón North American Endurance Cup Teams	Magnus Racing	Audi R8 LMS GT3
Tequila Patrón North American Endurance Cup Manufacturers	Audi	Audi R8 LMS GT3
VLN Speed Trophäe	Montaplast by Land-Motorsport	Audi R8 LMS GT3

2017

24H Series Drivers Rookies	Max Edelhoff (D)	Audi R8 LMS GT3
24H Series Continents Championship Driver Rookies	Max Edelhoff (D)	Audi R8 LMS GT3
Australian GT Trophy Series	Steven McLaughlan (AUS)	Audi R8 LMS GT3
Blancpain GT Series Asia Silver Cup	Marchy Lee/Shaun Thong (HK/HK)	Audi R8 LMS GT3
Blancpain GT Series Sprint Cup Teams Overall	Belgian Audi Club Team WRT	Audi R8 LMS GT3
Canarian Hill Climb Championship Clubs	Auto-Laca Competición	Audi R8 LMS GT3
China GT Championship Teams	Kings Linky Racing	Audi R8 LMS GT3
Intercontinental GT Challenge GT3 Manufacturers	Audi	Audi R8 LMS GT3
Pirelli World Challenge TC Teams	C360R	Audi RS 3 LMS
Thailand Super Series Super Car GTM Plus	B-Quik Racing Team	Audi R8 LMS GT3

AUDI R8 LMS CUP

2012	Marchy Lee (HK)	Audi R8 LMS GT3
2013	Adderly Fong (HK)	Audi R8 LMS GT3
2014	Alex Yoong (MAL)	Audi R8 LMS GT3
2015	Alex Yoong (MAL)	Audi R8 LMS GT3
2016	Alex Yoong (MAL)	Audi R8 LMS GT3
2017	Alessio Picariello (B)	Audi R8 LMS GT3

AUDI SPORT TT CUP

2015	Jan Kisiel (PL)	Audi TT cup
2016	Joonas Lappalainen (FIN)	Audi TT cup
2017	Philip Ellis (GB)	Audi TT cup

BEDEUTENDE SPRINT-EINZELSIEGE / SIGNIFICANT SPRINT RACE WINS

2011

Macau GT Cup	Edoardo Mortara (I)	Audi R8 LMS GT3

2012

Macau GT Cup	Edoardo Mortara (I)	Audi R8 LMS GT3

2013

Macau GT Cup	Edoardo Mortara (I)	Audi R8 LMS GT3
Baku World Challenge	Stéphane Ortelli/Laurens Vanthoor (MC/B)	Audi R8 LMS GT3

2014

Baku World Challenge	Cesar Ramos/Laurens Vanthoor (BR/B)	Audi R8 LMS GT3

GESAMTSIEGE BEI LANGSTRECKENRENNEN / OVERALL VICTORIES IN ENDURANCE RACES

2010

12h Ungarn / Hungary	Thomas Gruber/Philip König/Walter Lechner/ Niki Mayr-Melnhof (A/A/A/A)	Audi R8 LMS GT3

2011

12h Bathurst	Marc Basseng/Christopher Mies/Darryl O'Young (D/D/HK)	Audi R8 LMS GT3
24h Spa	Mattias Ekström/Greg Franchi/Timo Scheider (S/B/D)	Audi R8 LMS GT3
24h Zolder	Enzo Ide/Bert Longin/Xavier Maassen/François Verbist (B/B/B/B)	Audi R8 LMS GT3

2012

12h Bathurst	Christer Jöns/Christopher Mies/Darryl O'Young (D/D/HK)	Audi R8 LMS GT3
24h Nürburgring	Marc Basseng/Christopher Haase/Frank Stippler/ Markus Winkelhock (D/D/D/D)	Audi R8 LMS GT3
24h Spa	Andrea Piccini/René Rast/Frank Stippler (I/D/D)	Audi R8 LMS GT3
24h Zolder	Marco Bonanomi/Anthony Kumpen/Edward Sandström/ Laurens Vanthoor (I/B/S/B)	Audi R8 LMS GT3

2013

25h Thunderhill	Jeff Altenburg/Kevin Gleason/Robb Holland/ Roland Pritzker (USA/USA/USA/USA)	Audi TT RS

2014

24h Nürburgring	Christopher Haase/Christian Mamerow/René Rast/ Markus Winkelhock (D/D/D/D)	Audi R8 LMS GT3
24h Spa	René Rast/Laurens Vanthoor/Markus Winkelhock (D/B/D)	Audi R8 LMS GT3

2015

24h Nürburgring	Christopher Mies/Nico Müller/Edward Sandström/ Laurens Vanthoor (D/CH/S/B)	Audi R8 LMS GT3
12h Sepang	Stuart Leonard/Stéphane Ortelli/Laurens Vanthoor (GB/MC/B)	Audi R8 LMS GT3
25h Thunderhill	Guy Cosmo/Tomonobu Fujii/Darren Law/ Johannes van Overbeek (USA/J/USA/USA)	Audi R8 LMS GT3

2016

24h Dubai	Alain Ferté/Stuart Leonard/Michael Meadows/ Laurens Vanthoor (F/GB/GB/B)	Audi R8 LMS GT3
25h Thunderhill	Mike Hedlund/Darren Law/Dion von Moltke/ Johannes van Overbeek (USA/USA/USA/USA)	Audi R8 LMS GT3
12h Sepang	Robin Frijns/Christopher Haase/Laurens Vanthoor (NL/D/B)	Audi R8 LMS GT3

2017

24h Nürburgring	Kelvin van der Linde/Christopher Mies/Connor De Phillippi/ Markus Winkelhock (ZA/D/USA/D)	Audi R8 LMS GT3
24h Spa	Jules Gounon/Christopher Haase/Markus Winkelhock (F/D/D)	Audi R8 LMS GT3
12h Imola	Max Edelhoff/Horst Felbermayr Jr./Toni Forné/ Dimitri Parhofer (D/A/E/D)	Audi R8 LMS GT3
California 8 Hours	Pierre Kaffer/Kelvin van der Linde/Markus Winkelhock (D/ZA/D)	Audi R8 LMS GT3
25h Thunderhill	Tom Haacker/Charly Hayes/Darren Law/ Nate Stacy (USA/USA/USA/USA)	Audi R8 LMS GT3

KLASSENSIEGE UND TROPHÄEN BEI LANGSTRECKENRENNEN / CLASS VICTORIES AND TROPHIES IN ENDURANCE RACES

2009

24h Nürburgring SP9-GT3	Christian Abt/Jean-François Hemroulle/Pierre Kaffer/ Lucas Luhr (D/B/D/D)	Audi R8 LMS GT3
24h Spa G2	Marc Basseng/Marcel Fässler/Alexandros Margaritis/ Henri Moser (D/CH/GR/CH)	Audi R8 LMS GT3

2010

24h Nürburgring SP9-GT3	Marc Bronzel/Luca Ludwig/Dennis Rostek/ Markus Winkelhock (D/D/D/D)	Audi R8 LMS GT3

2011

24h Nürburgring SP9-GT3	Marc Basseng/Marcel Fässler/Frank Stippler (D/CH/D)	Audi R8 LMS GT3

2012

24h Trophy GT3 (Nürburgring - Spa)	Phoenix Racing	Audi R8 LMS GT3

2013

24h Daytona GT	Filipe Albuquerque/Oliver Jarvis/Dion von Moltke/ Edoardo Mortara (P/GB/USA/I)	Audi R8 LMS GT3
12h Sepang GTC	Ashraff Dewal/Jacky Yeung/Alex Yoong (MAL/HK/MAL)	Audi R8 LMS GT3

2014

24h Spa Coupe du Roi	Audi	Audi R8 LMS GT3
Petit Le Mans GTD	Matthew Bell/Christopher Haase/Bryce Miller (GB/D/USA)	Audi R8 LMS GT3

2015

24h Spa Coupe du Roi	Audi	Audi R8 LMS GT3
24h Spa Am-Cup	Ian Loggie/Callum Macleod/Benny Simonsen/ Julian Westwood (GB/GB/DK/GB)	Audi R8 LMS GT3

2016

24h Daytona GTD	Andy Lally/John Potter/René Rast/ Marco Seefried (USA/USA/D/D)	Audi R8 LMS GT3
24h Spa Coupe du Roi	Audi	Audi R8 LMS GT3
12h Sepang GTC	Daniel Bilski/Henk Kiks/Peter Kox (AUS/NL/NL)	Audi R8 LMS GT3

2017

24h Dubai TCR	Julian Griffin/Erik Holstein/Finlay Hutchison/ James Kaye (GB/IRL/GB/GB)	Audi RS 3 LMS
12h Mugello TCR	Hermann Bock/Max Partl (D/D)	Audi RS 3 LMS
Petit Le Mans GTD	Sheldon van der Linde/Christopher Mies/ Connor De Phillippi (ZA/D/USA)	Audi R8 LMS GT3

Chris Reinke
Leiter Audi Sport customer racing
Head of Audi Sport customer racing

AUDI SPORT CUSTOMER RACING

MITARBEITER STAFF

Armin Plietsch
Leiter Entwicklung
Head of development

Dirk Spohr
Leiter Kundenmanagement
Head of customer management

Michael Schäfer
Leiter Aufbau Renn- und Testfahrzeuge
Head of race and test car preparation

Dietmar Ponticelli
Projektleiter GT3 und GT4
Project leader GT3 and GT4

Hendrik Többe
Vertrieb GT3 und GT4
GT3 and GT4 Sales

Alexander Hecker
Projektleiter RS 3 LMS
Project leader RS 3 LMS

Detlef Schmidt
Technischer Projektleiter RS 3 LMS und Audi Sport TT Cup
Technical project leader RS 3 LMS and Audi Sport TT Cup

Garreth Greif
Vertrieb RS 3 LMS
RS 3 LMS sales

Philipp Mondelaers
Projektleiter Audi Sport TT Cup
Project Leader Audi Sport TT Cup

Eva-Maria Becker
Kommunikation
Communications

Kurt Gräfenstein
Kundenbetreuer
Customer support

Lukas Daum
Kundenbetreuer
Customer support

Martin Russegger
Kundenbetreuer
Customer Support

Johannes Trost
Kundenbetreuer
Customer support

Alfred Schweiger
Vertrieb Ersatzteile
Spare parts sales

Israel Martinez
Vertrieb Ersatzteile
Spare parts sales